Kuna Crafts, Gender, and the Global Economy

KUNA CRAFTS, GENDER, AND THE GLOBAL ECONOMY

KARIN E. TICE

UNIVERSITY OF
TEXAS PRESS

AUSTIN

I dedicate this book to the
mola *makers of Kuna Yala (San Blas)*
and to my daughter, Katherine

Library of Congress Cataloging-in-Publication Data
Tice, Karin Elaine, 1956–
Kuna crafts, gender, and the global economy / Karin Elaine
Tice.—1st ed.
p.   cm.
Includes bibliographical references (p.   ) and index.
ISBN 0-292-78133-4 (cloth : acid-free paper).—ISBN 0-292-78137-7
(paper : acid-free paper)
1. Cuna Indians—Industries. 2. Cuna textile fabrics.
3. Cuna Indians—Economic conditions. 4. Molas—Panama—
San Blas Coast. 5. Textile cooperatives—Panama—San Blas
Coast. 6. Women in cooperative societies—Panama—San Blas
Coast. 7. Economic development—Panama—San Blas Coast.
8. San Blas Coast (Panama)—Economic conditions. 9. San Blas
Coast (Panama)—Social conditions. I. Title.
FI565.2.C8T53 1995
330.97287'4—DC20   94-16152

Contents

Acknowledgments

This study would not have been possible without the support of the communities of Mansucun, Tupile, and Carti-Sugtupu and that of Los Productores de Molas R.L. (the *mola* cooperative). Although the list of people who shared their homes, food, joys, sorrows, and friendship with me is too long to include here, I would especially like to thank the López household, which treated me as if I were their own daughter. Carlos and Eneida López taught me a great deal of Kuna history. I am also especially grateful to the leaders of the *mola* cooperative, whose commitment to improving Kuna lives throughout San Blas has been an inspiration to me, both professionally and personally.

Research for this book began in 1981, when I was a first-year graduate student in the Joint Program in Applied Anthropology at Teachers College/Columbia University. Although I have learned from many people, I would particularly like to thank Lambros Comitas, George Bond, Charles Harrington, and Rayna Rapp for sharing their love of anthropology with me.

The research presented here was funded by the Inter-American Foundation, the IIE Fulbright Commission, the Organization of American States, and Sigma Xi. The Brookdale Institute at Columbia University provided financial support during part of the time I was analyzing data and beginning to write. John Seeley, president of FERA (Formative Evaluation Research Associates), hired me as an anthropologist in 1986 and provided a highly flexible, though intellectually challenging and demanding, work environment that allowed me time to complete my dissertation and this book. I am very grateful for all the support I have received.

In Panama, the Centro de Investigaciones Kunas, the Patrimonio Histórico, and the Instituto Nacional de Cultura gave me permission to conduct this study and provided access to important data sources. My Kuna colleagues Eligio Alvarado (sociologist) and Cebaldo de León (anthropologist) discussed the theoretical as well as the practical implications of this study with me at length. Arnulfo Prestán (anthropologist), Eugenio Walter (extension worker), and Francisco Herrera shared their knowledge of San Blas with me, as did Eligio and Cebaldo. Olga Linares asked me wonderfully helpful and usually difficult questions. Ester and Jack Goody visited me on the island of Tupile, shared their experiences with me, and made excellent suggestions for my own work. Anne Wensel, a longtime *mola* collector, opened her home in Panama City to me.

Lambros Comitas, George Bond, Eric Wolf, Libbet Crandon, Charles Harrington, and Bill Durham constructively criticized earlier drafts. The National School for Anthropology and CIESAS, an anthropology institute in Mexico City, invited me to present my work in a symposium on craft commercialization. Copresenters June Nash and Victoria Novelo offered helpful insights into this study and provided the intellectual stimulation that encouraged me to complete this manuscript.

Lynn Stephen, another anonymous reviewer for the University of Texas Press, and James Howe have given me very helpful suggestions for ways to strengthen this book. Alaka Wali and Nia Georges have been close colleagues and good friends throughout this lengthy process. Their insights have been highly valuable. Of course, I take full responsibility for the quality of this research.

I also appreciate my family's endless support. My extensively published father-philosopher, Terrence Tice, has provided endless encouragement and enthusiam and has read most of the drafts. To him I owe my love of books, of research, of reading, and of thinking across disciplines. My mother, Carol Tice, an innovator, has inspired and challenged me to think about the practical implications of this study. Jim Szocik, my husband, and Katherine, my baby daughter, have been patient throughout and have continually reminded me to enjoy life even as deadlines draw near. My grandmother and world traveler, Fern Hoff, taught me to ask questions, to pack for the unexpected, to wonder about the world, and to give something back.

1.
Introduction

Carti-Sugtupu, 1985. A steady stream of camera-laden tourists poured through the narrow path connecting the dock with the island's main pathway. The pathway was lined with Kuna women ready to sell their *molas.* As I wandered around, the cries of "twenty dollar" . . . "ten dollar" were accented by groans of "turista nued suli" (bad tourist, i.e., someone who did not buy a *mola*). One of my Kuna friends pulled me over and asked me to convince an indecisive tourist to buy a *mola.* She said, "If the ome sippu [white woman/tourist] doesn't buy my *mola,* my children will not eat fish."

Tupile, 1985. "Mormaknamaloe . . . mormaknamaloe" [go sew molas . . . go sew *molas*] . . . the cry became louder and louder until I saw my friend Rodolfina standing in the open doorway to the kitchen. "Tage Nagagiriyai . . . cooperativa anmarnae mormake" [Come on, Nagagiriyai—my Kuna name—we are going to the cooperative to make *molas*]. I went outside and joined a colorful stream of Kuna women and children walking in small groups all headed down the main path to the cooperative building. As the morning progressed, we sewed and we talked. The children played under our feet, crawled onto their mother's laps, and ran around. When the sun was nearly overhead, we started packing finished *molas* stored in a large wooden cupboard into a clean rice sack. A trusted friend of the cooperative was traveling to Panama City and would take the *molas* with him. The cooperative's administrator, a Kuna woman, would meet his plane and take the *molas* to sell in the cooperative's retail store.

Mansucun, 1985. Albertina, her husband, and their two young children had just returned from a day's long expedition to harvest coconuts. Their teenaged daughter, who had stayed behind to care for her tiny infant, greeted them when they entered the door. I had just returned from conducting household interviews and was sitting on a low stool in the space between the kitchen and the sleeping house writing up my notes. Albertina invited me to go to the store with her to buy cloth for a new *mola* she wanted to wear to an upcoming puberty ceremony. Before we went she ripped apart an old *mola* blouse. She asked me why *mergi* (people from the United States) like old, worn-out, faded molas instead of nice, brightly colored new ones. I said I didn't know. Albertina laughed and said, "Well, it's good for us anyway." In the store we were greeted by a Kuna man who asked Albertina if she had brought a *mola*. After some negotiation, Albertina exchanged her old mola for enough cloth to make a new *mola* and a little sugar. She was eager to start her new *mola*, so we hurried home.

When I arrived in San Blas in 1981, concerned with the effects of craft commercialization on women's access to economic resources, I had planned to study *mola* commercialization on the island of Tupile. During my initial three-month stay, a resort hotel illegally owned and operated by a North American family in San Blas was attacked. In the skirmish that followed, a Kuna man from Tupile, serving as a Panamanian National Guardsman, was shot and killed. Antiforeigner sentiment ran high within the Tupile community, and I was asked to leave for at least one month until the community had taken the needed time to process and mourn this man's death.

Members of the *mola* cooperative on Tupile were eager for me to begin my study and did not want me to leave. They made a formal request to the first *sakla* (head local leader) that I be allowed to stay. The *sakla* said no but made it clear that I was to return in one month and gave me an official travel pass so that I could travel to other Kuna communities with the status of a member of the Tupile community. The cooperative leaders quickly arranged an itinerary for me and sent me off to visit other local chapters of the cooperative throughout San Blas. This incident provided me an unexpected opportunity to travel extensively throughout the San Blas region. It quickly became obvious to me, as illustrated by the foregoing scenes, that the organization and effects of craft commercialization varied tremendously throughout the region.

This book is about the commercialization of Kuna women's clothing for sale in the global market. *Mola* blouses, worn by the Kuna women of San Blas, Panama, have been commercialized since the 1960s and in the 1980s provided a primary source of income for the entire San Blas region. I explore the effects on the division of labor by gender, social differentiation, and the commoditization of ethnicity of the shift from *mola* production for use to production for exchange. The political and economic history of the San Blas region is situated historically within a larger global context of international trade, political intrigue, and ethnic tourism.

The *comarca*, or district, of San Blas, often called Kuna Yala, lies along the northeastern coast of Panama. Kuna Yala literally means Kuna Land. The Congreso General Kuna has petitioned the Panamanian government officially to change the name of the region to Kuna Yala. Although this change has not yet been formally approved, many non-Kuna government officials have already begun to refer to the region as Kuna Yala. Like Howe (1986b:xiii), I fully support the use of Kuna Yala but agree that it does not adequately distinguish the coastal Kuna territory from other Kuna Yalas and so have decided also to use the name San Blas. San Blas comprises a long, narrow strip of mainland jungle extending two hundred kilometers along the coast and fifteen to twenty kilometers inland and an archipelago of 365 small islands. This area is home to the Kuna, one of Panama's three major indigenous groups.

In addition to the San Blas Kuna, or the island Kuna, as they are commonly called, there are Kuna who live outside of the *comarca*. Approximately 10,000 Kuna live in Panama City and Colón, the two major cities in Panama (Eligio Alvarado, personal communication). Many of these individuals still retain close ties with San Blas and consider the region their home. Seven villages with a total population of 804 are located in the Darién region near the hydroelectric dam (Wali 1984). A few other small communities are located in Colombia.

According to the 1980 Panamanian national census, the total population of San Blas was 28,567. There are fifty-four communities ranging in size from seventy to over two thousand inhabitants. Forty-two of these communities are located on small islands, ten are situated on the mainland coast, and two are inland on the riverbanks (see maps 1 and 2). All the inhabited islands are located no farther than one mile from the mainland coast and the mouth of a freshwater river. Proximity to the coast makes daily travel from the islands to the Kuna's agricultural fields, situated on the mainland, possible. Freshwater mainland rivers provide an easily accessible source of water for drinking, bathing, and washing clothes.

The Kuna are internationally known for their grass-roots, innovative approaches to the economic development of the San Blas region. They have received funding from international sources for projects to protect the rain forest from deforestation, to build an urban Kuna

Map 1. The Caribbean basin

village similar in style to their home communities, and to develop a crafts cooperative to improve women's opportunities for generating income. Other, locally funded projects have focused on retaining local control over the tourist industry, demarcating and protecting the boundaries of their land, supporting cultural events, and conducting social research on issues relevant to the social and economic development of the region. Indigenous groups worldwide have expressed great interest in learning about how the Kuna have achieved a considerable degree of economic, political, and social autonomy.

Kuna women's contributions to this process, although recognized locally, have been mostly ignored by economic development planners at the regional and national levels and even by other indigenous groups seeking to learn from the Kuna. Kuna women, although their interests sometimes conflict, have not accepted this passively. They have become active in national and local politics and have used the *mola* cooperative as a way to make their voices heard locally, regionally, and nationally. Cooperative leaders hope that this book will make economic development planners sit up and take notice of the potential income-generating opportunities as well as the exploitation of producers that comes with the commercialization of crafts made by women. One woman summed up how important craft sales are for many Kuna women: "For us women who speak no Spanish and who have not attended school, how else are we to feed and educate our children? If we go to the City [Panama City], we can only work as domestic servants . . . they abuse us. Selling our *molas* is the only way we can survive" (all translations are mine unless otherwise noted).

When I returned in 1984 for a year, my study had grown to include three Kuna communities. Whereas much of the literature at that time argued that, with a shift from a subsistence-based to a primarily cash-based economy, women, particularly women living in egalitarian-based societies such as the Kuna's, lost their former access to resources, this did not appear to be true for Kuna women. I hoped their experiences would contribute to the debate over the origin of women's oppression and would provide lessons about ways either to prevent or to begin to reverse the negative and unequal impact of economic development, often equated with modernization, on women relative to men.

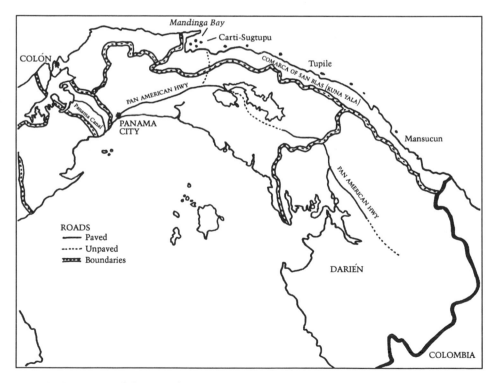

Map 2. Panama and the San Blas region

What I discovered, as have other researchers, is that the more we learn about women and economic development, the more complex the issues become. For the Kuna, the effects of *mola* commercialization have been mixed. Some men and women have benefited in specific ways at particular points in time. Others have not been so fortunate. The intersection of class, gender, and ethnicity is historically specific, changes over time, and defines Kuna women's and men's relationships to the global economy and to political forces at work within that context. Human agency, the involvement of people in creating their own social history, further complicates the picture.[1] Unfortunately, there is still an enormous gap between our theoretical understanding of how gender, class, and ethnicity operate and the practical application of those understandings to economic development policies and projects affecting and often further impoverishing women throughout the world. I intend this book to be useful to practitioners as well as to scholars by (a) discussing theoretical issues related to women and the commercialization of craft production; (b) raising policy issues; and (c) documenting a grass-roots-level effort to ensure that craft commercialization benefited impoverished, rural women.

The first six chapters situate San Blas and *mola* commercialization historically within the global political economy. These chapters contribute to theoretical debates related to gender, craft production, and the global economy by showing (1) the dynamic intersection of gender, class, and ethnicity at the regional, national, and international levels; and (2) the interrelationship between human agency, craft commoditization, and craft consumption. Chapter 2 provides a theoretical context for the book and some background information about San Blas. Chapter 3 is an ethnographic account of a Kuna woman's trip from Panama City to her home community in San Blas. This chapter provides contextual background and is an introduction to the region and the Kuna people. Chapter 4 reviews the history of San Blas and its increasing articulation with the world economy since the late 1800s. Chapter 5 presents the history of *mola* commercialization and its relationship to agricultural production, tourism, and the international market for ethnic crafts. Chapter 6 details shifts in the organization of *mola* production, marketing, and use and the implications of these changes for Kuna men's and women's earnings.

Chapter 7 describes the purpose, history, activities, and difficulties of the regionwide *mola* cooperative. Chapters 8, 9, and 10 present case studies of three San Blas communities, specific households within each of those communities, and the effects of *mola* commercialization on the division of labor by gender, household subsistence production, and access to cash income. Although some historical information is presented, these later chapters focus primarily on life in these villages in 1984 and 1985. Chapter 10 ends with a discussion of female-supported households in San Blas. Authority or power, decision making, and sources of economic support in female-supported households are discussed in the context of the three case studies. Chapter 11 presents the implications of the study, both theoretical and practical, for our understanding and for effecting social change at the global and local levels.

2.
Theoretical Framework

This study draws from and contributes to three overlapping bodies of literature. First, it contributes to the growing number of studies concerned with how women are affected by economic development. Second, feminist scholarship focusing on issues of class, ethnicity, and gender provides an important theoretical framework. Many of these studies draw from and contribute to the debates on women and economic development. A few focus on craft production, the third body of literature. The remainder of this chapter reviews theoretical frameworks useful for conceptualizing craft production and those related to women and development. Issues raised by feminist scholars will be woven into both discussions.

Artisan Petty-Commodity Producers

Artisans, or craft producers, have been defined to include a wide variety of individuals, including weavers, potters, brickmakers, lacemakers, tailors, and shoemakers (Bottomley 1965; Orlove 1974; Goody 1982; Mies 1982; Cook and Binford 1990). Within this wide array of artisan producers, there is a subniche called "artisans of the Fourth World." Graburn has defined the Fourth World as "the collective name for all aboriginal or native peoples whose lands fall within the national boundaries and technobureaucratic administrations of the countries of the First, Second, and Third World" (1976: 1). These artisans produce, among other things, items made from indigenous women's clothing for sale to tourists and for export.

Although the division of peoples into separate worlds tends to obscure class interests that cross national boundaries, it is useful to think about the commercialization of native people's arts, wherein ethnicity is manipulated in a different fashion and separately from the commercialization of bricks or shoes. For the purposes of this book, *ethnicity* is understood as "a concept used by a group of people in particular situations where they are trying to assert their status vis-à-vis another group of people, often for political, economic, or social reasons" (Stephen 1991a:11). Ethnic identity is defined and redefined within specific historical contexts.

"Artisans," however narrowly or broadly defined, cannot be categorized as a homogeneous population. Relations of production and circulation vary widely even within a particular region. Furthermore, noncapitalist relations of production can coexist alongside capitalist relations of production, even though both are tied into and dependent on a capitalist market (Novelo 1976; García Canclini 1982).

Approaches used to study crafts or artisans have both mirrored and influenced wider theoretical debates within the social sciences. Many of the early studies of craft production in Latin America were ethnographic descriptions of how crafts were made. These descriptions were ahistorical and did not discuss issues of class, gender, or ethnicity. Studies usually focused on single communities and did not discuss the distribution or consumption of crafts. Notable exceptions are two studies of the Otavalo focusing on social change and showing the interrelationship between landownership and craft production and sales (Collier 1949; Salomon 1973). Although the 1960s were characterized by a surge in the commercialization of indigenous crafts and the formation of craft cooperatives, largely through the efforts of Peace Corps volunteers, anthropologists do not appear to have published studies on the effects of these projects and policy developments during this period.

In the 1970s and the early 1980s, scholars using a dependency framework of analysis argued that in Latin America the commercialization of artisan products for export occurred as a result of "underdevelopment." Dependency theorists argued that Latin America and the rest of the Third World were being actively underdeveloped and impoverished through the exploitation of raw materials and cheap labor (Frank 1967).[1] When rural households were no longer able to subsist on agricultural production because of insufficient land, they were forced to supplement their incomes with the production and sale of crafts (Sabogal Wiesse 1978; Littlefield 1979; Garay Castillo and Medina Pérez 1981). Households with land often combined agricultural and craft production, while landless households depended entirely on income from artisan production (Sabogal Wiesse 1978). Although dependency theory aptly identified unequal relations between industrialized and the "underdeveloped" countries, it did not address issues of class, gender, or ethnicity. Neither did it illuminate how local populations were articulated with the larger political economy (Wolf 1982). Wolf writes: "Their [dependency theorists'] choice of focus thus leads them to omit consideration of the range and variety of such populations, of their modes of existence before European expansion and the advent of capitalism, and of the manner in which these modes were penetrated, subordinated, destroyed, or absorbed, first by the growing market and subsequently by industrial capitalism" (1982:23). Wolf challenged scholars to view the world as interconnected and to study these interconnections historically.

In the 1980s, scholars began to question Marx's assumption that precapitalist relations would disappear with the expansion of capitalism. Marx argued that "the handicraftsman or peasant who produces with his own means of production will either be gradually transformed into a small capitalist who also exploits the labour of others, or he will suffer the loss of his means of production" (quoted in McLellan 1977:398). Recent studies, however, have shown that in many areas of the world craft production continues to flourish and is well integrated into the larger capitalist system. Precapitalist relations of production coexist with capitalist relations of production (Novelo 1976; Goody 1982; Cook and Binford 1990). Precapitalist relations are characterized by ownership of the means of production. For artisans this includes tools such as looms or kilns and raw materials such as cloth or thread, production for personal or household use, and control over their own labor. Capitalist relations of production are characterized by lack of ownership of the means of production, the alienation of the producer from the product, and production for exchange on the market.

Studies of petty-commodity production and of the informal sector have contributed to our understanding of self-employed producers in rural and urban areas.[2] Despite the many contributions, there are three areas that have been only minimally addressed: (1) questions relating to gender oppression under capitalism; (2) the importance of commodity consumption for our understanding of the linkages between capitalist and precapitalist forms of production (García Canclini 1982); and (3) the role of human agency. Feldman (1991:74) notes that petty-commodity production research has been characterized by a "relative absence of women in analyses . . . and the neglect of women's contributions to home-based or family enterprises." Reasons for this include the following: (1) women's and children's unpaid work often remains invisible; (2) this work is defined as "unproductive work"; and (3) household members' interests are often viewed as homogeneous (Feldman 1991:66).

In addition to the lack of focus on women, few studies have focused on the consumption end of craft production.[3] Production knowledge has been defined to include not only the "how to" but also knowledge about the distribution and consumption of things (Appadurai 1986). In other words, it is important to understand not only how things, crafts, in this case, are produced and exchanged, but also how they are used.[4] How gender is embedded in patterns of craft consumption is an area of inquiry that has not been addressed.

Recent studies have begun to examine gender issues related to craft production (Mies 1982; Ehlers 1990; Stephen 1991a, b; Nash 1993). The extent to which women gain or lose economic control when crafts are commercialized varies by their class position (Ehlers 1990). Formerly egalitarian relations between men and women may become asymmetrical (Etienne and Leacock 1980). The ideology that defines women as "housewives" may support their exploitation as craft producers for the global market (Mies 1982). External ethnic identity, used to lay claim to the sale of certain crafts, may be contested internally among men and women from different social classes (Stephen 1991a, b).

The commercialization of crafts is an important topic of concern for practitioners as well as researchers. For example, some governments in Latin America have viewed the development of handicraft production as a solution to rural underemployment and the resulting migration to urban areas in search of wage labor (Bauch 1981; García Canclini 1982). In Mexico, Panama, and Peru, government actively promotes and supports the export of handicrafts. In the case of Peru, however, these "supports" have been criticized as benefiting the intermediaries and doing little to improve the income-generating potential of impoverished producers living in the rural areas (Bauch 1981). This study shows a similar pattern for Panama.

In 1978, Sistema Económico Latino Americano (SELA), an organization concerned with economic development in Latin America, formed a special committee to create a multinational organization for the express purpose of commercializing Latin American handicrafts. Fifteen of twenty-five member countries—Panama, Nicaragua, Costa Rica, Honduras, Guatemala, Mexico, Colombia, Ecuador, Peru, Bolivia, Guyana, Haiti, Jamaica, Barbados, and Cuba—financially supported and participated in this committee. The committee's first three years, 1978–1981, were dedicated to researching the realities of artisan production in each of the participating countries and to exploring potential markets for crafts. All of this research was coordinated in Panama. The next two-year stage, never implemented, was to be dedicated to the actual commercialization of crafts.

After extensive research, the committee concluded that Latin American craft producers were not ready for the increased commercialization of their products. The following reasons were given to support this conclusion: (1) the level of craft production in the member countries was too low to ensure a steady supply of goods to import-export companies; (2) the quality was highly variable and not dependable; and (3) the market for crafts was limited, since crafts are not consumable items.

Nonetheless, with or without government help and whether producers are "ready" to export their goods or not, the sale of handmade goods continues to provide an important source of income for many Latin American households, particularly those dependent on women's earnings. This is especially true in countries with large indigenous populations, such as Mexico, Guatemala, Ecuador, Bolivia, Peru, and Panama. Indigenous women's brightly colored clothing has been extensively commercialized for export. Mexican women's embroidered blouses, Guatemalan women's *huipiles* (blouses), and Kuna women's *mola* blouses, to mention a few, can be found selling for high prices in small ethnic arts stores, fancy boutiques, and art galleries throughout the United States and Europe. Unfortunately, more often than not, producers receive very low prices for the items they have so painstakingly made.

The Kuna, who are internationally known in certain circles for their innovative approaches to economic development problems, provide a case study of an indigenous people struggling with how to retain local control over economic resources including land, tourism, and *mola* commercialization. This book will contribute to the literature on craft production by extending our understanding of how access to resources from the commercialization of handicrafts is defined by relations of production, by the international market, and by the division of labor by gender.

Women and Economic Development

Research done in the 1970s drew attention to women's roles in economic development. Building on Boserup's (1970) work in Africa, researchers began to examine how men and women are differently affected by economic development in different ways. Studies drew from diverse theoretical frameworks to explain why women's lives are generally not improved by economic development efforts. Although men's lives are not always improved either, women often lost their former social and economic status through the development process (Nash et al. 1976; Etienne and Leacock 1980; Leacock 1981a). Relative to that of men, women's quality of life decreased (Bossen 1984).

One major area of debate has been over the origins of women's oppression. The hope was that if we could understand how and why women become oppressed, we might be better able to (1) prevent this from occurring in areas where symmetry among the genders still exists or (2) develop strategies to improve conditions for women. This debate is characterized by two main arguments: (1) that women's oppression is universal and that patriarchy is responsible; and (2) that women's oppression is linked to capitalist development. The former points to socialist and Communist societies where women are still oppressed despite the absence of capitalism (Croll 1981). The latter draws from Engel's work (1972) but argues that women are not universally oppressed. Advocates of this viewpoint have documented the fact that in egalitarian societies women have been known to hold equal standing with men. Also, some precapitalist societies, such as that of the Aztecs, were hierarchically organized and patriarchal. Colonialization and capitalist development often destroyed formerly egalitarian or symmetrical relations between men and women (Etienne and Leacock 1980; Leacock 1981a). This debate has never been resolved. The ethnographic material presented in this book shows that for the Kuna, gender symmetry remains in many areas of their lives, despite their direct involvement in the global capitalist economy.

Perhaps the most exciting thing about the debates that have evolved over the past two decades has been the concern researchers and professionals working in the field of women and development share for improving conditions for women worldwide. Disagreements over problem formulation and development of solutions and women's different political agendas, however, have created conflict among these people even as they work toward the same goal.

Unlike many areas of scholarship, the literature pertaining to women and development is multidisciplinary. Anthropologists, economists, sociologists, historians, and women at the local level have all contributed to this effort. Furthermore, there has been a relatively high degree of collaboration among scholars and professionals working in the development field. Economic development programs in the 1960s offered technological improvements, access to credit, and educational opportunities primarily to men. This began to change starting in the 1970s. In 1975, the first United Nations international congress of women was held in Mexico City, followed by international conferences in 1980 (Copenhagen) and 1985 (Nairobi). A surge of intellectual and professional activity during the 1970s and the 1980s resulted in increased attention to women's role in economic development. Many development organizations such as the

United States Agency for International Development (AID) and the United Nations created special subunits to focus specifically on "women's issues." During the 1970s and the 1980s, information networking and research centers were created worldwide to support the development of programs and policies that would benefit women.[5] These networks remain active in the 1990s. The remainder of this section highlights the underlying theoretical assumptions that frame my research.

Women are not a homogeneous group. Gender is crossed by class, race, and ethnicity (Gallin and Ferguson 1991; di Leonardo 1991). Class and gender systems are inseparable and are historically specific (Benería and Roldán 1987). Benería and Roldán (1987:10) write: "Although class and gender may be analytically distinguishable at a theoretical level, in practice they cannot be easily disentangled. The problem before us is to build a unifying theory and analysis in which material and ideological factors are an integral aspect of our understanding of gender subordination, while women's subordination is an integral part of our understanding of economic and social reality." For the purposes of this book, *class* is understood as the relations of the Kuna to others vis-à-vis the relations of production. *Gender* and *ethnicity* are viewed as interwoven into the process of class formation.

Women of different ages and generations may experience social change in different ways. Gailey (1987:9) writes: "Gender relations rarely are abstracted from other aspects of one's social identity in kinship societies. People exercise claims to specific relatives' labor or products, and work efforts may be organized on a relationship basis." She goes on to say that with class and state formation, "categories of gender, age, and skill [become] abstracted from their particular kinship connections and meanings" (p. 16). Women's status and their control over economic resources may vary within the context of their different roles (Sacks 1982). Women are not necessarily passive victims of colonization or of economic development (Nash and Fernández-Kelly 1983).

Division of Labor by Gender

The examination of changes in the division of labor by gender as a result of the expansion of capitalism has been widely used as an analytical tool for understanding the effects of that process on female access to resources (Leacock 1981a; Deere and León de Leal 1981; Nash and Fernández-Kelly 1983). *Gender*, in contrast with *sex*, which refers to genetic composition, is a socially constructed category. As such, the division of labor by gender, with the exception of biological reproduction, is based on socially defined tasks that determine men's and women's roles in productive and social reproductive activities (Weiner 1980; Stolke 1981; Sacks 1982). In this process, however, class differences in access to resources arise among women as well as between the genders (Stoler 1977; Bourque and Warren 1981; Bossen 1984).

Studies by feminist scholars focusing on the relationship between the division of labor by gender and the subordination of women have analyzed (1) the gender division of labor and the stages of industrial capitalism; (2) production and reproduction; (3) women and development in Third World societies; and (4) the division of labor by gender in socialist societies (Leacock and Safa 1981; Leacock et al. 1986). *Subordination* can be defined as "the relations between men and women within the social process as a whole and the way those relations work to the detriment of women" (Mackintosh 1981:2).

Nationally and internationally, women's work is often under-reported. Much of women's economic activity is unpaid and is therefore considered less valuable than any paid work. Part of the problem has resulted from the orthodox approach to economics, which stresses the quantification of exchanges within the capitalist market and excludes subsistence or use-value production, a great portion of which is done by women (Benería 1982). A Marxist approach to economics presents some difficulties as well. Although a Marxist approach would examine the underlying social relations, use-value production would still be viewed as "outside the sphere of political economy" (quoted in Benería 1982:129).

Feminist scholars have attempted to combine Marxist and feminist approaches by focusing on reproductive as well as productive activities. By "reproductive activities" I am referring not to biological reproduction but to the social reproduction of the labor force. This includes activities that fall under the general rubric of "housework," such as child care, food preparation and storage, cleaning, hauling water, and washing clothes (see Benería 1979; Harris and Young 1981).

Recent studies have focused on the international division of labor by gender (Nash and Fernández-Kelly 1983). Over the past three decades, there has been a shift of manufacturing jobs from declining industrial centers in the United States to the Third World. In the mid-1960s, industries in developing countries started producing components for export instead of goods for local consumption as multinationals relocated to take advantage of low-cost nonunionized labor and incentives offered by export-processing zones. Characterized as "footloose," these newly rootless companies can pick up and move to where profits are greatest. This mobility affects job stability and inhibits worker organization around labor-related issues. Much of this "new" work in the developing countries, especially in the clothing and electronics industries, is performed by women.

A new international division of labor by gender has been created in which women in the poorest countries are paid the lowest wages. Nash and Fernández-Kelly (1983:xi) argue that the "global integration of production further increased inequalities among women and men, minorities and dominant racial or ethnic groups." Recent studies have explored how cultural constructions of gender interweave with the shift of labor from industrialized to nonindustrialized countries and the effects on women's lives from the *maquiladora* sweatshops along the Mexican border to the electronics factories in the Philippines. Although some women have partially benefited from new wage labor opportunities, when corporations close or move on to locales where they can increase their profits, women are left with few employment options. They no longer have the handicrafts and business enterprises they had before entry into industrial wage labor (Nash and Fernández-Kelly 1983:xiv).

This raises several practical questions. What types of craft production and other businesses provide stable income for impoverished women and their households? What types of policies and innovative grant programs could be developed to support these activities, especially in areas affected by fleeing enterprises?[6]

Kuna Women of San Blas

Kuna women have caught the attention of explorers, anthropologists, and, in more recent times, tourists. Their dress is brilliantly colorful and absolutely exotic to the non-Kuna eye. Indeed, most of the anthropological studies that have focused on women in Panama were carried out in San Blas.[7] Much of the literature pertaining to Kuna women has used symbolic analyses to understand their role in Kuna society (Helms 1976; Howe and Hirschfeld 1981). Helms, following Lévi-Strauss, equates women with the procreative and unruly forces of nature. She argues that women's creativity must be controlled by men who produce "moral order." She views *mola* production and marketing as an extension of women's creative capacity. This role restores the "cosmological equilibrium which had been upset when women stopped participating in a major way in agricultural production" (Helms 1976:132). In contrast, Howe argues that Kuna women are clearly identified with culture rather than nature. In his

Belia sewing a *mola*

analysis of "the Star Girls" myth, he discovers that "Innatili is, after all, a culture hero in the full sense of the word—a culturizing or civilizing figure as well as a hero of the culture. By her teaching, she turns uncouth and half-civilized people, who could only mumble nonsense syllables as mourning, into more fully human and cultured beings" (Howe and Hirschfeld 1981:322).

Kuna myths and cosmology suggest that, symbolically, Kuna women hold high status (Helms 1976; Howe and Hirschfeld 1981). Howe (1981:320) writes: "Kuna women tend to be strong, purposeful and assertive, they enjoy considerable collective prestige, and they strongly influence household decisions." Most of the symbolic literature is ahistorical with one important exception. Nordienskiöld's analysis of Kuna creation myths suggests that prior to contact with Christianity only the "original mother" existed. Current myths refer to both *pab dummat* (the big father) and *nan dummat* (the big mother). He writes (1938:444): "The different versions of the creation myths among the Cunas and the greater significance of fatherhood in the versions which have not been preserved in the form of texts or in picture-writings, point to the fact that the conception has been shifted so that the original father has at least been given a more important role than he had earlier." Although these symbolic studies provide fascinating glimpses into the Kuna's mythical world, they tell us little about the realities of women's daily life in San Blas.

Most of the literature on Kuna politics and the social organization of labor focuses on men's work and men's political life (Howe 1974, 1986b; Stier 1979, 1982; Moore 1984; Bourgois 1988). Research on Kuna women done in the 1950s is primarily descriptive and ahistorical and assumes homogeneity throughout the San Blas region (Torres de Ianello 1957; Gamio de Alba 1957). More recently, several studies have examined changing "sex" roles. Judith Brown (1980), using secondary sources, traces changes in the division of labor by "sex" up to but not including the commercialization of *molas*. She does not discuss variations among islands. Costello (1982) presents important information about migration and changing "sex" roles in the community of Río Azúcar but, again, not much about the shift from *mola* production for use to that for exchange. Swain (1978, 1982) investigated Kuna women's changing roles on the island of Aligandi and the way ethnicity mediates these changes. Hatley (1976) provides us with a somewhat general but lengthy description of women's socially reproductive activities but does not relate them to women's productive activities. *Mola* commercialization is one of the most far-reaching social changes affecting Kuna women's lives in this century. Most of the literature, however, has focused on its symbolic impact or on Kuna ethnoaesthetics (see chapter 5 for a literature review).

This book takes the reader far beyond San Blas to understand the social, economic and political forces related to *mola* commercialization. I visited three Kuna communities and many homes to understand how Kuna women's and men's work, their access to resources, and their quality of life have been affected by, and have sometimes influenced, *mola* commercialization. Chapter 3 is an ethnographic description of a Kuna woman and an anthropologist (me) traveling to San Blas from Panama City.

3.
Traveling to San Blas

Dawn has not yet broken the stillness of the night. A taxicab pulls up in front of a small airport located on the edge of Panama City. A Kuna woman hands the driver two U.S. dollar bills and climbs out with a small child and six large cardboard boxes. The boxes are tied up with rough packing twine and have the name of her home island community scrawled on them in felt-tip marker. Two other Kuna women jump out of the cab to help her unload. One is dressed in *mola* while the other is wearing western clothes. I greet my friends and start helping them carry the boxes inside.

A Kuna man's voice greets the woman named Amma from the bench where he is sitting in shadow outside of the airport waiting room: "Amma pe nuedi?" (Amma, are you good?). "Nuedi, nuedi" (Good, good), she answers, stopping to adjust the large bright-red scarf with yellow designs that is draped over her head.

Amma is a member of the Kuna women's *mola* cooperative and is returning home to the island of Tupile after a week's buying trip to Panama City. The other two women are also members of the cooperative. They live in Panama City and tend to the cooperative's store. Cooperative members from Tupile sent Amma to buy thread, children's clothes, *saburrettes* (wraparound skirts worn by most Kuna women), *musues* (red scarves), and candies for an upcoming celebration. The cooperative women on her island each sewed four *molitas* (little *molas*) "for the cooperative" to raise the capital for this shopping trip.

Inside, the waiting room is already packed with Kuna men, women, children, boxes, bags, and bundles. Two tourists stand in the middle of all this looking quite perplexed. To the outsider there is no apparent order, and the numerous announcements about travel arrangements, all in Kuna, are completely unintelligible to English and Spanish speakers. Several people from different islands greet me in Kuna and ask me where I am going. We exchange travel plans and send greetings to friends on other islands. One person hands me a letter to deliver.

For many of the estimated ten thousand San Blas Kuna living in Panama City, the airport is the main link between the city and their home communities in San Blas. Letters, messages, and money as well as bundles of clothing, school supplies, and other needed items are sent with travelers. Some people who are in the waiting room will wait for other flights, hoping for news of their families and friends from passengers returning from San Blas. Kuna high school students, both male and female, studying in Panama City anxiously await money sent to them from San Blas. Many Kuna mothers partially or completely support their children's studies with income generated from *mola* sales.

Amma, our two friends, and I check the boxes at the weigh station and join a couple of Kuna men, political leaders, who have made a space for us on a bench. They want Amma to take a message from them to the Tupile *congreso*. As cooperative leaders, Amma and her friends are well known and respected throughout San Blas. I am also well known as the anthropologist who studies *mola* commercialization.

Amma launches into a long speech, half angrily, half jokingly, reprimanding these men for not including any cooperative leaders in the last regional economic development planning meeting. Amma found out while in Panama City that representatives, all Kuna males, from the Panamanian Departments of Education, Agricultural Development, and Health, among others, had been invited, as had the four Kuna representatives to Panama's Congress and the PEMASKY (Project for the Study of the Management of Wildlife Areas of Kuna Yala) staff, also all male, with the exception of a female secretary.[1]

Amma reminds the men, in no uncertain terms, that the *mola* cooperative is a regionwide organization approved as such by the Congreso General Kuna. The Congreso General Kuna comprises one or more leaders, or *saklas*, from each local Kuna community. Local communities usually have several *saklas*, an *arkar*, or "chief's spokesperson," and several Kuna *sualipet*, or police officers (Howe 1986*b*:12). The Congreso General Kuna meets about every six months to discuss political, economic, and social concerns facing San Blas. As an officially recognized group, the cooperative has the right to send representatives and to speak at the meetings but not to vote. Local *congresos* usually meet daily.

After twenty-five minutes of talking, without giving the men a chance to get a single word in, Amma falls silent. Long stretches of uninterruptible speech are a common and acceptable form of com-

Boarding a plane to Panama City

munication for both Kuna men and women.[2] The men answer, however, rather meekly giving what the women consider weak excuses mixed in with jokes. Amma makes a few additional emphatic points, also mixed in with jokes. She then turns to me and somewhat exasperatedly says: "Tell these men why *molas* are important and why cooperative leaders *must* be included . . . tell them what your study shows!" So I start talking (first in Kuna and then in Spanish) about the preliminary findings from my study. The men finally agree that the cooperative should be included in future economic development planning meetings and again say rather sheepishly that they had not intended to leave out the women . . . it just never occurred to them to include cooperative leaders.

Amma's name is called along with the names of the other passengers, including Amma's young daughter and me, traveling to Tupile and to Playón Chico, a neighboring island. We go outside and hop into a bright yellow-orange sixteen-seat airplane ready to take off. The sun is just peeking over the horizon.

As the plane gains altitude, we can see the tall white skyscrapers rising from the city below. Panama City is an exciting place, but Amma says that she is always glad to leave the hustle and bustle of the commercial center, where she spends most of her time, and return home to Kuna Yala. The city is expensive and everything costs money. She comments, "If you do not have money you go hungry and might have to sleep outside on the street."

In Amma's community people are very proud, as are the Kuna throughout San Blas, that no one goes hungry or lacks a roof. Visitors from other islands and even those from foreign countries are often fed and sheltered at no cost. Even so, visitors usually, but not always, do contribute something (food, labor, or money) to the household they visit.

As the skyline fades, urban sprawl gives way to a long stretch of naked deforested land. Visually, it is a relief to reach the thickly carpeted jungle of green that lets us know we are nearing San Blas. Looking down, we see plantain fields, coconut *fincas* (farms), and scattered fruit trees. Despite the commercialization of coconuts, *molas*, and lobsters and income from wage labor opportunities, subsistence production has been, and continues to be, the mainstay of life for most Kuna households in San Blas. Slash-and-burn agriculture, crop rotation, and intercropping are the primary techniques used.

Plantains and bananas, rice, corn, yucca, coconuts, and a wide variety of tropical fruits make up the main crops.[3] These are grown on the mainland and provide the bulk of the Kuna diet. Fish and game supplement these and provide high-quality protein in an otherwise starchy diet. Aside from an occasional pig or chicken, kept on the island near its owner's house, the Kuna raise no livestock.

Amma points out the muddy brown ribbons of river winding their way sluggishly toward the sea and starts telling me about how she used to paddle her *ulu* (dugout canoe) daily from Tupile to the mainland river to fetch water, wash clothes, and catch river crabs. That was before the women convinced the men to build an aqueduct to bring fresh water to the island from the mainland river. Her life was very different then. Food was more abundant, and her young children's father was still living with them in her mother's household. He planted plantains, corn, and rice and provided them with fresh fish.

Amma tells me that her husband decided to go to Panama City to find a paying job. At first, he sent ten dollars every now and then, but soon the money stopped coming. She heard from her friends living in the city that he had found another woman. Amma's father was old and could not keep up with all of the agricultural labor. Amma began to sell her *molas* so that they could buy a little rice occasionally. In those days there was no cooperative and store owners paid only two dollars per *mola*. Amma was not making any money, so when the *mola* cooperative started, she joined. It had been a struggle, but without the money she made from selling *molas* through the cooperative, her children would have gone hungry. Many women were in her same situation; it seemed that more and more often they needed money in order to eat.

Turning the plane, the pilot heads straight out over the sea. The plane enters a thick, white, puffy cumulus cloud, and for several moments we cannot see a thing. We burst out of the cloud and see Mandinga Bay dotted with tiny islands. Some islands are large, others small. I am intrigued by the variance in size and shape. Many islands are fairly round while others are oblong. Some have rather odd, irregular shapes, because the shallow areas surrounding the islands are often filled with dead coral, stones, and sand to provide more living space for growing populations on crowded islands.

Equally small, sandy, uninhabited islands planted with coconut trees dot the seascape. Coconuts are sold or traded for goods with Colombian traders who travel up and down the coast. They provide an important source of income for most households in San Blas. From above, we can clearly see the numerous coral reefs and atolls below the ocean's surface. The sea's color ranges from crystal blue to deep aqua-green, depending on the depth of the water.

The accumulation of coral reefs varies along the coastline and affects the abundance, type, and accessibility of fish in communities like Amma's. Amma tells me she is envious of the women who live in Mandinga Bay (within the Carti region), located west of her community, because they eat "lots of fish." Mandinga Bay has numerous coral reefs, which are home to a great variety of tropical fish. These reefs provide a protected area for fishing year round. Farther to the east, the coastline becomes rocky, mountainous, and exposed to the open sea. Different types of fish inhabit these waters, and fishing becomes impossible during the dry season.

The dry season lasts from December to April. During this time, communities located on the mainland coast are often shut off from contact with the rest of the region for weeks at a time. The northeast trade wind blows fiercely, and the ocean becomes so choppy and the waves so high that access by sea is impossible. No supplies or people can move in or out of these communities until the wind dies down, nor can men or women go fishing. Island communities with few or no barrier reefs nearby to provide protected waters for fishing are also limited by the dry season.

Like fishing, agricultural production varies throughout San Blas. The eastern part of the region has rich soil, which produces an abundant supply of plantains, bananas, coconuts, and avocados. The middle region also is noted for its agricultural production (see map 2). In contrast, the Carti region to the west has poorer soil. The Kuna living in this area plant crops, although avocados and plantains are brought each year from the eastern part of Kuna Yala to supplement their harvests. In 1984–1985, the area was struck by a blight and nearly all the plantains and bananas had to be imported.

Amma's daughter Kikkatiriyai, who has been sitting quietly until now, exclaims: "Look! Look! Our boat!" I direct my gaze to where Amma's small daughter is pointing and see the *San Ignacio* chugging along the coastline. The *San Ignacio* is collectively owned and operated by the Tupile community. It is one of several trade boats that travel the length of the San Blas coast, stopping at most of the larger inhabited islands. Each boat is collectively owned and operated by community members of a specific island. Goods flow unidirectionally, though passengers may travel in both directions. Typically, once a boat has unloaded its merchandise—flour, kerosene, canned goods, sodas, beer, soap, dishes, and furniture—it returns to Colón empty except for a few passengers.

The *San Ignacio* is coming from Colón. Stopping frequently to unload cargo, it will take the *San Ignacio* two full days to travel between Carti-Sugtupu (an island located in Mandinga Bay) and Tupile, its home community. Amma has made the three- to four-day boat trip from Tupile to Colón several times. I went part of the way once. Panama City is only about two hours from Colón by bus or train. Traveling by boat costs about one-fifth the price of an air ticket (twenty-five dollars one-way to Tupile), but many people (Kuna and anthropologists alike) fear the long stretches of open sea, where the boat is tossed from side to side by waves so large that the passengers can see nothing but dark green-gray sheets of water. Then the boat is picked up by the wave, riding along its crest until it plunges again into another valley. Many passengers get seasick.

As the plane continues down the coast, we can see a number of Colombian schooners. These vessels are longer and thinner than Kuna trade boats and have sails as well as motors. Each schooner has a capacity for fifteen thousand to one hundred thousand coconuts. About forty of these large schooners pass through San Blas every month. They travel up and down the coast from Colombia to Mandinga Bay, bringing goods from Colombia such as sugar, rice, gasoline, hammocks, children's clothes, coffee, and powdered cocoa. These products are sold or exchanged for coconuts grown by the Kuna for export.

Smaller Colombian boats called *chalupas* also travel up and down the coast. Many are not involved in the coconut trade with the Kuna but, rather, in piracy. These modern-day pirates are armed and ride the high seas in search of plunder. So far, their assaults have been on

Colombian schooners, but the Kuna are still very wary of these marauders.

Circling back over the jungle, the plane begins to descend. Small patches of felled trees, coconut groves, and plantain *fincas* appear amidst green jungle vegetation. For a moment it seems as if we will crash into the trees, but as always the grassy runway comes into view and the plane lands, stopping only feet from the sea.

A small concrete room with two large, square, empty spaces for windows and a wooden bench outside serves as the airport terminal. Inside, the room is completely empty. The airport attendants are waiting, as they do every day, to take arriving passengers out to the island. Amma's little girl kicks off her stiff city shoes and runs barefoot to the motorized *ulu* waiting to take us home. All the boxes are loaded onto a long, slightly raised plank at the bottom of the boat and are carefully covered with sheets of plastic so they will not get wet.

Amma and I shove the boat away from the shore, climbing in only when the water has reached our knees. When the boat picks up speed, the spray drenches everyone on board. It is a pleasant feeling on a hot, sunny day. Tupile, at first a mere speck on the horizon, draws steadily closer. In about fifteen minutes we can see the familiar shapes of houses built within feet of the water's edge. There are several two-story concrete houses. Most houses are made from locally found materials, cane walls bound together with jungle vines and covered with thatched roofs. Although to an outsider they all look the same, the airport attendant knows exactly which house is Amma's and heads straight to it. By this time, the motor has been heard on the island and most of the people in Amma's four-generation extended household come running out to help unload the boat. They have been expecting her because Amma has sent word that she is coming with someone traveling to Tupile who stopped in at the *mola* cooperative store in Panama City.

The cooperative store in Panama City serves as the hub of a large network of Kuna men and women from many islands. As they do at the airport, people stop at the cooperative to learn when and where people are traveling and to leave messages, money, or small packages to be taken to their home communities. The cooperative administrator, a Kuna woman, often goes out to the airport to pick up *molas* coming in from cooperative chapters on different islands and to send cloth, messages, or money back to the islands.

Amma lives in a matrilocal household that includes her grandmother, mother and father, three sisters, two younger brothers, and her four children. Two of Amma's sisters have children. One child's father works in Panama City and sends them money and clothing every now and then. The other father, who also lives and works in Panama City, sends nothing. Her third sister is still single and has no children.

Amma's mother and sisters help Amma and the airport attendant unload the *ulu*. One of her sisters and all of the little girls, including Amma's own ten-year-old daughter Kikkatiriyai, wear western dress. Amma is trying to save money so that her daughter can change into *mola*, but she cannot change until everything is purchased. Gold earrings, costing ten dollars per pair, and a fifteen dollar gold necklace with Kikkatiriyai's name engraved on it have already been bought. *Wini*, the long strands of multicolored beads that wrap around the lower legs and forearms, have yet to be made. These *wini* are made right on a woman's body, so that the complicated geometric designs, handed down through the generations, will come out just right. A complete set of *wini* costs about twelve dollars.

Several sets of *saburrettes* and *musues* must also be purchased. Each *saburrette* costs $5.00, the *musues* $1.50. Perhaps most important of all are the *mola* blouses that have to be painstakingly hand sewn and the *asuolo* (gold nose ring) that has to be purchased. No Kuna woman wearing *mola* looks dressed without an *asuolo*. The size and styling of the *asuolo* change from generation to generation, however. Kikkatiriyai's grandmother wears a rather large, heavy ring that reaches to her upper lip. Women in Amma's generation generally wear a smaller, somewhat flatter (less round) version of these larger *asuolos*. Several years ago Amma and many of her friends had taken their larger *muu* (grandmother) rings to the jeweler to be made into smaller and "more fashionable" ones. Kikkatiriyai would wear an even smaller ring, the latest rage in nose ring fashion among women in their teens and early twenties. In a way, her mother explained, it is just as well, because the smaller *asuolos* cost around forty dollars in contrast with the eighty dollars she would have to pay for a *muu*-sized ring.[4]

Many women from Tupile who have grown up wearing western dress are now saving to change into *mola*. Like Amma, these women also want their daughters to wear *molas*. Wearing *mola* is a visual statement of Kuna pride, especially since the resurgence of Kuna "traditions" resulting from the 1925 Kuna revolution (see chapter 4).

Mola refers to *mola* panels in the blouses worn by Kuna women as well as to the entire blouse. To "wear *mola*" implies that a woman is dressed in full Kuna attire. Some women wear western dress most of the time but occasionally wear a *mola* blouse and a *saburrette* without the *musue,* gold jewelry, and *wini.* Although this is acceptable on many islands, these women are not considered fully dressed "in *mola.*"

Dress code varies from island to island. On some islands, including Tupile, what a woman wears is considered her own business, and women wear western dress, *mola,* or a combination as they see fit. On other islands, however, women and girls of all ages are required by their local *congresos* to wear *mola* (full Kuna dress). This is considered a symbol of resistance to acculturation into western, or non-Kuna, culture.

Amma climbs out of the *ulu* and heads for the house only yards from the water's edge. She calls to me: "Tage Nagagiriyai, anmar koboe" (Come, Nagagiriyai, we will drink). We go in the "back" door, ducking under rows of hammocks slung side by side. Briefly, we greet her sisters who are sewing *molas* and her sickly grandmother and go out through the "front" door onto Tupile's main sandy path. Amma's household lives in two houses, one for sleeping and the other for cooking, eating, and processing food. The "kitchen" is located directly across the path from the sleeping house. Amma enters and sits down on one of the small, low wooden seats carved by her grandfather. Her mother sits tending the fire, deftly peeling and cutting up plantains for lunch with an old steel blade. By now, I know to find a stool and sit down without waiting to be invited.

Amma's sisters come into the kitchen, with the *molas* they are working on, to hear the latest news from Panama City. All the children in Amma's household have also gathered in hopes that Amma has brought them a treat. Some neighbor women drift in, and steaming hot cups of *olikwa* are passed around to everyone in the kitchen. *Olikwa* is a sweetened drink made from ground corn and roasted, ground cocoa beans. Amma pulls two rectangular loaves of soft white bread out of a box and gives everyone a slice. She always brings either bread or saltines from the city as a treat. Small French-type loaves of freshly baked bread are made daily by bread collectives on the island, but the children especially like the soft city bread. I pull out a jar of peanut butter to share.

Amma's father, who has gone fishing, does not think much of city bread. In fact, he does not like bread at all. Bread, he claims, is not even food. Only plantains can be considered "real" food. Her father has also said that he wishes they could drink *olikwa* every day, as he did when he was a child. Then Kuna men provided Kuna women with the ingredients to make a wide variety of hot drinks. Now they usually drink *ochi* (a sweet drink), usually hot chocolate made from purchased cocoa powder mixed into water and sweetened with store-bought white sugar.

Amma launches into a long, animated monologue describing what she had to eat and drink on her trip. I am also asked to describe what I consumed in Panama City, and we start talking again about the high cost of eating in Panama City. Food and hospitality are considered important to the Kuna, and it is rare for anyone coming back from a trip to the city or from another Kuna community not to comment on both. As we talk, people drift in and out of the kitchen. Several friends come walking down the main path, stick their heads in the doorway, enter, and without a word sit down and are immediately brought cups of *olikwa*.

Amma and her friends, also members of the *mola* cooperative, decide to call a general meeting of the cooperative. Her friends go off to find Belia, the woman who usually calls the meetings, while Amma and I, tired from our trip, rest in hammocks in the sleeping house. Belia has a good voice and walks around the island quite literally "calling" women to the cooperative meeting. Kuna women call their cooperative meetings in the same fashion that Kuna men call men and women to the local *congreso*.[5]

Congresos on Tupile used to be held nightly and were attended by both men and women. I have learned through my trips to other islands that this is still the case in some communities, although on many islands, including Amma's, men and women now meet separately. On Tupile, men meet in the evening primarily to discuss sociopolitical concerns. Women meet twice a week during the day to listen to the *saklas* chant Kuna religious stories and give them advice on how to behave properly. "Mormaknamaloe," which means "Go sew *molas*," is the cry used to call women to the *congreso*.

As Amma and I lie swinging in our hammocks, Amma talks with her sister about her ideas for raising money for Kikkatiriyai's *inna muttikkit*, an *inna*, or *chicha* celebration, that is to be held when Kikkatiriyai reaches puberty. Amma is also hoping to save enough to hold an *inna suit*, where Kikkatiriyai will have her hair ritually cut and the entire community will celebrate for three to five days. This ceremony is often held before a girl reaches puberty, but not always. Once they have reached puberty, girls who have gone through this ritual can wear their hair shaved up the back in the traditional fashion. Adult women who have not undergone the haircutting ritual may wear their hair short, but not shaved close to the scalp in the back.

The birth of a female child is cause for celebration in San Blas. In past years, the entire community would celebrate by holding an *ikko inna*. This *chicha* is a one-day ritual celebration during which the baby's nose is pierced and her birth rejoiced in. Although these celebrations are no longer held in the majority of Kuna communities, including Tupile, some communities in the eastern part of San Blas still hold them. No similar ritual is held for the birth of a male child, nor are any other community celebrations held for boys, as they are for girls.

No matter what the cause for celebration, when an *inna* is held, every household is expected to contribute firewood, fish, and plantains to be consumed during the festivities. Women of all ages work together to cook food in large vessels. Male specialists prepare large pots of *inna* or *chicha*, alcoholic beverages made from fermented sugarcane and parched and blackened corn and consumed during the *chicha* celebrations.

Puberty ceremonies last for only one day. In Tupile they are held in a *chicha* house constructed especially and exclusively for celebrating *innas*. The entire community is invited to come to eat and drink. In the past, these celebrations involved little capital outlay on the part of the girl's household. Now this custom is changing; although the community still provides many needed items, Amma's household will have to purchase white sugar, white rice, and rum, among other things, for the occasion.

Amma and her sister are discussing the idea of forming a small *sociedad*, or collective, to raise money for the celebrations. They would ask members of the household to join, each putting in five dollars. Amma and her sister would each buy Kikkatiriyai a share in the *sociedad*. With the combined capital they could buy kerosene from the Colombian traders who travel regularly up and down the San Blas coast buying coconuts and selling or trading goods. Then the kerosene would be resold and the profits distributed equally to all of the members.

Mola sales through the *mola* cooperative produce more income for the women than selling kerosene, but the money generated from *molas* is needed to purchase things for the household such as sugar, powdered cocoa, salt, and rice. Amma also uses her income from *mola* sales to buy clothing and personal items for herself and her children and to purchase the children's school supplies. Amma's mother, sisters, and, occasionally, her unmarried brother also help with household expenses. Amma's father generally stores up his coconuts to trade with the Colombians for needed household items such as hammocks, metal storage bins, large steel cooking pots, or one-hundred-pound sacks of sugar.

A main pathway on one of the islands

"Cooperativa se nae!" (Go to the cooperative!) The midafternoon sun is high in the sky and searingly hot. Our stomachs are rumbling, but Amma's father has not yet come back with fish for the daily meal, so we gulp down cups of *ochi* and join some of the other women heading for the cooperative.

The *mola* cooperative is an attractive two-story concrete building painted green and yellow and decorated with two enormous *cambombia* seashells. This building, constructed primarily by the cooperative members themselves, is fancier than the buildings most local chapters of the cooperative have. Most chapters have only a small traditional house with no windows. Cooperative members on Tupile worked very hard to construct their building. They carried sand and rocks from the mainland river and learned how to mix cement and to use a hammer. They also sewed many extra *molas* in order to raise funds for materials and to pay the Kuna carpenter (male) to supervise the construction.

Even with the new building, not all of the 160 members fit inside when general meetings are called. Women stand outside in bunches, gathered around the open windows in order to hear. The brilliant reds, oranges, blues, and greens in their clothing produce a riot of color against the wall of the cooperative. Crowded inside, women of all ages stand or sit on benches. Ramón and three male friends sit giggling in one corner with some women. These four young men are *omekit* (womanlike) and are the only male members of the cooperative. Although sewing *molas* is definitely considered "women's work" by Kuna men and women alike, *omekits* sew *molas*. In addition, they participate in a wide range of women's activities. Everyone has brought a *mola* to work on during the meeting.

The main purpose for calling this meeting is to fill everyone in on the cooperative news from Panama City and to discuss when the sale of the clothes, towels, and toys Amma has purchased on her trip to Panama City will take place. Christmas is only two months away. The cooperative will sell the goods at a slightly higher price than their cost in Panama City but they will still be less expensive than similar items in local stores. The profits will be spent on a special Christmas meal for all the island's children so that no child will go hungry on Christmas.

Amma starts the meeting by reminding members about the cooperative's latest contract. A Panamanian man who owns a chain of supermarkets in Panama City and is interested in supporting artisans by selling their handicrafts in one of his stores has requested five thousand small Christmas tree ornaments and some other holiday-related items. Each local chapter is responsible for producing a certain quantity before the holiday season. The Tupile chapter is making *mola* Santa Claus pillows and *mola* Christmas stockings. Amma reminds everyone not to fall behind on their sewing. After hearing all the news from the city, the women go on to discuss plans for the clothing sale and for the upcoming Christmas celebrations. The meeting lasts about an hour.

By the time Amma and I return from the cooperative, her father has returned and the *tule masi*, the main meal of the day, is ready. For this coconut-based soup, fish are steamed in coconut milk, which is then poured over large chunks of boiled green plantains. Salt, lime juice, and hot chile pepper are added by each individual for flavor and the steamed fish is served to the side. Although there are many heavy, low wooden stools in Amma's kitchen, there are only two tiny, low wooden tables, so we must take turns eating.

After eating, Amma sits tending the fire for her mother, who is smoking the extra fish caught that day. Her sisters sit in the kitchen, too, sewing their *molas* and talking with Amma and me. The sun is low in the sky by the time Amma suggests that we go out back to bathe. Her mother is washing some clothes, using part of an old *ulu* as a wash basin. The children are all out back, playing and pouring cold water over themselves. The spigot is on full force and the large red plastic basin underneath is rapidly filling. We bathe, in turn, in a small bamboo enclosure and change into clean clothes. It is a Kuna custom to bathe first thing in the morning and then again in the evening.

Most evenings Amma spends sitting at home with her children sewing *molas* by the light of a small kerosene lamp. Sometimes Amma, her mother, and her sisters sit up until the wee hours of the morning sewing and sleep only briefly before getting up to start the new day. Other evenings Amma visits relatives and friends or goes to the cooperative to sew. As Christmas approaches, groups of women from the cooperative will chip in money to buy kerosene for the cooperative's pressure lamp, and they will sit up together all night sewing.

Tonight, Amma is tired from her trip. She lies swinging gently in her hammock, talking softly with her children and other household members. I sit on a low bench next to a small kerosene lamp that will remain lighted all night to keep away vampire bats. I open my notebook, arrange the sandwich of blank and blue carbon papers, and begin to write up my notes from the day. The lamp casts a dim light, and it is not long before I am squinting and yawning. I go sit in my hammock and write a little while longer by flashlight. It is not long before everyone is in their hammocks discussing the day's events. A neighbor's child is crying and we can hear voices and occasional laughter from the households on either side. I hear Amma's father return from the *congreso,* wash his feet in the metal bucket always kept next to his hammock, and lie down. He tells us about what happened at the meeting. Amma's father always talks with Amma, her sister, and her mother at length about what goes on in the nightly community meetings.

One by one people drop off to sleep, and the night becomes increasingly still and quiet. Finally, only the ever-present rhythmic sound of the waves breaking against the shore and the wind rustling through the fronds of the coconut palm out back can be heard. The moonlight filters through the cracks in the bamboo walls and, finally, I too fall asleep.

4.
Political Economy of San Blas

Although still geographically isolated from the interior of Panama, San Blas has been drawn rapidly into the international economy through the commercialization of coconuts, lobster, and *molas*, and through wage labor migration and tourism. These new economic activities have stimulated changes in Kuna social, economic, and political organization. This chapter analyzes these changes, with the exception of *mola* commercialization and tourism, and their effects on the division of labor by gender and on access and distribution of economic resources within the region, among households, and between the sexes. Taking a historical perspective, I analyze regional change as a complex, dynamic process intricately connected to and affected by national and international change. Chapter 5 focuses on how *mola* commercialization and tourism fit into the region's history.

San Blas, 1600–1925

When the Spaniards arrived, the Kuna lived primarily near the gulf of Urabá in what is today Colombia. According to Kuna oral historians, the Kuna fled from the Spaniards up the jungle rivers and moved into the Darién region of what is now Panama. Contact with the Spanish starting in the 1600s has been characterized as violent and trade was limited (Langebaek 1991).

Subsequently, the Kuna engaged in lucrative trade with the Scots, the French, and the British colony of Jamaica. Kuna chiefs learned European languages and traveled throughout the Caribbean. The Kuna also traded with pirates as early as the 1600s, perhaps even earlier (Stout 1947:53). A Scottish colony was established in 1698. Alliances and trade relations with Kuna communities were established and maintained until the 1700s, when the Spanish drove out the Scots for good (Langebaek 1991).

In the 1700s, the French began to trade with the Kuna and to forge military alliances that protected both parties from the Spanish and the British (Stier 1979; Langebaek 1991). Relations were so good that intermarriages occurred. In the 1740s, however, the French began to cultivate cacao for export and soon thereafter to use Kuna labor (Stier 1979:78–82). Relations between the two groups deteriorated until the Kuna rebelled and attacked the French settlers and drove them out of the region (Langebaek 1991). The Kuna took over the production of cacao (an estimated seventy-three properties with about one hundred thousand trees; Cuervo 1891:258, cited in Langebaek 1991) and began to trade with the British for guns, ammunition, tools, and cloth. By the 1850s, maritime trade with pirates and merchants was well developed; it has continued to provide the Kuna with a steady source of goods to the present.

By the early 1900s, most Kuna villages were located in three distinct areas. A few small communities remained in Colombia, three others were near the headwaters of the Bayano River in the Darién region, and most were located along the San Blas coast. The Bayano region was relatively isolated from Panama's urban centers between 1890 and 1940 (Wali 1984:67). "Money was practically unknown in the Bayano. Items such as salt or kerosene were obtained through barter from San Blas villages, with whom close ties were always maintained through trade and inter-marriage" (Wali 1984:72).

Until the mid-1800s, Kuna villages were located on the banks of freshwater mainland rivers and not on islands, as most communities are today.[1] The Kuna were egalitarian and lived in extended matrilocal households. Land was plentiful and subsistence agriculture, hunting, and fishing were the mainstays of life. Men hunted and fished while women were primarily responsible for agricultural production. In the late 1600s, a surgeon-explorer on a pirate ship who lived for several months with indigenous people in the Darién described the division of labor by gender thus: "The men first clear the Plantations, and bring them into order, but the Women have all the trouble of them afterwards; the digging, hoeing, planting, plucking the Maize, and setting Yams, and every thing of Husbandry is left to them, but only the cutting down of Trees, or such Work that requires greater Strength. The Women also have the managing of Affairs within Doors, for they are in general Drudges of the Family" (Wafer 1903:150).

Over the last half of the nineteenth century, four major interrelated changes occurred that affected articulation of the region with the international economy, the division of labor by gender, and Kuna households' access to resources. Coconuts were commercialized,

Kuna communities began to move gradually out to the coast and onto islands located near the mouths of freshwater rivers, Kuna males took over the formerly female-based subsistence production activities, and a property ownership and inheritance system was developed.

Coconut Commercialization

Coconuts grew wild along the shore of San Blas and on the sandy islands just off the coast. Until the late 1800s, they were traded along with tortoiseshell, vegetable ivory, cacao, and ipecac, which were "gathered, fished for, or furnished from the food crops already on hand" (Stout 1947:73). By 1870, however, increased demand by traders for coconuts led to their planting and commercial exploitation. With the decline of the market for ipecac, vegetable ivory, cacao, and tortoiseshell, coconuts rapidly became the principal medium for trade and an increasingly important source of income for the Kuna (Stout 1947:74).

Beginning in the mid-1800s, entire Kuna villages started gradually to move out to inhabit the sandy islands located near the mouths of freshwater rivers. Anthropologists' explanations for the move point to epidemics, probably due to malaria-carrying mosquitoes. They also argue, however, that with commercialization of coconuts, moving to the islands gave the Kuna easier access to traders who traveled up and down the coast by boat (Stout 1947; Holloman 1969; Stier 1979). Movement to the coast also brought them closer to their coconuts. "At the turn of the century, Kuna in many parts of San Blas industriously planted every suitable uninhabitable island to palms, along with great stretches of mainland shore" (Howe 1986*b*:14).

Concurrent with commercialization of coconuts and relocation of many mainland villages to the islands, Kuna men from these islands increasingly took over subsistence agricultural production while women turned their attention to the coconut trade. This shift did not occur in all of the Kuna communities, nor did it happen all at once. Some of these differences will be described and explored in chapters 8, 9, and 10 within the context of specific communities. Still, despite the variations, overall, men took increasing responsibility for plantain, corn, rice, yucca, fruit, and sugarcane production.

Both men and women planted, weeded, and harvested coconuts, but the women from each household were usually the ones to exchange them for goods or cash. Women continued to be responsible for child care, food preparation, food preservation, and other tasks related to household maintenance. They also sewed *molas* for them-

Kuna canoes approaching a Colombian trade schooner

selves, their daughters, and elderly mothers with failing eyesight. Men continued to hunt, fish, and craft many needed household items such as baskets, fans, stools, and ladles. They often still sewed their own clothes, although increasingly, men wore purchased western clothing.

Why this shift from female- to male-centered agriculture occurred is not clear. One anthropologist, working from secondary sources, argues that the increasing distance of fields from the village may explain why agricultural production became male- instead of female-centered. Population growth forced men to clear fields located deeper in the jungle (Brown 1980). Some fields were up to five miles from the village, so that cultivators were required to spend the night there (Marshall 1950: 92, cited by Brown). Brown assumes that women did not want to travel so far from the village.

In contrast with Brown's findings, the present study shows that the shift in division of labor by gender was not homogeneous throughout the region and that, even though men took over primary responsibility for agricultural production, some women continue to participate even today. Moreover, in 1985 women from several communities reported that they regularly traveled such distances (usually with male relatives), and elderly women remembered that when young they had walked for two and three days to visit Kuna communities located in the Darién. Thus, the increased distance of the fields does not sufficiently explain women's decreased participation in agricultural activities. Both elderly men and women, interviewed in 1985 about changes in the division of labor by gender in their communities around the turn of the century, agreed that distance was not a factor but could not provide any alternative explanations.

A missionary's description of women's work in the 1940s also provides evidence that the shift from female-centered to male-centered agricultural production was not complete. His decription is as follows: "[Women] Sweep the street in the morning, carry water two or three times a week and wash clothes . . . Help their husbands with work in the jungle: harvest coconuts, rice, sugarcane, cacao; plant corn, yuca, ñame [and other crops] . . . they process sugar cane every day" (Puig 1948:51).

When women decreased their agricultural activities, their husbands, sons, and other affinal male relatives took over the cultivation of subsistence plots and coconut groves. Women, however, continued, to own their own land and to control the produce from their own subsistence plots as well as that from their husbands' plots. Initially, neither the commercialization of coconuts nor the resulting shift from female to male responsibility for subsistence production substantially altered Kuna women's access to or control over resources.

Property Ownership and Inheritance

Private property did not exist among the Kuna until the mid- to late nineteenth century. Increased population pressure and the cash cropping of coconuts precipitated this change (Howe 1976). Inheritance of land is bilateral. Although sons and daughters inherit approximately equal amounts of land, men have greater possibilities for acquiring land than do women. Women inherit, but do not lay claim to, new plots of land. Only men clear uncultivated land. For example, virgin jungle may be claimed by clearing and cultivating a plot. Whoever clears the land retains usufruct rights, which are passed down to his children. Spouses do not inherit land from one another.

Coconut groves, located on the mainland coast or on uninhabited islands, may be inherited by an individual or by a "cognatic descent-based corporation" (Howe 1976:158). Cognatic descent-based corporations in San Blas consist of groups of descendants of a male or female ancestor that collectively own and exploit coconut groves and sometimes agricultural lands. For example, if a senior woman gives a coconut grove collectively to her six children, these children and eventually their children would form the cognatic descent-based corporation or group. The usufruct rights to harvest the coconut trees on that plot would rotate among them. In this particular case, each son or daughter would probably take a two-month turn every year. If one of the heirs has four children, they, in turn, will inherit their parent's two-month harvesting period. They might split the two months into week-long harvesting rights or, alternatively, divide it up into one-month periods every other year (Howe 1976:155–157). On uninhabited islands rights to harvest coconut trees and usufruct rights to sand, entitling the "owner" to catch sea turtles that come to lay their eggs on the beach, may belong to different parties.

Assimilation and Revolution

Panama, previously part of Colombia, became an independent nation in 1903. The new government did not have sufficient resources to subdue and incorporate the Kuna who inhabited several dozen villages along the San Blas coast (as well as a few on rivers well inland) into the new nation (Howe 1990:144). They turned to missionaries for help. Father Leonardo Gassó went to San Blas in 1906, to the island of Nargana. He gained some support until he left in late 1911 or 1912 but "threw the community into turmoil, sending shock waves throughout the region and provoking antagonism and conflict" (Howe 1990:146). He attempted to suppress *chicha* ceremonies and the Kuna's sacred gatherings. In 1913, Anna Coope, a nondenominational Protestant missionary, secured permission to establish a mission school on Nargana. In contrast to Gassó, Coope was willing to "put up with a great deal of native custom" (Howe 1990:153).

Missionary attempts to subdue the Kuna were not successful. Howe (1990:162) writes: "The most important effect of mission rivalry up to 1920 on the later secular struggles was to establish in the minds of police and bureaucrats that the contest was not just between civilization and savagery, but in part between Panamanian and North American culture. . . . What is most striking is the way in which Kuna converts appropriated missions for their own purposes, and the degree to which mission rivalry affected the consciousness, not of the Kuna, but of the administrators and police sent to pacify them."

In early 1915, the government created a new administrative unit, the Circunscripción de San Blas, and installed a governor on the island of El Porvenir, located at the western end of San Blas. Government schools and police detachments were sent to Nargana, Nusatupu, and two other villages (Howe 1990:154). During the years that followed, local *congresos*, political-religious meetinghouses of the

Kuna, were shut down in many communities; a few were burned. Traditional Kuna women's dress, methods of healing, and other forms of sociopolitical expression were prohibited. Those who refused to comply were fined, jailed, and sometimes beaten. On many islands schools were established where Kuna children were expected to learn Spanish.

A group of conservative and moderate Kuna responded to the Panamanian government's attempts to "assimilate" them by revolting. An uprising known as the Revolución Tule (Kuna Revolution) was planned in secret and became a reality in February of 1925 (Falla 1979b; Herrera 1972; Howe 1974, 1986a, 1986b, and forthcoming). All of the colonial police who did not flee were killed. Kuna rebel leadership declared San Blas an "independent republic" (Howe 1986a:63).

Interestingly, the U.S. government played an important role in facilitating the negotiations between the Kuna and the Panamanian government following the revolt.

> The U.S. Minister, John Glover South, put together a mixed Panamanian and North American party on the USS Cleveland, a cruiser of the "Special Service [i.e., intervention] squadron" and sailed for San Blas. . . . After interviewing the Indian leaders and coming to sympathize with their plight, Minister South flew back to Panama to fetch the Panamanian Minister of Foreign Affairs, H. J. Alfaro. . . . With South as a mediator and witness, the Kuna and the Panamanian government rapidly came to a peace agreement, under which the Indians renewed their allegiance to Panama while the police withdrew. (Howe 1986a:63)

Through the revolt the Kuna procured the right to practice their socioeconomic and political traditions without direct interference from the Panamanian government. The Kuna Revolution was the start of a negotiation process between the Kuna and the Panamanian government over who has the right and power to make decisions that affect the San Blas region.[2] Kuna women's right to wear their "traditional dress" was at the heart of the revolution.

Postrevolutionary Change, 1925–1968

Major social changes occurred after the 1925 revolt. The Revolución Tule marked a turning point in Kuna history when the Kuna began consciously to struggle for self-determination and local participation in and control over economic, social, and political processes. These struggles continue to the present. The Kuna effected changes in land-ownership, political organization, and the social organization of village life and entrepreneurial activity. Concurrently, the San Blas Kuna became rapidly incorporated into the cash economy through wage labor migration, tourism, and the commercialization of coconuts, *molas*, and lobster. Information about tourism and the commercialization of *molas* is not presented in this chapter but will be the focus of chapter 5.

Political and Social Organization

After the Revolution, political leaders, who had previously operated more or less independently of one another, joined forces in order to negotiate as one unit with the Panamanian government. Local meetinghouses were rebuilt, Kuna authorities reinstated, and a general Kuna *congreso*, comprising local authorities representing each village, was established. The Congreso General Kuna created a unified political entity that can negotiate with the Panamanian government. Today this general *congreso* meets approximately every six months; emergency sessions are called if a crisis occurs. Different islands take turns hosting meetings.

Kuna leaders viewed ownership of land as the first essential step toward an indigenous path to "economic development" that would celebrate and support their ethnic identity while giving them increasing control over resources at the local level. The Congreso General Kuna has attained a number of important achievements that support their rights to self-determination. In 1930, partial autonomy for San Blas was affirmed through negotiations with the Panamanian government (Falla 1979*b*:87–89). In 1938, the region was officially recognized as a Kuna reserve, and the new constitution known as the Carta Orgánica de San Blas was approved in 1945 (Stout 1947:87; Holloman 1969:453–454).

Legal recognition of San Blas as a territory collectively owned by the Kuna people had implications for the economic organization of the region. The Carta Orgánica prohibited non-Kuna from purchasing, renting, or otherwise using land within Kuna territory. This law has been used by the Kuna to ensure that all enterprise within the San Blas region is owned and operated by Kuna and not by outsiders. A subsequent law (Ley 16) passed by the Panamanian government in 1953 further delineated the reserve's boundaries as well as political and economic relations between the Kuna and the national government.

Since 1938 all lands located within the *comarca* of San Blas are owned collectively by the San Blas Kuna, though they do not own subsoil rights.[3] The Kuna recognize individuals' rights to land. According to Kuna law, whoever first clears a plot may pass the land down to heirs. Since only men clear land, women generally inherit easily accessible, already-producing fields. Women's brothers are expected to clear unclaimed land and often inherit fallow plots. Heirs retain their rights to land even if it has not been cultivated for many years.[4]

Nele Kantule was a major revolutionary leader. He is particularly noted for viewing the assimilation process as destructive to the Kuna way of life (Holloman 1969). After the 1925 revolution he and, according to some informants, Cimral Colman, another Kuna leader (Howe 1986b:115), were instrumental in encouraging villages to return to what were considered ancient "traditional" Kuna forms of sociopolitical and economic organization, including communal landownership and collective labor arrangements. Some of these forms, however, like the collectivization of small business, were new to the Kuna.

Many communities added "chiefs of things," each responsible for a specific communal task. These new offices included "a 'house chief' (*ney sakla*) to supervise home building; an 'eagle chief' (*sulup sakla*) to handle marriage ceremonies; a 'chicha chief' (*inna sakla*) to manage chicha ceremonies and other female rites of passage; . . . a 'path chief' (*ikar sakla*) to lead communal clearing of mainland paths; a 'cemetery chief' (*uan sakla*) to supervise maintenance of village burying grounds; and a 'canoes chief' (*ur sakla*) to organize the work parties that in those days dragged roughed-out hulls from the forest to the water" (Howe 1986b:114).

In more recent years, collaborative work parties have been organized through the *congresos* for a wide variety of community improvement projects, including the construction and maintenance of aqueducts and boat docks (Holloman 1969). Activities are divided by gender, with each activity coordinated by a member of the appropriate sex. For example, men are responsible for house construction while the task of women is to provide them with food, drink, and certain building materials. Women often haul heavy loads of sand and rock.

Initially, social pressure was sufficient to ensure that all adult community members participated in these projects. Eventually, a system of fines was developed to punish those who did not cooperate and to ensure that community members living in Panama City and those with full-time jobs, like schoolteachers, contributed.

Communities also began to clear land for collectively owned and collectively exploited subsistence crops and coconut plantations (Howe 1986b). The harvest was either consumed during community festivities or distributed among households. Likewise, income from coconut sales was distributed, used to finance projects, or invested in other community enterprises such as running a store or purchasing and operating a trade boat.[5] Community activities were organized through the local *congresos*.

Small collective entrepreneurial groups were also encouraged. These groups, named *sociedades*, or voluntary associations, were aggregates of friends, relatives, and neighbors (Holloman 1969; Shatto 1972). Members contributed initial capital in the form of shares and, subsequently, labor. *Sociedades* were organized around specific economic activities such as selling gasoline or operating retail stores, restaurants, and trading boats, to mention a few. Membership could be all male, all female, or mixed. In 1985, mothers often paid for shares and worked in one or more of their children's names. The "children's" profits from *sociedad* activities, distributed among members, were saved for a particular purpose. Financing *chicha* celebrations, changing into *mola,* and buying educational supplies were popular uses for these savings. Since the 1930s, *sociedades* have become one of the principal forms through which economic activities are carried out in the region.

Sociedades were also organized to clear land for subsistence production and for coconut cultivation. This new way of organizing production had implications for women's use and inheritance of land. The rights to harvest a coconut grove or subsistence plot cleared and planted by a *sociedad* are passed down in the same way as are coconut groves belonging to cognative, or nonunilineal, descent groups (Howe 1976). Rights to part of the *sociedad* harvest are alienable, however. Regular participation in maintenance-related tasks such as weeding, clearing paths, and, in the case of subsistence plots, planting and harvesting is required in order to retain inherited rights.[6]

Introduction of *sociedades* and communal entrepreneurial activities expanded both men's and women's access to resources while retaining egalitarian characteristics of Kuna social organization even as San Blas moved rapidly into the cash economy. As will be discussed in greater detail in chapters 8, 9, and 10, however, not all women were affected by the shift from subsistence-based to cash-dependent economy in the same way. Furthermore, although women continued to own land and harvest rights, they could lose their inherited rights in *sociedad* subsistence plots and coconut groves more easily than could men.

During World War II, changes in the coconut trade led to decreased subsistence agricultural production in many San Blas communities. The United States turned to Panama when its primary source of coconuts in the Philippines was cut off by the war (Chapin 1983:463). One merchant offered the Kuna ten cents for coconuts as compared to the five cents per dozen to a penny per coconut that the Kuna had been receiving (Chapin 1983:463). On many islands, *sociedades* that previously planted subsistence crops began to plant coconuts instead. Even when the market for these coconuts dropped (Philippine plantations came back into production), the *sociedades* did not return to planting subsistence crops (Chapin 1983).

Household Organization

At this point, before discussing wage labor migration, a description of household organization and the organization of labor within households would be useful. The prototypical Kuna household as described by Stout (1947), Holloman (1969, 1976), and Howe (1985) is matrilocal, comprising a senior couple, one or more married daughters with their husbands and children, and the senior couple's unmarried children. Researchers have disagreed about what is most important for our understanding of Kuna household organization. Stout (1947) viewed female ownership and inheritance of the house to be key. In contrast, Holloman (1976:137) argues that "the most important functional attribute of the Cuna household is that it is the unit of subsistence production, and agricultural work organization is based upon relationships among males." She views female household ownership as a "complementary but restricted theme" (Holloman 1969:182). Costello (1982:82) argues that "household organization is not best seen simply as the application of norms. Rather, individuals with different household statuses have different and somewhat conflicting interests, resources, and strategies."

Building on Costello's work, my research argues that households and the individuals with sometimes conflicting, sometimes converging interests, resources, and strategies who make up those households must be situated within a larger political-economic and historical framework. How the region as a whole, communities within that region, and households within those communities are articulated with the global economic system through migration, commercialization, and political intrigue at specific or different points in time affects Kuna household organization. Discussing households in isolation from this larger framework presents only a partial picture and makes it difficult to explain the high degree of variation within the San Blas region.

Households may reorganize any number of times within the life span of any given generation. For example, women may return to their mothers' households each time their husbands go to Panama City to work. Also, kin, unrelated children, visitors, teachers or other government-paid employees working in the village, and even an anthropologist or two may join any given household for several days, months, or even years.

Sleeping houses where husband, wife, and children sleep are considered independent households only when their residents cook their own food and do not depend on another household to provide for their daily needs. One elderly Kuna man commented that the young people wanted to be independent (i.e., to sleep separately from the rest of the household), but they always returned at mealtime. In his view, the young men did not work hard enough to raise crops necessary to sustain their wives and children.

In the past, young people did not choose their own partners. The girl's father and mother chose a young man, based on his ability to work, and made arrangements for the marriage, usually without the knowledge of either young person. Today, young people usually choose their own partners. Couples may marry in the hammock—a short ritual considered to be the "traditional" form of marriage. Alternatively, they may present themselves to the *congreso* and state their intention to marry. Unmarried men who move in with women are considered "married," and such couples are expected to notify the *congreso*. Some of the younger women who meet their husbands in Panama City marry there according to civil law. Religious ceremonies either in San Blas or in Panama City are another possibility. Any child resulting from a union uses the biological father's surnames. If the biological father refuses to recognize his baby, the child uses the mother's name. No apparent stigma is attached to children bearing their mother's name or to their mothers. Women retain their own names.

No money, food, land, or other goods are exchanged between households before, during, or after the marriage. Husband and wife each retain rights to their own property and other resources. If one spouse dies, the dead spouse's property cannot be inherited by the survivor but is distributed among the deceased's offspring. If a man marries a woman from another community, he must often pay a fee to her *congreso* to help ensure that he is serious about the commitment. For example, on one island in-marrying men are charged one hundred dollars, half of which is refundable if the couple is still married after two years. Some *congresos* also require a letter from the man's home village certifying that he is single.

Once married, a man is expected to reside in his mother-in-law's household and to work under the direction of his father-in-law. Any fish caught, game hunted, or produce harvested must be given to his mother-in-law to distribute. This is true even regarding food harvested from fields to which he owns the rights.

Wage Labor Migration

Unlike in the rest of Latin America, male, not female, out-migration predominates in San Blas (Stier 1983). Migration of Kuna men from San Blas began long before the turn of the century. Kuna men traveled around the world working as sailors on European and U.S. trade boats.[7] In the early 1900s, young boys from several islands were sent to secular and religious schools in Panama City, the United States, and Venezuela (Howe 1990: 144, 150, 152).[8] These educational experiences laid the groundwork for wage labor migration.

Beginning in the 1930s, the numbers of Kuna men moving to Panama City and to Colón in search of wage labor increased. "Since about 1930 a rapidly increasing number of young men have been working in the Canal Zone, as laborers and as mess boys in the U.S. Army posts. During the same period thousands more have found employment in Colón and Panama City, usually in restaurants and bars; and several hundred young women, mostly from Nargana and Corazón de Jesús, have gone to the cities where they often work as housemaids" (Stout 1947:57).

Throughout the first half of the 1900s, Kuna parents often sent their children to live and work in a *waga* (non-Kuna) household so that they could attend school. Both boys and girls were sent. Arrangements varied from households in which the youths were treated as members of the family to those in which children were exploited as domestic servants, beaten, and sometimes not even allowed to attend school.

According to the 1950 and 1960 censuses, 1,058 and 2,096 Kuna, respectively, lived outside of San Blas (Howe 1986b: 15). In the 1980s, there were an estimated 10,000 Kuna living outside of San Blas, primarily in Panama City and Colón, Panama's two major cities (Eligio Alvarado, personal communication). Many Kuna men also migrate to Changuinola, a banana plantation located in western Panama (Bourgois 1988).

In Panama City, the Kuna encountered a hierarchical division of labor by gender, with lower-paying jobs defined as "women's" work (Torres de Araúz 1975). Ethnicity also defined possibilities for men and women in different ways. For example, Kuna women who continued to wear *molas,* symbolizing their identity as Kuna women, in general had a difficult time finding jobs. In 1985, one Kuna woman who wore *molas* taught at the university. Nonetheless, most women who continued to wear *molas* in Panama City, as many did, worked as domestics, sewed *molas* for sale, or worked for primarily Kuna projects such as the *mola* cooperative and a Kuna housing project (directed by a Kuna woman). Kuna women in Panama City who worked as secretaries or store clerks wore western clothing. Most Kuna men wear western clothing.

More detailed research on the differential impact of migration on Kuna men and women is needed to fully understand the relationship between gender, ethnicity, and access to resources. Temporary or permanent absence of men who left children to be supported by their mothers and grandparents was a widespread pattern in the 1980s and has not yet been discussed in the literature on San Blas. How men's migration affects women's access to resources, their need for cash income, and their role in *mola* commercialization will be discussed, among other important factors impinging on the life of Kuna households, in the chapters to follow.

Overall, men have access to better-paying jobs outside of San Blas than do women. Costello's studies of migration patterns from Río Azúcar in 1970 and 1978 found that single males under thirty worked for short periods at unskilled jobs such as "kitchen helpers and janitors." Educated younger men and "middle-aged married men" sought skilled and semiskilled jobs with the Panama Canal Company, the U.S. military, or in the private sector. Young women worked as domestics, while educated women found skilled and semiskilled jobs in the garment industry, worked as secretaries and store clerks, or held "semiprofessional positions within the education and public health services of the national government" (Costello 1982:74). Sometimes Kuna children were sent by their parents to live in Panamanian households to work as house servants, with the understanding that they would also attend school.

In an attempt to prevent alienation, Nele Kantule encouraged the organization of *sociedades* in Panama City, each comprising members of a particular community (Holloman 1969:456). These *sociedades,* many of which are still in operation, were an extension of community organization. Individuals retained their membership in a particular community, now contributing money instead of labor to collective work projects.

Researchers differ in their descriptions of how migration has affected Kuna household organization. Holloman (1976) views Kuna household organization as remaining constant overall and supporting women and children when men migrate. Costello's 1970 and 1978 censuses of Río Azúcar, however, showed "a shift in residence patterns from matriuxorilocal (female-focused) to neolocal postmarital residence" (Costello 1982:70). In this community, women often migrated with their husbands. Stier (1983:20) notes that migration is a way for sons-in-law to escape the traditional authority of their fathers-in-law. Data for the three communities I studied (one of which was the same community that Holloman surveyed) support Holloman's observation. As in *mola* commercialization, one might expect also to find quite different patterns of migration and impact on households emerging within the region.

Different strategies for household maintenance are emerging within the region as well. Costello's 1970 census of Río Azúcar (another Kuna island community) revealed that most male migrants' spouses not only accompanied them to Panama City, but also worked full- or part-time in wage labor and helped support their households. Similar patterns were noted in 1978. Labor migration has been used as a way for young males to gain independence from extended matriuxorilocal households. In the process, however, women on Río Azúcar lost their ownership rights to house sites (Costello 1982:86).

My data show a different pattern emerging in the communities of Carti-Sugtupu, Tupile, and Mansucun. Many women are not accompanying their spouses to Panama City; they are remaining in or returning to their mother's households in San Blas. In some cases, these women are helping support their husbands and in-school children in Panama City as well as providing essential income to the households they live in.

Commercialization of Lobster

Lobster and, to a lesser extent, crabs and octopus began to be commercialized in the 1960s (Holloman 1969; Herrera 1972:121). Unlike coconut cash cropping, in which any man could be involved because it required no special tools or skills, diving for lobster is considered a young man's activity. Oxygen tanks are not used, and diving requires lung capacity that men over the age of thirty-five rarely have. Equipment needed for diving includes a spear gun and a mask; flippers are optional. In the 1980s, the Congreso General Kuna actually prohibited the use of oxygen tanks. Few divers have their own equipment. Most borrow spear guns and masks from their friends in exchange for a portion of the catch. In 1985, spear guns cost forty dollars in the local stores.

Diving for lobster is done almost exclusively in the rainy season, when the sea is relatively calm. It is combined with men's responsibilities for agricultural production and fishing. Divers usually spear fish for their households, in addition to lobster, when they dive.[9] Men usually work in pairs, one partner diving while the other waits in the boat. If a motor is available, a group of men may go out together. Sometimes men will go to a distant island where lobsters are known to be abundant. They may stay there for several days or weeks diving. Profits are divided evenly among all the men who go, the boat owner, and the man who owns the motor. Thus, if one man went diving and allowed the group to use his boat and motor, he would receive three shares.

Lobsters are purchased in San Blas by non-Kuna agents who travel weekly to the region in their private planes. Kuna store owners with freezers also serve as brokers, buying lobster and octopus from divers on their own and sometimes on other islands. Lobster commercialization has become an important source of income for young men on many islands. In the late 1960s, the price for lobster varied between $.25 and $.40 per pound. By 1985, Kuna divers were receiving $4.00 per pound for lobster tails and approximately $2.50 per pound for whole lobsters.

Income from lobster sales contrasts sharply with that from coconuts in the way it is utilized. While coconut income is expected to be contributed toward household expenses, most men consider income from lobster sales their own and pocket it. Although many men do contribute part of this income to household expenses, this appears to be the exception rather than the rule. Young wives complain that their husbands spend all their money on clothes, beer, and eating out. Mothers-in-law and fathers-in-law echo this view. In 1985, tape decks, athletic shoes, wristwatches, and T-shirts with pictures of rock stars and the Olympic games were among the visible consumer items purchased by young men. Several divers I interviewed in 1985 felt that they worked hard for their money and had a right to spend it as they pleased as long as they provided plantains, fish, and firewood for their households.

Political and Economic Change, 1968–1985

In 1968, Lt. Col. Omar Torrijos took charge of Panama's national government. In 1972, a new constitution was implemented, bringing about political changes of an ideological, structural, and organizational nature that markedly affected the political administration of San Blas. Under the new constitution, new political boundaries were drawn throughout Panama. San Blas became politically and admin-istratively separate from the province of Colón. Government minis-tries, previously administered through Colón, opened regional of-fices in San Blas. The *comarca* of San Blas was divided into four subareas called *corregimientos*. Each *corregimiento* was to be re-sponsible for electing one representative to the newly formed Asam-blea Nacional de Representantes de Corregimientos. These represen-tatives, in turn, were to be responsible for economic development planning within their respective areas. They also were to administer government funds toward that end.

Changes in the political-administrative structure went beyond the election and activities of these four area representatives. Due to the nature of the new political boundaries, in 1980 the Kuna were able to elect a Kuna representative to the national legislature. Thus, for the first time in history the Kuna, as a group, were officially repre-sented in politics at the national level.

The possibility of influencing local representation at the national level stimulated Kuna men and women to participate actively in na-tional political parties. Local chapters of a wide range of political par-ties were organized within Kuna communities. In most villages, women organized their own chapters and activities separately from the men's, even within the same political party. In 1985, on some islands fund-raising and other activities continued all year, even in the absence of electoral campaigns. Organized like *sociedades*, these groups often ran small businesses. For example, one chapter ran a store, another baked and sold bread, and a third sold cooked food. Usually, each had its own house, which served as a social meeting place.

In the 1970s, a new position titled "administrative *sakla*" was cre-ated by the national government for San Blas. These new *saklas*, paid a small stipend by the national government, were responsible for po-litical, economic, judicial, and administrative tasks. Religion, on the other hand, was left to the care of the "traditional *saklas*." Before the 1970s, every village in San Blas had four to six traditional *saklas*, who were considered political as well as religious leaders. The cre-ation of this new administrative position divided up leadership re-sponsibilities. It also created severe conflicts among the leadership of many communities. Subsequently, many islands decided to ap-point one person to both positions, an innovative solution that re-solved many of the conflicts.

These changes in political organization affected the region's access to economic resources and the extent of men's and women's political participation. For the first time in history, the Kuna controlled government funds appropriated for the region's use. Administrative and economic development funds became tied to party politics, however. Under pressure from the four representatives, the Congreso General Kuna divided the budget into four equal parts. This prevented coordinated regionwide projects from being organized. In the 1980s, some Kuna leaders were concerned that funds were being used selectively to further party solidarity and to ensure candidates' reelection. For example, funds were often used to buy stoves for local political party chapters or to fund the construction of a cement boat dock or landing strip, all popular requests from local communities. Using funds in this way did little to address the many serious economic and social problems facing the region.

Although both Kuna men and women became active in national politics in new ways, these changes were greater for women than they were for men. Kuna women gained opportunities to hold formal political leadership positions, which they had not had in the local political structure. For example, at least one woman has served as the administrative *sakla* of her community; at least two Kuna women have run as candidates for representative to the Asamblea Nacional, though neither won; and in the mid-1980s, a woman was selected by the Congreso General Kuna as temporary governor of San Blas.

Although women have gained new opportunities for political participation, they are still left out of regional and local economic development planning activities. For example, although the *mola* cooperative was officially recognized as a regionwide Kuna organization by the Congreso General Kuna, as of 1985 its representatives had not been invited to participate in regionwide economic development planning meetings. Similarly, women were often left out of other important meetings in their home communities where economic development strategies for the region were discussed. As a result, even as late as 1984, the sale of *molas* was usually not even mentioned when male political leaders and development planners discussed the major economic resources and problems affecting the region. In general, women's economic contributions and needs were rarely discussed.

From a national perspective, the Torrijos government viewed modernization as the path to development. In addition to the changes designed to encourage greater popular participation in politics through representation at the local level, the Torrijos government focused on providing transportation, health, and educational facilities and services to the rural areas. By 1985, the San Blas region had a hospital, approximately fourteen airstrips, at least four secondary schools, primary schools in nearly all communities, and a number of community health centers. Much of this infrastructure was built during the 1970s by the Torrijos government.

As schools and health centers were built, new jobs were created in San Blas. Initially, these new jobs were filled by non-Kuna Panamanians; however, as more and more Kuna received training in the fields of health and education, they increasingly took over these jobs. Thus was created a small group of Kuna living in San Blas who received steady salaries from the national government.

Aqueducts bringing fresh water to the islands from mainland rivers were also constructed during this period. Women on islands without aqueducts would spend many hours per day fetching water for drinking, cooking, washing, and bathing. The construction of aqueducts has contributed to a decrease in women's involvement in agricultural and gathering activities. While this new technology considerably increased women's available time for sewing *molas,* it resulted in a decreased variety of foodstuffs in the Kuna diet. As will be described in greater detail in the last half of this book, Kuna women often hunted river shrimp and crab and gathered snails and fruit on their trips to the river for water.

Education took on new importance to the Kuna during the Torrijos years. Construction of schools on the islands allowed more children the possibility of receiving a primary and secondary (junior high school) education without going to Panama City. Before the 1960s, Kuna children had often been sent to live with a non-Kuna household to work and attend school. Starting in the 1960s, fathers began to accompany their children to the city. Because the fathers had low-paying jobs, these urban households were often supported by income from women's *mola* sales. For example, in 1981 José had three school-age children. He found a job as a kitchen helper in a restaurant in Panama City and rented a one-room apartment in a run-down neighborhood where many Kuna lived. His three children lived with him and attended school. José's wife remained in San Blas with the younger children, sewed *molas,* and regularly sent money to Panama City to help support her children's studies. In some households, entire nuclear components moved to Panama City. Younger children were often left with grandparents. With the exception of working as a domestic or as a prostitute, few jobs were available to uneducated Kuna women living in the city, so these women continued to sew and sell their *molas* to help maintain the household.

An increasing number of Kuna students started attending the university and studied a wide range of subjects, including medicine, nursing, education, history, archaeology, and dance. A smaller number of Kuna pursued graduate studies abroad. In 1985, there were two anthropologists, a sociologist, a linguist, and a medical doctor, to mention a few, who had completed graduate degrees

Overall, the San Blas region became increasingly interconnected with the national government during the Torrijos years through educational, political, and economic activities. The economic and political structures developed under Torrijos have remained intact.

Access to Resources in the 1980s

In the 1980s, Kuna men and women had access to resources as community, *sociedad*, and household members. As was described in the previous section, access to resources was also defined vis-à-vis regionwide efforts to keep resources in and to channel them to San Blas, primarily through the national government. Profits from community enterprises and fines were channeled into projects that benefited the entire village. *Sociedades* might have all male members, all female members, or a mixed membership. Participation in this form of social organization was accessible to any person, man or woman. Household resources, as was mentioned earlier in the chapter, were also available to both sexes. Men and women both inherited land, though women distributed food. Overall, access to these basic resources was symmetrical among community members and between the sexes.

This did not mean that variations among households did not exist. Households or individuals had different amounts of land and money. These differences, however, did not translate into differential access to labor or to power. Furthermore, as was discussed previously, inheritance patterns prevented wealth accumulation and ensured the redistribution of usufruct rights to land and to coconut trees among households across the generations.

In 1985, within San Blas wage labor opportunities were equally accessible to Kuna men and women. Salaried government positions such as teacher and health worker were filled by both sexes. A few positions, such as air traffic controller, national guardsman, and agricultural extension worker, were occupied only by men. Community salaried positions such as airport attendant, accountant, and store clerk, however, might be given to either a man or a woman. A few jobs, such as boat captain, sailor, and mechanic, were filled exclusively by men. They received salaries similar to those paid to other community workers, however. Thus, with the exceptions of diving for lobster and sewing and selling *molas*, inheritance of land and possibilities for participation in most income-generating activities in San Blas were symmetrical between the sexes.

Outside of San Blas, however, wage labor opportunities were stratified by gender. While highly educated women had job opportunities
similar to those of their male counterparts, possibilities for minimally educated men and women were quite different, and women
generally earned lower wages than did men. Men and women who
did not speak Spanish had very few income-generating opportunities
available to them in Panama City.

Socioeconomic Differentiation in San Blas

Stout's (1947:33) description of two social classes, "rich and poor,"
each with different amounts of wealth (canoes, coconut plantations,
clothing, and jewelry), has been challenged by subsequent researchers. Holloman (1969) and Howe (1986b:28) argue that distinct strata
do not exist. Some researchers have argued that inheritence patterns
ensure that accumulated wealth gets distributed among different
households a few generations later (Holloman 1969; Hirschfeld 1976:
52). Howe (1986b:28) is not convinced that this leveling of wealth
pattern works.

This difference of opinion must be settled by empirical data. Given
what we know about regional and subregional differences in San Blas,
it would not be surprising if the pattern of wealth distribution across
the generations works in some communities or households and not
in others. Household case studies that I conducted indicate that who
controls wealth and to what ends vary by the source of wealth as well
as by age and gender differences (see chapters 8, 9, and 10).

Some Kuna are definitely wealthier than others. Factors affecting
socioeconomic differentiation include amount of land a household
controls (Stier 1982:534); ancestors' levels of industriousness in
planting coconuts and the extent to which current household members have planted coconuts; opportunities for paid employment
(Howe 1986b:28); and income from *mola* sales (Tice 1982). Age is
another key variable for understanding differences in wealth: "young
migrant laborers can get consumer goods and lumps of cash, older
men and women hold most of the land" (Howe 1986b:28). Store
ownership does not appear to be clearly linked to migration. Whereas
on the island of Río Azúcar stores were established with savings from
wage labor outside of San Blas (Costello 1975:215), on the island of
Tubuala store-owning households spent less time working outside of
San Blas than did other households (Stier 1983:20).

Stier writes the following about landholding in the community of
Tubuala: "The data available on land inheritance suggests that much
of the land planted to subsistence crops was inherited by males from

their fathers, which would mean that father's landholding, the number of sons who survive to adulthood, and the migration histories of sons are important influences on the amount of land a household controls" (Stier 1982:534). I would argue that, although this may be true, Kuna women's landholdings are equally important to our understanding of the amount of land a household controls. Although sons may not inherit land from their mothers or wives, they do work their wife's lands and may also farm the land passed down to their unmarried sisters. Data are needed on women's landholding and inheritence patterns and how these have been affected by migration and the decreased amount of time women spend on the mainland due to aqueduct construction and *mola* commercialization.

Differences in wealth among households in San Blas do not translate into political power (Howe 1986*b*:29), nor do they usually translate into wealthier households appropriating the labor of poorer ones.[10] Most agricultural labor in San Blas is organized collaboratively at the community and *sociedad* levels and by the senior male or female at the household level. All appropriate-age males and females are required to participate in community labor projects and are fined if they do not. Women sometimes barter agricultural produce or fish in exchange for male labor from another household. Kuna women maintain critical kin, neighbor, and friend-based social networks essential to access, distribution, and consumption of food. Costello (1971:428) notes that "individual profit-making is subservient to community service in commercial activity whenever the two arc in conflict."

Following Marxist-oriented scholars who focus on the relative importance of demographic factors, position in the labor force, and access to productive resources in the process of class formation, class relations among the Kuna are only beginning to emerge (Bourgois 1988). If a wider angle lens is used, however, Kuna producers come into contact with merchants, and class relations become apparent. Bourgois (1988:331) argues that class and ethnicity "cannot be conceived as distinct dimensions, however, because class and ethnicity are not characteristics, but social processes that define one another. Both shape the same 'material reality,' the same structure of power relations and conflict, which also produces them." This study will also assume that class and ethnicity are inseparable, but that gender is interwoven as well. The research presented in the following chapters shows that *mola* commercialization has resulted in variations in wealth among women dependent on their access to capital and on various markets for *molas*. Chapter 5 presents the history of *mola* commercialization.

5.
Mola Commercialization

Our grandmothers did not need to sell their molas *because the land, the animals living there and the sea provided everything they needed to sustain life.*

Carlos Lopez

The sale of *molas* has become one of the most important sources of income for Kuna households in San Blas. This chapter tells the history of *molas* and contextualizes their commercialization within a larger set of social, economic, and political changes, including increased international trade, revolutionary change, decreased agricultural production, the development of national and local tourism, and new interest in and demand for *molas* internationally.

To date, research on *molas* has provided information about the Kuna social context of *mola* use (Sherzer and Sherzer 1976), ethnoaesthetics (Salvador 1976a, 1976b, 1978), and the symbolic importance of *molas* (Helms 1976; Hirschfeld 1976) among the Kuna. In addition, types and variations in *mola* designs have been photographed, described, and categorized (Salvador 1976a, 1978; Parker and Parker 1977; Hartmann 1980). Little attention, however, has been paid to the effects of *mola* commercialization on Kuna social and economic organization. This is surprising, since *mola* sales provide one of the two most important sources of income for the entire region. One notable exception is Swain's (1977) study of *mola* sales in the tourist area of San Blas. She concludes that *mola* commercialization has been a cohesive force, a way for Kuna women to maintain their ethnic identity. Hirschfeld (1976:52) argues that *mola* sales "are a means for maintaining egalitarianism in the distribution of resources." This book argues that, far from being a cohesive force, *mola* commercialization has resulted in an unequal distribution of resources among Kuna women residing in different parts of the re-

Mola cooperative leaders counting income from *mola* sales

gion and between the sexes. It has been one of the most important, yet least studied, social changes to occur in San Blas in this century.

Early *Mola* History

"Mormaknamaloe" (Go sew *molas*) shouted the town crier as he strode around the island. In his wake, a few women, myself included, began to leave our homes and walk to the *congreso*. Once seated on the high-backed wooden benches in the *congreso*, we took out our *molas,* began to sew, and waited for the *sakla* to start chanting. Bamboo walls and a thick thatched roof made the *congreso* quite cool even though the midday sun was blistering outside. Many of the young children who had come with their mothers played in and around the *congreso.* Half an hour passed and fewer than thirty women were sitting in the *congreso.* The *sakla* sent the village policemen to find the rest of the women. Soon thereafter, more women began to arrive. When the *congreso* was nearly filled with women, all bent intently over their unfinished *molas,* the *sakla* began chanting the stories of Kikkatiriyai and Nagagiriyai, two important women in Kuna history. The *sakla* chants in metaphoric language, which the general Kuna population does not understand. The *arkar's* job is to translate what the *sakla* has said into everyday Kuna and to talk about the meaning of the stories and their relation to daily life. Here is one *arkar's* translation of the history of Kikkatiriyai and Nagagiriyai.

Before the arrival of Ipeorkun and Kikkatiriyai, Kuna women wore animal skins decorated with parrot, guacamaya, and other bird feathers. Ipeorkun (male) and Kikkatiriyai (female) were great Kuna teachers who lived about the same time as Jesus Christ. Kikkatiriyai organized a school where she taught other Kuna women to make cloth from a particular tree bark by soaking it in seawater for several days. Fibers from other plants such as *urduk, guiba, naba,* and *ikor* were also used to make cloth. They made the cloth into longish dresses and colored them with black, blue, red, and green dyes made from *mageb, goga, abgi,* and *diskela,* all plants found in the jungle.[1] The dresses had a white, red, and blue border around the bottom. Kikkatiriyai also taught them to weave hammocks and to craft ceramic ware. These objects were all plain solid colors; none were decorated with designs. Designs were discovered at a later time by Nagagiriyai, a great female Kuna *nele.* Nagagiriyai discovered *mola* and other designs in Kalu Duibis, a mythical dwelling made of white rock that only women may enter. Nagagiriyai went to Kalu Duibis in her dreams; there she discovered colorful, geometric designs painted all over the walls. She memorized the designs and their corresponding names in order to teach them to the other Kuna women on her return.[2] The designs were used to decorate *molas, bicha* (interior skirts), hammocks, *wini,* baskets, and ceramic vessels. Each item had its corresponding designs. *Mola* geometric designs were usually patterned and named after common household items and were painted onto bark cloth or onto Kuna women's bodies with natural dyes. (In the 1980s, *molas* with geometric designs were called *muu,* or grandmother, *molas.*)

According to Kuna legend, Nagagiriyai was one of eight great *neles* who taught the Kuna their current customs, traditions, and values, and she was the only female *nele*. Although these teachers lived before the Spanish Conquest, their lessons still serve as guides for behavior.

Men also produced crafts. While Kikkatiriyai was busy teaching the women, Ipeorkun taught the men how to fashion and decorate hunting, fishing, and household tools. These tools included items used by men such as spears, bows, arrows, and canoes (*ulus*). Men also made (and continue to make) baskets, ladles, stools, and fans to keep the fire going for women. They learned to make their own clothing. Men's clothes included a solid-colored shirt with pleats in the front and a pair of pants also without designs. (Some Kuna men continued to make their own clothing in 1985, though most purchased western style clothing.)

Once the story had been interpreted, the *arkar* reminded the women of their responsibilities to sweep, cook, and make *molas*. They were also reminded to be good community members and to collaborate on upcoming work projects.

It is clear from this account that both men and women designed and created beautifully crafted objects that were used in daily life. Men and women did not fashion the same objects, however, nor did they use the same designs. Male and female creative spheres were distinctly separate. *Mola* designs, belonging to the female sphere, existed long before scissors and needles, tools used today to sew cloth *molas*, were available.[3]

The *arkar* does not separately discuss *omekits'* participation in early craft production or how *omekits* fit into the Kuna's conceptualization of gender. (See the section on gender crossing at the end of this chapter for a more detailed discussion of *omekits*, gender, and the division of labor by gender.) In 1985, *omekits* did not wear *molas* themselves but might sew a *mola* for sale or as a gift for a female relative. Anthropologists described *omekit* involvement in making *molas* as early as 1926, before *molas* were commercialized. "In Nargana there is a man who has bathed his eyes with water in which he had placed the leaves of this plant and he draws like a real artist and makes all kinds of beautiful baskets. He can also cut unusually beautiful *molas*" (Nordenskiöld 1938:414). *Omekits* have likewise participated in a wide range of other female tasks.

The first description, by outsiders traveling to the area, of what are today known as *muu mola* designs is similar to that given by the Kuna *arkar*. In 1680, an explorer described the geometric designs painted by the Kuna on their bodies (Wafer 1903). In 1827, a trader described the Kuna women's dress as follows: "they were clothed in wrappers of blue baftas, or stripped cotton of their own manufacture, reaching from the breast to a little lower than the calf of the leg" (Roberts 1827:43). *Mola* designs were not applied to cloth much before the 1900s.

Access to Cloth

From existing accounts it is not clear precisely when cloth, needles, scissors, and thread became available to the Kuna or exactly where they learned the technique for cutting and sewing the layered designs that emerged in the early 1900s. We do know, however, that friendships and commercial relationships were established between the Kuna, pirates, and merchants as early as 1600, perhaps even earlier.

Pirates had the most contact with the Kuna from 1675 to 1725 (Stout 1947:51). The pirate circuit, which included Jamaica, Lesser Antilles, and the Mosquito Coast of Nicaragua, extended down the entire Panamanian Atlantic watershed to the region bordering the Gulf of Urabá near where the Kuna lived. The Kuna often aided pirates entering the Atrato River, providing them with food, water, and a sheltered place to repair their ships in exchange for goods (Torres de Araúz 1974:12). Stout, an anthropologist who worked in San Blas, wrote (1947:51): "it appears probable that nearly every pirate active in the Caribbean and the Bay of Panama during the latter 17th and early 18th centuries was in contact with the Cuna." Trade with English, Dutch, and U.S. trading ships was recorded as early as 1698 (Rose 1929:215). Vessels from Cartagena, Curaçao, Jamaica, and Porto Bello also sailed the San Blas coast during the 1700s and the 1800s (Cullen 1853:70; 1868:169–170). "By the 1850's trade was well developed and though some of it was contraband, it has continued steadily until the present" (Stout 1947:53).

Settlers may also have provided the Kuna with cloth and other goods. A group of Scots seeking wealth in the new world attempted to settle in 1698 and again in 1699 in Anachucuna Bay, located in the eastern part of the region. Malaria and other hardships caused both attempts to fail (Torres de Araúz 1974). In the early 1700s, French Calvinists successfully settled along the San Blas coast, where they planted cacao plantations. They lived in relative peace with the Kuna, trading goods and even marrying Kuna women until 1750, when the Kuna revolted against them. All of the French either fled the region or were killed by the Kuna. French exploitation of Kuna labor on their plantations was one of the underlying causes for the revolt (Severino 1956–1957:312, cited by Stier 1979). Missionaries were also present in the region during this time, though their attempts to convert the Kuna were unsuccessful. Repeatedly, missionaries were killed or expelled from the region.

Although it is clear that the Kuna had at least sporadic access to cloth as far back as the 1600s, there is no known written record of cloth *molas* until the 1800s. In 1868, another explorer described *molas* as "short sleeved chemises extending to the knees" (De Puydt 1868:97). In 1887, yet another traveler wrote: "on the bottom part [of the chemises worn by Kuna women] there is a band of about 10 centimeters with red and yellow designs" (Restrepo Tirado 1887).

Stout provides us with a more detailed description of cloth *molas*. He wrote (1947:67): "Sixty years ago [in the late 1880s] this *mola* was of plain, usually dark blue material with a simple band of red cloth around the bottom. It reached to the knees and was worn with a knee-length underskirt painted with geometric designs. Forty to fifty years ago [1890–1900] women began to use brighter colored cloth when it became accessible through the traders and to decorate the blouse along the hem with a simple applique of contrasting colors."

Decoration of *mola* blouses steadily increased until by the 1920s Kuna women covered all but the yoke and sleeves of their blouses with designs. In the 1920s, *molas* were again described as almost knee-length chemises. They consisted of two decorated panels (two layers thick), sleeves, and a yoke. The same cotton cloth was used for the sleeves, yoke, and bottom panel. This cloth was printed with tiny dots, flowers, or some other pattern, in two contrasting colors. The second, top layer of the panel was one solid color of cloth. Patterns were cut out of this top layer, partially revealing the patterned cloth below. Raw cloth edges were painstakingly folded under and whipstitched into place. Designs were still basically geometric, though *molas* with flowers and animals were also sewn (Brown 1925).

Molas and Revolution

As described in chapter 4, conservative and moderate Kuna successfully revolted in 1925. Though many factors contributed to the revolt, the treatment of Kuna women was a key factor leading to the decision to take action against the colonial police (Howe 1986a).[4] Prior to the Revolution, Kuna women in a number of Kuna communities had been forced to take off their *molas*, to wear western clothes, to remove their nose rings and *wini*, and were prohibited from painting their noses. Kuna women on one island remembered a schoolteacher having told them not to wear their gold nose rings because they looked like pigs. Furthermore, young women were forced to attend obligatory western-style dances and dance with the colonial police. *Chicha* celebrations were prohibited.

Forcing women to change from *mola* to western dress was considered by many Kuna as a way of stripping them of their identity as Kuna people. Not all Kuna, however, agreed on this point. On the island of Nargana the administration forced women to abandon native dress completely. This was not accepted passively: "many inhabitants once again fled to unpacified islands to the East. . . . A few days after the ban on native dress, when police pursued a woman fleeing the policy to the nearby island of Kwepti or Río Azúcar, Claudio Iglesias was killed during a melee in the dark" (Howe 1990:156). Claudio, a young Kuna Catholic, was "fervently nationalist and modernist" and sided with the government teachers and police in their efforts to suppress indigenous customs (Howe 1990:154). Although Coope, the British Protestant missionary, supported the ban on women's traditional dress, she thought it should be done voluntarily and gradually. She completely agreed with the conservatives on other issues like viewing dancing as immoral.

Wearing *molas* has come to symbolize Kuna ethnic pride tied to a "traditional" way of life (Swain 1982:114). *Molas* are "THE Cuna ethnic boundary marker par excellence in that for both Cuna and non-Cuna it is a constantly visual, striking sign of *Cunaité*" (Sherzer and Sherzer 1976:27).[5] After the Revolution, the majority of Kuna women living in the communities where the colonial police had been stationed proudly and defiantly dressed in *mola* and their *asuolos*. Most women living on Nargana, however, the island most heavily influenced by missionaries, continued to wear western clothing (this was still true in 1985). Since the revolt, wearing *mola* has been seen by conservative and moderate Kuna (both male and female) as an important symbol of the Kuna people's right to self-determination.

World War II

The Second World War opened the way for *mola* commercialization. During World War II, the U.S. Air Force set up stable camps near the communities of Carti-Sugtupu, Aligandi, and Pito. Several airstrips built by U.S. forces increased the accessibility of the region. Servicemen purchased *mola* blouses already worn by Kuna women or girls as curiosity pieces to send to their friends and relatives back home. In many cases, friendships were established between Kuna households and U.S. military personnel. When the war was over and the camps were dismantled, many U.S. military and air force men settled down to live with their wives and children in the Canal Zone. Many friendships and contacts that had developed in San Blas continued. Through these contacts new opportunities opened for Kuna men to work in the Canal Zone's military kitchens. This activity, in turn, created a small but steady market for *molas*. Tourists, curious to see these people who wore rings in their noses and beads around their arms and legs, started to visit Mandinga Bay around this same time and also began to purchase *molas*. Their numbers were small, however, and, unlike tourists today, buying *molas* was not the primary focus of their visit.

During the 1940s and the 1950s, in spite of the developing market for *molas*, women continued to sew them exclusively for personal use. The sale of used *mola* blouses was carried out through Kuna women's personal and kinship networks with Kuna men who had contacts with U.S. citizens stationed in the Canal Zone. Kuna women gave their used blouses to their own male relatives or to female friends' male relatives working in Panama City to sell. Men were expected to bring or send back the full sale value of the *mola* to the producer.

Kuna women began to use designs in their *molas* that reflected the socioeconomic changes that were occurring as a result of the increased movement of people, cash, and consumer goods between San Blas, Colón, and Panama City. *Mola* designs became increasingly varied and complex. Pictures of fishnet twine labels, matchbox covers, and shotgun shell boxes, among other things, were copied and embellished (Parker and Parker 1977).

Mola commercialization and the shift from production for personal use to production for exchange did not occur all at once; rather, it has been a process that started in the 1950s and has continued ever since. While few changes related to *mola* production occurred in the 1940s and the 1950s, shifts in the region's articulation with the international market in the 1960s profoundly affected *mola* production and sales. The history of this process, closely tied to the development of the national tourist industry and intertwined with changes in agricultural production, coconut cash cropping, and labor migration, will be the focus of the rest of this chapter.

Mola Commercialization and Agricultural Production

Coconuts provided the Kuna with their major source of cash income throughout the first half of the twentieth century. During the 1950s and the 1960s, however, coconut palms were affected by a severe blight, so that coconut production sharply decreased. Initially, the blight affected only the eastern side of San Blas, but it moved quickly westward until the entire region was affected. An anthropologist working on Tupile during the time of the blight wrote (Holloman 1969:122): "the combined effect of decline in the total number of trees and of decreased production from blighted trees accounted for a decline in coconut income among Tupile residents of nearly 80 per cent over the decade 1957–67, and even greater decline in total production." Thus, the primary income-generating activity was decreasing at the same time that the market for *molas* was beginning to expand. This decrease in overall income, combined with increased migration of Kuna men in search of wage labor and the subsequent decrease in subsistence farming and fishing, had an enormous impact on households in San Blas. In many households, women began to purchase items such as rice, sugar, and fish, which men had previously provided.

Women began to trade their *molas* for needed goods such as sugar, salt, kerosene, and cloth in local Kuna stores and with Kuna petty traders. The store owners and itinerant traders were all Kuna men. Foreign intermediaries and tourists, both male and female, provided an additional but infrequent option for selling *molas*. Both tourists and foreign intermediaries paid higher prices for *molas* than did the local Kuna store owners and traders, but this alternative was available only to Kuna women living in Mandinga Bay (see map 2). Tourism is concentrated almost exclusively in this area.

It is difficult to pinpoint an exact date for the broader commercialization of *molas* because the Kuna tend not to remember dates, integration into the international market occurred at different times on various islands, and it was a process that took place over a number of years. It is clear, however, that a major shift in the organization of production and marketing relations occurred during the 1960s, when *mola* commercialization became articulated with the international market in a major way. In this decade we find a shift from production for use, with a few incidental sales, to production for exchange on the international market. Intermediaries began purchasing *molas* by the hundreds at very low prices: $2.00 to $2.50 each. Many Kuna women became desperate to sell or trade their *molas*. Households came to rely increasingly on the sale or trade of *molas* to meet their daily needs.

In the 1960s, the sale of *molas* took place through already-existing patterns of exchange. With the decrease in coconut production and new availability of places to sell *molas* in Panama City, San Blas store owners and itinerant traders began to accept both *molas* and coconuts in exchange for merchandise. These Kuna men served as the principal intermediaries between producers of *molas* in San Blas and the non-Kuna store owners in Panama City. Unlike those Kuna men who sold small quantities of *mola* blouses directly to consumers in the Canal Zone as favors to their female relatives, these intermediaries began to purchase *molas* by the hundreds from women on their own and surrounding islands. Store owners in Panama City wanted individual *mola* panels and not whole blouses, so women ripped apart their beautiful blouses before trading or selling them.

Although women recall having been pleased at first to receive cash for worn-out *molas*, they soon realized that they were being exploited. As immediate stores of worn *molas* became depleted, grandmothers started to sell their fine old *molas* and women of all ages felt pressured to sell *mola* blouses with good wear still left in them. Some women began to notice that store owners' profits were two-tiered. First, they earned a percentage selling or trading the merchandise in their stores, then they sold the *molas* at a higher price in Panama City.

Desperate to sell their *molas*, but unwilling to accept the low prices offered by intermediaries, Kuna women actively looked for alternative markets. If a woman was lucky enough to have a relative in Panama City, she would send her *molas* there to sell. The relative in the city would go door to door in the Canal Zone, try to sell in the street, or else draw on any contacts he or she might have with U.S. citizens living or working in Panama. One woman knew a secretary at the U.S. embassy who let her go with her sister from office to office selling their *molas*. Women with no city contacts were dependent primarily on local store owners in San Blas. Women's realization that they were being exploited by intermediaries created conditions for the organization of a *mola* cooperative, which will be discussed in chapter 7.

National Tourism

Without a market, even the highest-quality products cannot be commercialized in any major way. The commercialization process is, in effect, a complex dialogue between the producer and the market. Therefore, it is important at this point to turn our attention to the dynamics of the market for *molas*. Expansion of tourism in Panama and increased demand for indigenous handicrafts in the United States are two factors that stimulated *mola* commercialization.

Tourism has been promoted by the Panamanian government since 1939, but not in a systematic fashion until 1962, when the Instituto

Panameño de Turismo was organized as a department of the national government. Before the 1960s, tourist literature featured non-Kuna, Panamanian women wearing *polleras,* handmade lacy dresses, known as the Panamanian national costume. During the 1960s, *molas* became a national symbol and Kuna women in their "exotic" dress were prominently featured in Panama's tourist literature along with non-Kuna women wearing either *polleras* or bikinis. Foreigners came to identify both *molas* and the Panama Canal with Panama.

Panama's nightlife and shopping opportunities have been, and continue to be, heavily emphasized in the tourist literature (Chapin 1990:44). Starting in the 1960s, promotion of Panamanian crafts became another prominent strategy used by the government to attract tourists to Panama. Government support of the *mola* industry, however, has been minimal, even though two ministries have implemented major projects designed to support the commercialization of Panamanian handicrafts. In 1966, the Servicio Nacional de Artesanías y Pequeñas Industrias (SENAPI) was formed by the Panamanian government. SENAPI's primary objective was the commercialization of Panamanian handicrafts. This ministry provided technical and administrative assistance to Panamanian artisans and attempted to organize cooperatives in other parts of Panama, but it was unsuccessful. For two years SENAPI worked with a United Nations project (PNUD—Pan 8) designed to assist in the formation of national level institutions to foster the development of artisans. The United Nations project sent seven consultants experienced in the production and marketing of artisan products made from leather, fiber, ceramics, and wood to work jointly with SENAPI staff. Because *molas* were already commercialized, they were not included in this project and the *mola* cooperative received no assistance.

SENAPI was disbanded in 1969, and its functions divided among various governmental departments, including the Ministerio de Comercio, the Ministerio de Trabajo, and the Instituto Panameño de Turismo (IPAT). Artesanías Nacionales was set up as a department of the Instituto Panameño de Turismo, making very clear the relationship between artisan production and tourism. Indigenous handicrafts, especially *molas,* were part of a marketing strategy used to draw tourists to Panama.

In 1985, Artesanías Nacionales operated three stores in Panama City geared specifically to tourists and featuring handmade items from all over Panama. Although a government department, it was expected to be primarily self-supporting, and most of its operating funds came from the sale of handicrafts. This created conflict between its primary goal, which was to support local artisans, and the need to be self-sustaining. *Molas* are purchased by Artesanías Nacionales from male Kuna intermediaries in Panama City. Occasionally, the staff travels to San Blas to buy directly from producers. Artesanías Nacionales pays approximately five dollars for an average *mola* panel and ten dollars to fifteen dollars for a fine *mola*. An average *mola* is resold for twenty dollars. Of this twenty dollars, 5 percent goes to pay store employee salaries, 45 percent goes to the stores' operating expenses such as rent and electricity, 10 percent is given as a discount to consumers on large purchases, and the remaining 15 percent is profit. Given these figures, it is questionable how much support artisans actually receive from Artesanías Nacionales. Products are promoted and special projects are sometimes undertaken; however, the organization functions primarily as an intermediary.

Private sector tourism-related infrastructure increased during the 1960s and created new markets for *molas*. The Panama Hilton, for example, thought of by many as Panama's finest hotel, was built in 1961. At this time, a store featuring indigenous handicrafts, the first of its kind in Panama City, was opened in the hotel. The owner discovered that *molas* were the perfect souvenir or gift for tourists or traveling businesspeople who wanted to take home something specifically Panamanian. Unlike bulky baskets or ceramics, *molas* are light, nonbreakable, and take up very little room in a suitcase. Furthermore, *molas* are unusual, a conversation piece at the least, and, to those with a trained eye, fine works of art. Another ethnic arts store opened about the same time. Although the two stores carried a wide range of handcrafted items, *molas* sold faster than other items. Both store owners amassed substantial fortunes from *mola* sales.

Prices received for *molas* sold vary so widely that is not possible accurately to estimate earnings from *mola* sales from national census data on *mola* production. Data from the *mola* cooperative, however, provide accurate details about the amount of income produced from sales through the cooperative. In 1973–1974, cooperative earnings totaled $8,900 for 398 members. By 1979, the cooperative had sold $42,791 worth of *molas*. In 1980, sales jumped to $65,182. Leaders of the *mola* cooperative report steady drops in sales after 1980. Sales through the cooperative represent only a fraction of the total income from *molas* regionwide. Still, it is clear that the *mola* industry brings substantial income into the region.

Reflecting *molas'* emerging importance as a source of income, questions about *mola* production and sales were included, for the first time, in the 1960 national census. These national census statistics on *mola* sales in San Blas show an upward trend paralleling that

Table 1. Mola *production and sales, San Blas, 1960, 1970,* *and 1980*

	1960	1970	1980
No. of households answering survey questions	1,826	2,404	2,930
Molas produced	31,706	92,411	101,900
Molas sold	414	39,229	60,239

Sources: "Cuadro 34 Producción y venta de la industria doméstica, en las áreas indígenas de la república: censos de 1950, 1960, 1970 y 1980," in Censos nacionales de 1980: Cuarto censo nacional agropecuario 17 al 24 de Mayo 1981 (Panama City: *Dirección de Estadística y Censo,* 1981:59–60). Information about *mola* production and sales was not collected in 1950. Informants were asked about the number of *molas* produced and sold over a one-year period.

of tourism. Thus, the number of *molas* produced reportedly increased over threefold from 1960 to 1980, and the ratio of *molas* produced to those sold also increased (see table 1).[6] Visitors to Panama increased steadily, from 132,786 tourists reported in 1969 to 392,062 in 1980. After 1980, Panama experienced a steady decline in tourism. In 1983, 78,000 fewer tourists visited Panama than in 1980.[7] Tourism to Panama in the 1990s is virtually nonexistent (Ann Wenzel, personal communication).

Global political events have had an impact on Panama's tourist industry and, consequently, on *mola* sales. Upheavals in Guatemala, El Salvador, and Nicaragua throughout the 1980s resulted in dramatic declines in tourism throughout Central America, Panama included. In 1989, the United States invaded Panama in an attempt to capture General Manuel Noriega (see the end of this chapter for more details). Media images of Panama City burning did nothing to promote tourism. In the 1990s, the tourist hotels are relatively empty. Informants living in Panama City tell me that since the invasion Kuna women are desperate to sell their *molas* because there are relatively few tourists in Panama City. Although cruise liners continue to stop in San Blas, only Kuna women living in one area of San Blas sell to these tourists (see chapter 8).

Adventure and ecological tourism are now being promoted by the Panamanian government. Several agencies have developed eco-tours to the Darién jungle for tourists interested in learning about the rain forest (Ann Wenzel, personal communication). Adventure tours to explore the jungle rivers and other natural areas are another focus for tourism. This new type of tourism represents a dramatic shift in the way tourism is focused. So far, opportunities for buying *molas* are not part of these new tours.

Craft producers are directly linked to or affected by the global political economy through the sale of goods. Both Kuna men and women are vulnerable to external forces beyond their control. Whether the Kuna *mola* producers, merchants, and intermediaries will find another product to sell or find new markets for *molas* remains to be seen.

Tourism in San Blas

Tourism in San Blas is concentrated in the Carti region, where transatlantic cruise ships have been stopping in increasing numbers since 1939. For several decades cruise ships were the primary way that tourists entered the region. These ships came from a wide range of places, including the United States, Holland, Germany, and Great Britain. Initially, tourists aboard these ships did not buy *molas*; they came to view an "exotic" indigenous people and their way of life.

Tourists began to buy *molas* in the 1960s, and by the 1980s, viewing and purchasing *molas* was their primary activity. Between January 1984 and December 1985, no fewer than thirty-two such vessels disembarked at Carti-Sugtupu. Within that period, two cruise ships started disembarking passengers on a weekly basis (from November to April) on other islands. One ship, the *Great River Explorer*, carries several hundred passengers and makes stops at the islands of Aquadup and Naranjo Grande. Another carries up to thirteen hundred tourists, who disembark on the island of Naluneka, where there is a beach so that tourists can swim in addition to buying *molas*.

At least eight hotels were constructed between 1930 and 1985, providing a second way for tourists to visit the area (see Falla 1979a: 45–49). In 1985, four hotels were still operating in the Carti area. Two, located on populated islands, were privately owned by Kuna men. The hotel on Wichubwala was a medium-sized, two-story concrete building. The hotel on Naluneka consisted of a handful of small Kuna-style houses made from local materials and a house where guests ate their meals. A third hotel was located on the relatively unpopulated island of El Porvenir. It had been illegally owned and operated by a non-Kuna Panamanian for many years. Now it belongs to the San Blas Kuna and is administered jointly by the governor of the region and the Congreso General Kuna. This hotel also consisted of less than a dozen small Kuna-style houses. The community of Carti-Sugtupu itself built a small hotel in 1983 or 1984; it caters primarily to Kuna travelers and is not connected with the tourist agencies in Panama City. Local materials were used to build this hotel, with the exception of a corrugated tin roof, donated by a U.S. general who also provided all of the beds and other furniture.[8]

Outside of the Carti area, hotels can be found on at least two islands. The Hotel Anay is now owned and run by a *sociedad* on the island of Aligandi (see Holloman 1969:214–216; Swain 1977:76; Howe 1986b:209). Although relatively few foreign tourists come to stay in the hotel, it has a restaurant that is frequented by the Kuna who live on that island. In sharp contrast, the hotel located on Nargana, which also had a restaurant, rarely served anything but coffee, beer, and soft drinks. It too had few guests, although traveling Kuna occasionally stayed there.

Increased availability of hotels has made it easier for foreign intermediaries wishing to buy *molas* to travel to San Blas. Visitors can arrange weekend tour packages, including airfare, hotel, and sightseeing, through non-Kuna travel agencies in Panama City. Planes land twice daily on a relatively unpopulated island where one hotel is located. Three out of four hotels provide English-speaking guides who take visitors on excursions to other Kuna communities where they can buy *molas* and to unpopulated islands where they can swim and snorkel. Foreign intermediaries who come to buy *molas* simply rent an *ulu* (with a motor) and a guide who will take them to visit islands where they can purchase *molas*.

Control over tourist facilities has been a constant source of concern and conflict for the Kuna (Falla 1979a; Howe 1982a; Chapin 1990:43; Tice n.d.). In the 1960s, two U.S. citizens constructed two small tourist resorts, Islandia and Pidertupu, in San Blas in spite of a law that prohibits non-Kuna from engaging in commercial activities that require land within the territory. Subsequently, in 1969 and 1981, respectively, attempts were made to burn both hotels and the operators were forced by the Kuna to leave (Holloman 1969:475; Howe 1982a; Chapin 1990; Tice n.d.). John Mann, another U.S. citizen, who had operated tours of the islands for tourists on a small scale since 1968, was also asked to leave. In the early 1970s, IPAT instituted a multimillion-dollar project to turn the Carti region into an international tourist center (Swain 1977:74). The project would have involved construction of an international airport and high-rise hotels. The Congreso General Kuna was strongly opposed to this project and after a long struggle succeeded in having it dropped (see

Stier 1979:108–110; Howe 1982a:16; Chapin 1990:43; Prestán n.d.). The *mola* cooperative has been active in these struggles.

International Context

Interest in ethnic arts in general, and *molas* in particular, increased during the 1960s and the 1970s in the United States and Europe. *Molas* became increasingly sought after by museums, galleries, fashion designers, and home decorators in the United States. They were exhibited in various places, including the Field Museum of Natural History in Chicago, the Pan American Union in Washington, D.C., and several university art departments. Art galleries in several cities, notably Miami and New York, also featured *molas*. Newspaper articles appeared acclaiming *molas* as genuine works of art and urging people to buy quality *molas* while they still could.[9]

Molas also became visible in the realm of fashion, design, and home decoration. For example, in 1970, a *mola* skirt was featured on the cover of the Nieman Marcus Christmas catalogue. From 1966 to 1978, no fewer than four popular books about *molas* were published in English. These ranged from "how-to" books to those destined for display on coffee tables. During this period, numerous articles appeared in home decorating and craft magazines describing how *molas* could be used as pillows and wall hangings to beautify homes. Promotion of interest in *molas*, whether as part of a commercial endeavor or a cultural event, resulted in increased demand.

How *molas* were used by the people who bought them varied tremendously. For some, *molas* were fine works of art; for others, they were raw materials with which to create other objects such as pillows, quilts, and bags. How the changing context for *mola* use affected Kuna women's designs, choice of color, and relationship to their art will be explored in chapter 6.

International political intrigue has also had an impact on the market for *molas*. In 1986, senior Reagan administration officials expressed concern about evidence linking Panama's Gen. Manuel Noriega to drug trafficking, money laundering, and the death of a political opponent (*New York Times*, June 13, 1986:8). In 1988, the U.S. Justice Department indicted Noriega for trafficking in drugs, for accepting millions of dollars in bribes from drug traffickers, and for turning Panama into the "capital of international cocaine smuggling" (*New York Times*, February 6, 1988:1). Over the next two years, the U.S. government imposed severe economic sanctions on Panama in hopes that Noriega would relinquish power and leave the country. For example, nearly seven million dollars in revenue generated by the Panama Canal was witheld (*New York Times*, March 12, 1988:1). President Reagan ordered all payments to the Panamanian government by American citizens or U.S. corporations or their subsidiaries to halt (*New York Times*, April 9, 1988:1). As a result, Noriega ordered all banks in Panama to close. Checks and credit cards were no longer honored (*New York Times*, March 12, 1988:6). The *New York Times* (June 9, 1988:1) reported that "economic activity in Panama has been cut in half as a result of American confrontation with General Manuel Antonio Noriega."

In 1989, President Bush ordered U.S. troops into the streets of Panama to capture Noriega (*New York Times*, December 20, 1989:1). Ten thousand troops were involved, but Noriega was not captured. In the process, scores of Panamanians were killed, hundreds wounded, and widespread looting occurred (*New York Times*, December 21, 1989:1). A twenty-six-thousand-member U.S. military force attempted to reestablish control in Panama (*New York Times*, December 23, 1989:13).

In 1990, Noriega surrendered to U.S. authorities (*New York Times*, January 5, 1990:1). Panama's new president, Guillermo Endara, went on a hunger strike, saying that the "Panamanian economy is in even worse condition than before the American invasion that overthrew General Manuel Antonio Noriega; unemployment is above 30 percent, many people are going hungry and businesses are in ruins" (*New York Times*, March 12, 1990:1).

Needless to say, tourism and trade were dramatically affected by the events just described. Kuna women were desperate to sell their *molas* (Ann Wenzel, personal communication). Global political and economic events—in this case, outside the Kuna's control—dried up the market for *molas* overnight. To what extent marketing routes have been restored is an area for future research. What this incident clearly highlights, though, is women's vulnerability to both political and economic global forces.

Gender Crossing

Gender, in contrast with biologically determined sex, is a socially constructed category. Gender crossing has been noted in many parts of the world (Ortner and Whitehead 1981; Williams 1986). In indigenous North American cultures, gender crossing "consisted of the permissibility of a person of one anatomic sex assuming part or most of the attire, occupation, and social—including marital—status of the opposite sex for an indeterminate period" (Ortner and Whitehead

1981:85). Commonly refered to in the literature as *berdache* (the French word for male prostitute), males would participate in women's productive labor, cross dress, and take on mannerisms and speech patterns commonly attributed to women. Choice of sex partner is a less-important defining feature of the gender crosser: "its salience is low; so low that by itself it does not provoke the reclassification of the individual to a special status" (Ortner and Whitehead 1981:97). For example, males who are not defined as *berdache* might regularly engage in sexual activity with a *berdache* (Williams 1986). Female gender crossers, sometimes referred to as "amazons" (Williams 1986), have also been observed but appear to be less common and less fully institutionalized than male *berdache*.

The Kuna have four gender classifications: male, female, *omekit* (womanlike [man]), and *macharetkit* (manlike [woman]). Male gender crossing among the Kuna is characterized primarily by choice of productive labor and demeanor and only secondarily by sexual orientation. According to interviewees, *omekits* are usually identified as such as children. These boys talk and sing like little girls and always want to play with girls, not boys. They also are interested in "female tasks" such as cooking, sewing *molas,* and sweeping.

In the 1980s, *omekits* straddled both men's and women's activity spheres. They participated fully in women's activities such as *mola* sewing and cooking. They were members of the *mola* cooperative and were well known as highly competent *mola* sewers. On at least one island, however, *omekits* were required to participate in collective men's labor tasks. Some also occasionally worked in the *monte* (countryside) with the other men in their households. *Omekits* always danced the men's part in the traditional Kuna dances. During one *chicha* celebration, I observed that all of the *omekits* started out sitting with the men. As the celebration wore on, however, they moved over to join the women. I noticed that early on some women also crossed over into the men's space. After having quite a bit to drink, the division between men's and women's spaces dissolved.

Unlike what has been observed elsewhere in North America (Ortner and Whitehead 1981), I did not see *omekits* in San Blas who regularly cross dressed; they almost always wore men's clothing. Although I never saw an *omekit* wearing a *mola,* I saw several men occasionally wearing a *saburrette.* I also observed several young men setting and curling each other's hair. One woman told me that an *omekit* friend of hers dresses like a woman when he goes into Panama City. She had seen pictures. It is possible that *omekits* used to cross dress more. Ortner and Whitehead (1981:88) note, however, that "it was possible for persons to maintain the gender-crossed status by occupation alone while dressing, in response to white pressure, as befitted anatomic sex." It is possible that pressures from missionaries and the homophobic Latino population in Panama City have influenced cross dressing in San Blas.

Some *omekits* married women but had sexual relations with other men as well. Our neighbor, a middle-aged man, had been married four times (to women), but his wives left him because he was continually going after other men. Other *omekits* "married" men. None of the three communities where I lived, however, allowed *omekits* actually to live together as a married couple. Overnight visits were ignored. *Omekits* openly referred to their partners as "an ome" (my woman), in the same words that a man might use to refer to his wife. I know of one case in which an *omekit* went to Panama City to marry another man. When this news reached his home community, the *sakla* sent someone to find him and bring him home.

Kuna men I interviewed who had not spent time outside of San Blas seemed much more tolerant of *omekits* than the Kuna men who had spent considerable time in Panama City. The latter spoke negatively about *omekits*, pointed to same-sex relations as morally wrong, and compared the *omekits* to the homosexuals in Panama City. Kuna women I interviewed, regardless of time spent outside San Blas, thought that any woman who had an *omekit* son was very lucky indeed.

An *omekit* joined me and a number of other members of the *mola* cooperative on a trip. On the way back, we stopped at an island to visit. The *omekit* met his friend/lover and decided to stay the night. His friend came to get his bag out of our boat and the two of them walked away together. Normally full of jokes, the women's only response was to say "Panemaloe" (See you tomorrow).

Female gender crossing has been noted in thirty-three North American groups (Blackwood 1984). The Kuna recognize a category called "*macharetkit*," or manlike (woman). From the little information I could gather, *macharetkits* are defined by their productive labor and their demeanor. One day a grandmother commented that her grandaughter, a girl about eight years old, was a *macharetkit*. I asked why this was so and the girl's mother explained; "She plays just like a boy . . . climbs around, gets into everything, takes things apart and beats the dog." One adult married woman told me she was *macharetkit* because she was strong and when her husband migrated to Panama City she put on his boots and pants and worked in the fields just like a man. Other women who performed men's work were not called nor did they define themselves as *macharetkit*. Mostly, people changed the subject whenever I asked questions. Missionary and other outside influences that condemn gender crossing have resulted in people's disguising and not discussing their identities with outsiders (Williams 1986). The impact of missionaries and increased contact with Panama on the social construction of gender in San Blas is an area in need of futher research.

Sewing *molas* is a "woman's" task whether performed by a biological woman or a man who is socially defined as womanlike. This has not changed as a result of *mola* commercialization. For the remainder of this book, when I refer to women and *mola* production, I am refering to both biological and socially defined (*omekits*) women. How *mola* production is affected by gender, class, and the changing consumption of crafts will be addressed in chapter 6.

6.
Mola Production, Exchange, and Use

The bus left us standing coughing in clouds of black smoke on one of Panama's main commercial streets. Adela, the cooperative's administrator, and I were in search of stores carrying mass-produced cloth printed with *mola* designs. The street was a collage of stores selling everything from electronics to clothing. As we pushed our way along the crowded sidewalk, we heard our names called out in Kuna and saw two members of the *mola* cooperative dressed in full *mola* waving to us. After we explained what we were doing, they joined us. Soon we found several stores selling bolts of *mola* cloth. The women talked with me at length about how angry it made them to have their *mola* designs stolen and mass-produced. Adela told me that she had heard about a law that prohibited the sale of goods competing with handcrafted items made in Panama and told me that if I could find a copy of this law she personally would visit Panama's vice-president and demand that the law be enforced.[1]

The shift from sewing *molas* for personal use to producing them for exchange on the global market has affected *mola* sewers and their relationship with their craft profoundly. This chapter details the relations of *mola* production, exchange, and use in the mid-1980s and explores how gender, ethnicity, and class intersect. Of special interest is how producers' and buyers' knowledge of how *molas* are used within specific social contexts has affected both. Except where otherwise noted, the information presented in this chapter was collected in 1984 and 1985.

Mola **Production for Personal Use**

In the 1980s, Kuna women of all ages, girls (starting around five years of age), and *omekits* sewed *molas*. Women sewed their own *mola* blouses and blouses for their daughters and their elderly mothers, if the latter were unable to sew. Sisters might help one another to finish a *mola*, particularly if it was to be worn at a special event such as a *chicha* celebration.

As of 1985, no internal market had developed in San Blas for *molas* made to be worn by a Kuna woman (*omekits* did not wear *molas*). If a Kuna woman sewed a *mola* for another Kuna woman, it was generally done as a favor. Very rarely, a woman would pay a female relative or friend to sew a *mola* for her. This happened more frequently on some islands than on others. For example, on Tubuala, women were required by the *congreso* to wear *molas*, which were often sewn by machine. On this island, women participated actively in agricultural production and had no time to sew *molas*. Women with sewing machines often sewed *molas* for their friends at no cost. Requiring women to wear *molas*, however, does not necessarily result in their sewing *molas* by machine. For example, on the island of Tigre, women were also required to wear *molas*, but they did not use sewing machines. Tigre was known throughout San Blas as a community that valued and supported Kuna "tradition."

All the materials needed to sew a *mola* (cloth, thread, a needle, a pair of scissors, and a thimble) could be purchased or traded for at one or more local store in every San Blas community. Bolts of coarse cloth, generally used only as the bottom layer of a *mola*, were acquired by store owners from Colombian traders. Most of the cloth, however, was purchased in Panama City and came from Japan, China, or England. Thread, also purchased in Panama City, was imported from France and England. Scissors came from West Germany and China.

Assuming that a woman had scissors, a needle, and thread, the minimum cost for starting a *mola* blouse was roughly $3.00. Cloth cost from $2.25 to $2.80 per yard, and it took about one and a half to two yards of cloth to make two three-layered *mola* panels for a blouse. Cloth for the sleeves and yoke of a blouse was usually purchased once the two panels were completed. The satinlike cloth fashionable in 1985 cost $4.00 per yard. The cost for finishing a blouse depended on the price of the cloth and the size of the woman. Small folding scissors from China cost $1.00 a pair, needles cost $0.05 each, and thread ranged from $0.20 to $0.65, depending on the quality and size of the spool.

A *mola* panel can take from two weeks to many months to complete. The amount of time it takes to sew a panel depends on the number of layers, the type of design, and panel size. Other factors include the amount of time a producer has to spend sewing, how fast she sews, the fineness of her stitching, and how many other *molas* she is working on at the same time. Women generally agreed that it takes about a solid week of work, sewing most of the day and well into the evening, to complete one *mola* panel (a *mola* blouse requires two panels).[2]

Women and girls sewed *molas* for their own use primarily in the late afternoon and evenings. Attending local *congreso* meetings provided several hours at a time when women could concentrate on sewing *molas*. Except at the *congreso*, women and *omekits* sewed primarily at home.[3] Partially completed *molas* were also taken along on visits to friends' or relatives' households.

The measurements of the two panels that *mola* blouses require vary, depending on the size of the woman who plans to wear the blouse and her preferences for style and comfort. *Mola* panels are usually three layers thick but may range from two to six layers. A design is cut in the second layer of cloth. The raw edges are then turned under and sewed onto a cloth backing, preferably with a matching color of thread. When the first two layers are complete, the third layer is basted down. The top layer is then selectively cut away to reveal the designs underneath while adding an additional color. Women use their sense of feel to tell where to cut. Again, the raw edges are tucked under, creased with a fingernail to keep them in place, and stitched in place.

Once the three layers and the basic design are in place, a second creative stage begins, that of embellishing the *mola*. Small pieces of cloth in any number of different shapes, sizes, and colors may be appliquéd onto the *mola*. Tiny triangles, squares, or other shapes may be cut into one or more layer of cloth to reveal a drop of color from below. Alternatively, embroidery thread may be used to stitch on animal eyes and bird feathers or to give texture to an otherwise "uninteresting" area of the *mola*. Not all *molas* are embellished.

Once the two panels are completed, women purchase cloth for the sleeves and yoke. The blouse may be finished either by hand or by sewing machine. Some women sew multiple layers of cloth or purchased trim on their blouses to further decorate the sleeve cuffs and yoke border. If a woman does not have a sewing machine in her household, she may ask a friend who does to finish the *mola* for her. As with cutting *molas*, no money is exchanged; however, whereas anyone may ask a skilled producer to cut a design, only friends of a woman with a sewing machine will ask her to complete their *molas*.

As described in chapter 5, early *mola* designs were geometric and represented items used by Kuna men and women in their daily lives. Certain women in each community were known to have *kurgin* (special gifts or abilities) in the realm of design. Special medicinal leaves with geometric veins were often used by these women to enhance their abilities. These leaves were soaked in water and placed over the artist's eyes. Leaf-cutting ants were also used as medicine to make the needleworker's hands work harder (Sherzer and Sherzer 1976:39). Women with artistic talents were sought out by other *mola* makers to cut new designs or to copy old ones. These artists gave freely of their time, skills, and creativity. Like most Kuna, they believed that if they cooperated and helped others on earth, they would be repaid in the afterlife. Popular designs were copied and recopied, sometimes spreading throughout the entire region. *Mola* makers copied designs they liked that were worn by friends, relatives, or visitors from other islands. Original artists were soon forgotten and only very recently cut designs could be traced back to their creators. A woman's design might come to her in a dream or she might use her imagination to create one.

Women draw their inspiration from a wide range of visual images, life events, and abstract concepts. In the 1970s, Sherzer and Sherzer (1976:32) noted: "*molas* do not represent Cuna ancestors, mythical beings or scenes, or good or bad spirits of a supernatural nature. Nor do they contain designs or motifs that have a magical value." Women have sewn *molas* drawing design elements from electric fans, televisions, underwear, designs on matchbox covers. As new commercial goods entered the region, *mola* producers incorporated these items into their *molas*. In the 1940s, *mola* makers began to incorporate advertisement, trademark, and package label designs into their *molas*. [*Mola* makers have also drawn inspiration from sporting events, Canal Zone and U.S. military themes, Christian religious imagery, illustrations from books and magazines, flight images, western clothing and common objects, and games and entertainment (Parker and Parker 1977).] In the 1960s, when the Kuna were drawn increasingly into national-level politics and the role of the Panamanian national government expanded in San Blas, *mola* blouses began to be used as one way women could express their opinions on political and economic issues. For example, women sewed their favorite presidential candidate on their blouses (Parker and Parker 1977). Sometimes *mola* designs mix reality and abstraction. For example, in 1984, a fourteen-year-old girl's mother made a *mola* blouse for her daughter, who was about to go off to Panama City to study. The *mola* showed an airplane taking off within the outstretched wings of a large bird. The mother hoped that the bird, which for the Kuna symbolizes luck, would ensure her daughter a safe journey.[4]

In the 1980s, highly skilled *mola* makers and designers had gained prestige within their own communities. Some had become known throughout the region for their special abilities; a few were known by *mola* buyers abroad. Kuna women use intricacy of design, use of color, and fineness of stitching to judge their own and each other's *molas*. Producers talked among themselves about *molas* in process. They shared ideas and pieces of cloth, and critiqued one another's designs and color combinations.

Understanding who wears *molas,* why they are worn, and within which social contexts illuminates the ways women's dress defines Kuna ethnic identity and is used symbolically as a means for resistence. While most adult women in San Blas wore full Kuna dress daily during the 1980s, wearing *mola* did not mean the same thing to all women. For some women, wearing *molas* was symbolic of their social and political autonomy as indigenous people. Older women in some communities had been forced by the colonial police to don western clothes before the 1925 revolution. They spoke with pride when they talked about wearing *molas.* Some younger Kuna women who attended the university in Panama City wore full Kuna dress very consciously and proudly as a symbol of their ethnic identity. For other women, wearing *molas* was tied to a way of life. These women wore western clothing if they left San Blas to procure an education or a job. For example, Reina had two young daughters, ages seven and ten. She was planning to send the youngest to Panama City to continue her studies. This daughter would not change into *mola* at puberty. The other daughter did not like school and wanted to remain in San Blas and follow in the footsteps of her mother and grandmother, both highly skilled and respected women in the community. Reina was already saving up to buy her a nose ring and all the other necessary items for changing this daughter into *mola* when she reached puberty. This girl would go through the three-day haircutting ceremony while only a one-day puberty ceremony would be held for her sister.

In some communities, women and girls were required by their local *congreso* to wear *molas* (i.e, "traditional" Kuna dress). These *congresos,* comprising both men and women, had decided that this was an important way of upholding and valuing their traditions and therefore their identity as Kuna people. In the majority of San Blas communities, however, women were free to choose what they wore.

Often girls would wear western clothes until they reached puberty, at which point they were able to choose between western and Kuna dress. Some young girls and adult women shifted back and forth, wearing mixtures of western and Kuna dress, depending on their mood. Adult women usually made a clear choice one way or the other, however. There was a trend among Kuna women for those who had been wearing western dress to change into *mola*. *Omekits* did not wear *molas, wini,* or any other piece of traditional Kuna women's clothing. This contrasts sharply with what has been described for *berdache* in North America, who are in part defined by cross dressing (Ortmer and Whitehead 1981; Williams 1986)

Wearing *molas* also provided women with a public medium for social commentary, a means for describing and recording social changes, and a way to organize socially and to define their relationships with other Kuna women in their communities. Older or less intricate *molas* were usually worn during the day while women were working. Newer and finer *molas* were worn to *congreso* meetings and on special occasions. *Molas* could be worn to make a political statement, such as indicating support for a political candidate or for a particular issue. One *mola* I saw showed a Kuna woman placing a ballot into a ballot box with other women lined up behind her. The symbol for one of Panama's national political parties was prominently featured on another *mola*. Socially relevant statements were also made. For example, one *mola* showed the male figure of a missionary being cooked in a large pot by a big fish, who was stirring him into the brew. Another *mola* depicted a child being eaten by an alligator. This *mola* documented an actual occurrence and was used by the mother to impress on her children that alligators are dangerous.

Molas may also define the status or cohesion of a group of women within a community. Often groups of women would sew the same *mola* to wear for a special occasion. For example, Sippu and her husband were organizing an *inna muttikkit* (puberty ceremony) for their daughter. Sippu asked her daughter's female relatives who planned to participate in the celebration to sew a special *mola* and to purchase matching *saburrettes*. As is customary, these women sat in a special place in the *inna neka* (the house where the celebration took place) and were expected to drink until either the *inna* was all gone or they passed out. Although the entire community was invited to help drink and celebrate, these women had special responsibility for drinking. By wearing identical dress, they were set off visually from the rest of the women present.

Chicha celebrations were a good time for women to show off their *molas,* so women tried to have one new *mola* for each day of the *chicha.* Young women would try to attract the attention of young men by wearing an especially well sewn or beautiful *mola.*

Styles of *molas* worn varied among women of different generations. For example, sixteen-year-old Albertina's *mola* blouses were so tight that she had to wriggle and tug to get them over her head and torso. She liked flower and animal designs, especially those designs that her friends were wearing. The yoke and sleeves of her *mola* were made of chiffon. In contrast with the tight-fitting body of the blouse, the sleeves were gathered and puffed out about six inches away from her arm. Albertina's grandmother wore what is commonly referred to as a "grandmother *mola.*" Her *mola* was quite loose fitting, with modest sleeves. Most of her *molas* were decorated with geometric designs, though some also had flowers or animals on them. The yoke and sleeves were made of cotton cloth or of brightly colored polyester. Although not all sixteen-year-olds wore see-through chiffon yokes, younger women did tend to wear their *molas* tighter and their sleeves puffier than did older women.

Women were highly conscious of changes in Kuna fashion, and fads in clothing and jewelry would sweep through the entire region. During my stay in San Blas in 1981, a certain type of beaded necklace that had gone out of style was rediscovered by some young women. This new craze quickly spread throughout the entire region. Granddaughters were begging their grandmothers to dig through old cardboard boxes, baskets, or suitcases perched high on the rafters of houses to find these old necklaces. Some young women learned how to make the necklaces while others depended on their grandmothers to make them new ones. Some fads, like the one just described, were originated by the women themselves; however, itinerant traders and store owners also stimulated changes in fashion. *Saburrettes* and cloth for *mola* yokes and sleeves with new combinations of colors and designs were brought from Panama City and displayed prominently so that women would want to buy them.

Despite their commercialization, *molas* are still produced for personal use and continue to have meaning within a social context. As clothing they serve a functional purpose. Wearing *molas* symbolically expresses Kuna ethnic identity and, for many, a desire for autonomy from the non-Kuna world. *Molas* are a medium for social commentary, for personal creativity, and for fashion. Kuna women gain prestige through their sewing and design skills; however, *molas* do not differentiate women socially with the exception of *molas* displaying style differences that might be worn by different generations.

Mola **Commercialization**

In the 1950s and the early 1960s, *molas* continued to be produced almost exclusively for personal use. Used *mola* blouses might be sold, but *molas* were not produced for sale. This changed in the late 1960s, when *molas* began to be produced, exchanged, and consumed as commodities. Commodity production coexisted with production for personal use. In the late 1960s, as before, *molas* made for a woman's personal use could still be worn and then sold or traded. These *molas* can be considered commodities by metamorphosis: "things intended for other uses that are placed into the commodity state" (Appadurai 1986:16). Many Kuna women thought it rather odd and quite humorous that tourists, whom they perceived as having lots of money and hence able to afford a nice, new *mola*, would want their worn-out, faded *molas*. Not all *mola* blouses that are sold, however, reach the worn out and faded stage. One thirteen-year-old Kuna girl loved to eat rice. She regularly sewed *mola* blouses for herself, but her hunger for rice always took precedence over her wish for more than one change of clothing. Every time a new blouse was finished she took another barely worn blouse to the local store to trade for rice.

With their commercialization, *mola* makers started producing *molas* intended specifically for sale. Appadurai (1986:16) has defined these as "commodities by destination, that is, objects intended by their producers principally for exchange." Throughout the 1980s, different sizes and shapes of *molas* were produced for sale, though women still sold their used blouses. Women sewed *mola* panels (approximately fourteen inches by seventeen inches), *molitas* (little *molas* roughly six inches by seven inches), and round *mola* patches about three inches in diameter. While the panels used in *mola* blouses might vary by several inches, the size of *mola* panels, *molitas*, and patches produced for sale varied little and these were recognized throughout the San Blas region as distinct size categories. During the 1980s, in Mandinga Bay, the area of San Blas frequented by tourists, women started sewing parrots and the words "San Blas" onto T-shirts to sell to the tourists.

In the 1980s, Kuna women had several options for producing and selling their *molas:* they could sew *molas* for sale as independent producers, as part of a piecework system, or through the *mola* cooperative. In each case, the organization of *mola* production, exchange, and consumption was distinct and bore implications for access to cloth, choice of colors and designs, and prices received by producers. Although it is useful conceptually to separate these three categories of producers, in 1985 *mola* makers or sewers could be members of the cooperative and independent producers or sewing piecework and selling *molas* independently. Kuna women did not, however, engage in piecework production (special requests excepted) and sell their *molas* through the cooperative. Mass production of items with *mola* designs will be discussed later in this chapter.

Independent producers sewed the majority of *molas* for sale. These women ranged in age from nine years to over sixty. The extent to which the very young and the very old were involved in sewing *molas* for sale varied throughout the region and among households. In the area frequented by tourists, more elderly women and young girls sewed *molas* than elsewhere. Household-level factors will be explored in later chapters that describe the communities of Carti-Sugtupu, Tupile, and Mansucun. Independent producers did not have a guaranteed market for their *molas*. Unlike piecework producers and cooperative members, independent *mola* makers needed capital to purchase cloth. They had the most choice in *mola* sizes, colors, and designs but lacked information about what buyers liked and the effect of taste on sales. Prices received by producers depended on the options available to them for selling *molas* where they lived. Kuna women generally would not bargain with buyers, although if a woman were in desperate need of cash, she might sell a *mola* for less. Otherwise, women waited for buyers who would pay them "decent" prices.

In 1985, piecework production and special requests were not widespread in San Blas; nonetheless, they did exist. Kuna women were asked to produce pockets, collars, yokes, and other parts needed by non-Kuna female fashion designers. Sewing piecework was attractive to some Kuna women because they did not have to spend any of their own resources on cloth and were guaranteed the sale of their *molas*. Most women, however, thought that piecework sewing was boring because they had very little choice over color and design.

The following account describes the largest of three known piecework operations located in Panama City. María, a middle-aged Panamanian woman, was the initiator and owner of a successful fashion clothing business. She worked out of her home, an apartment located in one of Panama's better neighborhoods. One room had six sewing machines operated by non-Kuna women. A second workroom was used for storage and for cutting patterns and cloth. A showroom displayed fashionable women's and children's clothing. All the clothes had *mola* yokes, cuffs, collars, or patches incorporated into their design. A few vests were completely covered with *mola* designs.

María worked closely with Eliana, a Kuna woman who coordinated a group of women on her home island to sew pockets, yokes, and other pieces. María paid Eliana a small salary for serving as an intermediary. She gave Eliana cloth already cut into the correct shape and smaller pieces of cloth to be used in creating the designs within the overall larger shape. Producers had some flexibility in how they would arrange the designs and smaller pieces of color on a pocket or yoke, though María specified whether she wanted geometric designs, animals, rainbows, or some other general design category. María commented to me that "you can tell them to sew a fish, but do not try telling them what kind of fish to sew or you will not get back good *molas*."

Special *molas* were requested through contacts, either personal or through their husbands, with U.S. citizens living in the old Canal Zone. Most Kuna women I spoke with about special requests had mixed feelings. They liked them because they could charge higher prices, but, like piecework production, requests were not much fun to sew and left no room for the creative process; designs and colors were already specified.

Although cooperative members had more choice than pieceworkers over color and design, their choices were still dictated by the market. For example, if the cooperative administrator in Panama City should send word that the store had too many fish but needed toucans, everyone would be expected to collaborate and sew toucans. Members said they would sew toucans not because they were required to but because they wanted the cooperative to be successful and felt that this was best accomplished through cooperation.

Although Kuna women had always used a wide variety of sources to give them ideas for *mola* designs, when they began to sew *molas* specifically for sale, designs began to be imposed from outside. This was especially true for piecework production, in which intermediaries specified not only the designs to be sewn but the colors, sizes, and shapes, and for special requests. Special requests might include company logos sewn into *molas* to give as presents to employees, the Panamanian flag to hang in bank lobbies and government offices, and Christmas tree ornaments. In some cases, the producer would have no idea what she was sewing. Increasingly, producers were trying to understand the social context of designs that had meanings for consumers, and in doing so, to produce items that would sell. These *molas* produced specifically for sale were not worn by Kuna women; they were valued because they generated income.

Piecework production increased dramatically in the 1990s. The drop in tourism after the United States invaded Panama (1989) left Kuna women with few markets for their *molas*. Responding to that void, at least three new small *maquiladora*-type industries have opened in Panama City that produce women's fashion clothing with *molas*. Requests for *mola* collars, pockets, belts, and other pieces of clothing are sent to San Blas. Panamanian (non-Kuna) women are employed at the factories and use sewing machines to incorporate the *mola* pieces and to complete the garments.

Mola designs were used illegally throughout the 1980s to mass-produce souvenirs for sale to tourists. Importation of items into Panama that compete in any way with locally produced handicraft items has been illegal since January 30, 1967. This law, however, has not been adequately enforced, so that mass-produced items have continued to be imported and to compete with the sale of *molas* produced by Kuna women. In an attempt to address this ongoing problem, Kuna legislators, encouraged by the *mola* cooperative leaders, worked to pass a law specifically prohibiting the import of mass-produced *molas* into Panama. The law reads: "ARTICLE 1.—It is prohibited to import *mola* cloth; prints that copy *molas*; imitations of *molas* and any other cloth or article that in one form or another copies or competes with the Kuna handicraft called *mola*" (Law 26—October 1984).

Despite this new law, mass-produced items were still available in stores throughout Panama City in 1985. Large bath towels and other beachwear featuring *mola* designs were being mass-produced in El Salvador and sold in high-priced ladies' fashion stores in Panama City. In addition to beachwear, "*mola*" cloth was being produced in Japan and sold in fabric stores by the yard. Kuna women living in Panama City reported that dresses made from this material had been featured in the fashion sections of Panama's major newspapers. One store owner, who owned a chain of stores in Panama City at that time, would send photographs of *molas* to a company located in Taiwan. The firm would use the photographs to produce ashtrays, playing cards, and plastic shopping bags featuring the *mola* designs. These "souvenir" items would then be shipped back to Panama for sale to tourists. Mass-producing ashtrays with *mola* designs can be considered a misuse of Kuna ethnic symbols. I do not know what effect the decline in tourism in the early 1990s has had on the production and sale of mass-produced *mola* items.

Gender, Income, Ethnicity, and the *Mola* Market

A careful description of the chain from producer through intermediary to end buyer reveals social differentiation based on access to capital among the Kuna as well as between men and women (see fig. 1).

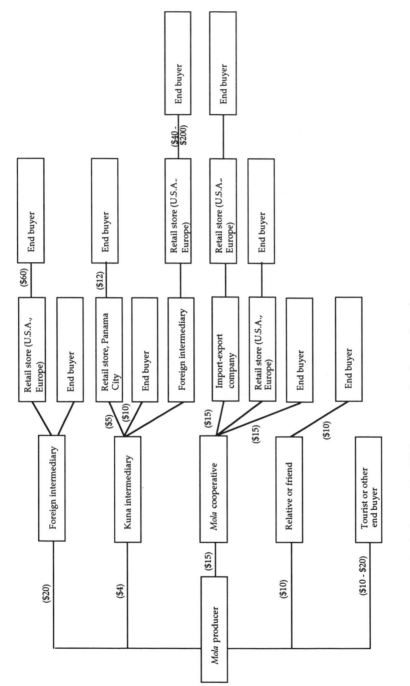

Prices are approximately what buyers paid in 1984 for an average three-layer mola panel

Figure 1. *Mola* marketing: From producer to consumer

Access to *mola* buyers in Panama City in the 1980s was defined by gender and had implications for resource distribution. Kuna men and women sold their *molas* in different places and at different prices. Several different types of intermediaries operated in Panama City, with Kuna men providing the link between the San Blas region and Panama City. Other intermediaries, including small independent entrepreneurs (both male and female) and Panamanian retail store owners (all male), sold *molas* to consumers in Panama and to intermediaries from the United States. Intermediaries from the United States (male and female) included representatives from import firms (all male) and owners of small retail shops specializing in ethnic crafts or in gift items (male and female).

Molas were purchased by consumers, intermediaries, and retail stores. The most direct transaction, and the most economically beneficial to the producer, was the sale of a *mola* by a producer to the end buyer. Tourists, whether in San Blas or in Panama City, have been the largest direct buyers of *molas*. The second largest group of purchasers have been U.S. citizens connected with the United States Army, Navy, or Air Force or with the Panama Canal. Until the 1990s, when it became fashionable for upper-class Panamanian women to wear clothing decorated with *molas,* Panamanians bought very few *molas.*

Retail stores in Panama often served as a link in the chain of intermediaries between producers and retail stores and consumers abroad. For example, individuals representing import-export companies might travel only occasionally to Panama. They would establish a relationship with the *mola* cooperative or with the owner of a retail store in Panama City who had a large selection of *molas* and was willing to ship orders. Museums and art investors searched for high-quality *molas* and were willing to pay relatively high prices. Some traveled to the islands. Others depended on retail stores in Panama. In one case, an investor owned a large chain of retail stores. He bought *molas* in bulk, culling out the finest ones for his personal collection.

In Panama City there were a number of places in the 1980s where *molas* could be sold directly by the producer or through an intermediary to the consumer. These places included Balboa Park, where fifteen to twenty Kuna women would congregate daily to sew and sell *molas,* the plaza in front of the national lottery building, and street corners. Balboa Park is located in the old Canal Zone. There was a circle just off of the road where Kuna women would go daily to sell and to sew *molas.* The circular bench there was located in a cool, shady area surrounded by trees. Tourists would wander around looking at *molas* and occasionally making a purchase. Also, Kuna women sometimes sold *molas* at the Miraflores locks (James Howe, personal communication).

Another very popular spot for selling *molas* was a public plaza where every Sunday the winning numbers for the national lottery were selected. Working-class Panamanians would turn out by the hundreds for this weekly event. Kuna and non-Kuna artisans alike would come to the plaza on Sundays to sell their wares. Some would bring *molas*, paintings, or jewelry that they had produced. Others would bring wares made by others. For example, one Panamanian non-Kuna woman had a table with items she had made from *molas*, including a bikini, visor hats, glasses cases, and small handbags. Others sold Panamanian straw hats, large ceramic flower pots, and jewelry made from beads, shells, and low-grade metals. Kuna women would sit beside small piles of *molas* and sew. Some Kuna men had piles of *molas* that they had purchased from women on their home islands or were selling for their female relatives.

A few women would sit out on sidewalks trying to sell their *molas*. This was not a common sight in the 1980s, though it could be a poignant one, as in the following scene: A lone Kuna woman sits in front of McDonalds, her legs stretched out in front of her. She has several *mola* panels and some beaded bracelets displayed on a blue piece of plastic beside her. All of her wares have been made by women in her household. She sews a *mola* as she sits waiting for people to stop. Next to McDonalds is a women's clothing store displaying the latest New York fashions in the window. One blond manikin wears a beach towel printed with *mola* designs.

Tourists often found the beach towel a more attractive purchase because they could use it. Several tourists commented that the woman's handmade *molas* were beautiful, but they did not know what they would do with one if they bought it.

The average price of a *mola* panel when sold directly to a tourist in the places mentioned above was ten dollars. Actual prices might range from five dollars to twenty dollars, depending on the quality of the *mola* and how desperately the woman needed to make a sale. Some women reported sitting for several days without selling anything. The marked drop in tourists visiting Panama during the 1980s had a profound impact on women's ability to sell their *molas* directly to tourists in Panama City. Some women sold their *molas* through personal networks to U.S. citizens living in the old Canal Zone. These buyers would generally buy only high-quality *molas* and would pay higher prices than the average tourist. Most tourists could not distinguish between a high- and a low-quality *mola* and did not like to pay higher prices.

Mola producers did not have the same access to store owners in Panama City as Kuna intermediaries did. Store owners preferred to buy large sackfuls of *molas,* paying three dollars to five dollars per panel, than to negotiate with individual producers. Store owners explained that Kuna women would demand higher prices and they would only go to retail stores when desperate for money because they would usually be turned away and could ordinarily get higher prices for their *molas* elsewhere. Also, because Kuna women tended not to speak Spanish, they had to find someone to accompany them or risk negotiating with what little Spanish they knew. Communication was difficult at best.[5]

For male Kuna intermediaries, the range of places to sell *molas* in Panama City was considerably larger than for female producers, and their ability to make a profit was greater. For example, at the time of my research, there were four or five Kuna men who sold *molas* regularly to the buyer for a chain of drugstores located in Panama City. They usually came twice a month and brought two hundred to three hundred *molas* at a time. The average price paid for a *mola* panel was $3.50. The owner of the chain started to collect *molas* in 1975 as a hobby and for investment. His personal collection was kept in a safe. In the process of searching for collector's items, he decided to try to sell lower-quality *molas* in his stores. Some of these *molas* were made into hats, handbags, pillows, scarves, wall hangings, and other items. Others were framed or were sold as individual panels. The director of the store calculated that by 1984 he had purchased about $50,000 worth of *molas.* In 1979 and 1980, during the tourist boom in Panama, he bought even larger quantities of *molas.* Five years later, with fewer tourists visiting Panama, sales to this chain of stores were down.

Molas were also sold in ethnic art stores in Panama City. These stores ranged from small shops located in the old and poorer section of town to stores in some of Panama's finer hotels. One woman, Rosa, formed a partnership with her brother-in-law in 1961 and opened a store. He provided the capital; she provided the labor. Kuna intermediaries came to Rosa with sacks full of *molas.* She often bought in bulk sight unseen. Sometimes women came into her store with individual *molas* for sale. She might pay five dollars per blouse, depending on the quality of the *mola.* Rosa preferred to buy *molas* from Kuna men, however. She sold framed *molas,* single *mola* panels, change purses, bags and purses of varying sizes, visors, tennis racket covers, dresses with small *molas* sewn onto them, and T-shirts with the words "San Blas" and a small patch of *mola* sewn on them.

Class, gender, and ethnicity all come into play when *molas* are sold. Gender stratifies access to income from *mola* sales. Although Kuna men and women sell directly to tourists, only Kuna men are intermediaries outside of San Blas. Differentiation along gender lines appears to be clear-cut: female producers sell their *molas* at low prices to male intermediaries who then resell the *molas* at a profit. If we return to San Blas and ask who these intermediaries are, however, and who controls their capital, the picture becomes more complex and we can begin to see the intersection of socioeconomic differentiation and gender.

Kuna intermediaries who buy and sell *molas* are typically store owners or itinerant traders. Although the men generally travel to Panama City, their wives are often "business partners." Wives tend the store, tell their husbands what to purchase, and, in some cases, keep and jointly control all of the capital. This follows the "traditional" pattern of how Kuna households organize and control the distribution of resources. The senior man and woman jointly decide what the household needs. The senior man organizes the junior men's labor to provide for those needs while the senior woman controls the distribution of resources brought into the household by men. (Chapter 10 discusses in greater detail the control and distribution of resources at the household level.) In some merchant households, senior Kuna women continue to control and distribute resources. In others, however, men have taken over this role and, although a woman may benefit from her husband's business, she has no control over the capital. Still, it is clear that socioeconomic differentiation among women as well as between the sexes is occurring.

If we widen our analytical lens to include retail store owners in Panama City and the United States, we can begin to see other ways that class, gender, and ethnicity intersect. Although Kuna merchant households earn more from *mola* sales than do individual producers, their earnings are still minimal compared with those of Latino store owners, itinerant traders, and piecework contractors in Panama City and store owners in the United States. It is interesting to note that the three ethnic arts stores I visited in Panama City and the six in the United States where *molas* were sold were all owned and operated by women. All of the chain stores in Panama City were owned by men. The four intermediaries I spoke with who purchased crafts to sell to the ethnic arts stores in the United States were men, and all were Latino. Some women (Panamanian, non-Kuna, and from the United States) functioned as intermediaries; however, they depended on interpersonal networks for both the purchase and the sale of *molas*. For example, one woman from the United States who has lived in Panama for years buys *molas* from Kuna households she knows and sells them to friends in Panama City and the United States.

Although I do not have systematic data on merchants who buy *molas*, the data I do have suggest that gender defines the global *mola* market. Women appear to be small-scale merchants whereas men appear to control the production and sale of mass-produced items made with *mola* designs and sold in the chain stores in Panama and the high-cost galleries in the United States where *molas* are often exhibited.

New Social Contexts for *Mola* Use

Whether people buy *molas* as examples of Kuna art, as souvenirs, or for personal use influences the type of *molas* that are produced as well as the producers' relationship to the productive process. *Molas* may be viewed as fine art to be viewed in galleries and museums, as financial investments, as designs removed from their social context to be used for interior decorating, as ethnic handicrafts made by the Kuna people, or as "souvenirs" from an "exotic" place. *Molas* may also decorate other usable items. For example, in 1985 there were a number of non-Kuna Panamanian women who created handbags, skirts, vests, change purses, and other such items with *molas*. Some bought *mola* panels already made and incorporated them into their designs; others contracted for piecework to provide them with particular shapes and patterns. Out of five of these women I interviewed, four had other women working for them sewing handbags and other items. One woman purchased mass-produced bags and other items and decorated them with *mola* patches.

In general, Panamanians have not decorated their homes with *molas* and have tended not to buy *molas* except to use as gifts when they travel abroad. Unlike in Mexico, where it has become fashionable in certain circles to decorate with indigenous crafts, the Panamanian upper class has had its sights firmly set on fashions from New York and Miami. One person explained that if an object was "made in Panama" people would automatically think that it was "no good." I observed some middle-class Panamanians in Panama City buying practical items such as *mola* handbags, visors, and glasses cases. The Panamanian poor could not afford to buy *molas*.

Interestingly, a new surge of nationalist sentiment, as a result of the United States invasion of Panama in 1989, has stimulated the upper class's interest in *molas*. In the 1990s, wearing clothing incorporating *molas* has become fashionable and a symbol of national pride (Anna Wenzel, personal communication).

Tourists bought *molas* mainly as souvenirs or to give as gifts. A survey of 123 tourists aboard a cruise liner visiting San Blas revealed that 76, or over half, had purchased *molas*. Forty of these planned to use them to decorate their houses; 27 planned to keep them as souvenirs of their trip; 25 were going to give them as gifts; 26 planned to use them for a functional purpose. Conversations with these tourists revealed that they knew little, if anything, about the Kuna people or about *molas*.

In addition to their appeal to tourists, by 1985 *molas* had become a well-recognized symbol of Panama. *Molas* were hung in prominent public places throughout Panama City. Large murals made from numerous *mola* panels sewn together covered entire walls in one of Panama's major hotels and in the lobbies of two banks. In 1985, it was not uncommon to find framed *mola* panels hanging in hotel lobbies, government offices, and banks. The Panamanian flag was a popular theme for these *molas*. In addition to cloth, materials such as paint and tile might be used to create these designs. One gas station had *mola* designs painted in bright yellow and orange on the columns next to the gas pumps. Another had a full wall painted with *mola* designs. Decorative ceramic tiles painted with *mola* designs were prominent on at least two public buildings in the city.

Molas produced specifically as public art might or might not be made by Kuna women. Sometimes designs would be copied from already-existing *molas*, and Kuna women were not involved in either the creation or the production of the items. At other times, Kuna women were asked to sew the *molas* needed for a particular project.

Producers' and consumers' knowledge about each other's social contexts is highly important; the availablity of knowledge, or lack thereof, can be used as a locus for negotiation and control over price, design, and sales. Appadurai (1986:42) has defined production knowledge as including both technical knowledge (the how-to) and "knowledge of the market, the consumer, the destination of the commodity." Knowledge about the social context within which *molas* will be used varies widely among producers. For example, an owner of a large chain of supermarkets in Panama City ordered one thousand small *mola* snowmen to be used as Christmas tree ornaments. One day a number of women were sitting together sewing these snowmen. One leaned over and asked me what snowmen ate, how big they were, and if they lived in the jungle or the sea. None of the women had the foggiest idea of what they were sewing. As we sat there with beads of sweat dripping down our necks, I attempted to

Mola animal pillows, patches, and Christmas tree ornaments

explain in Kuna, a language with no word for snow, all about snow-men. The only thing they knew about that was frozen were *bolis*, small plastic bags filled with frozen Kool-Aid. They tried imagining what shredded coconut as cold as *bolis* would look like coming down from the sky. The general conclusion was that snowmen were very strange indeed. The women thought they would die if they ever visited the United States when it was cold enough to snow. These co-operative members accepted sewing items such as snowmen without protest because they needed the cash.

At the other extreme, Kuna women who have opportunities to observe consumer behavior directly have developed very sophisticated knowledge about what sells. These women's use of color and design has been affected by buyers' likes and dislikes. This was especially true in the tourist area of Carti, where women would think very consciously about what sold when they chose their colors and designs. They explained and sometimes excused the repetitiveness of their designs in terms of needing to sew what the tourists would like. They knew that tourists liked toucans and parrots. *Molas* with orange as the dominant color would not sell well, especially to Europeans. Bright and contrasting colors such as pink and chartreuse green generally would not go over very well with tourists either. Producers in nontourist areas might not observe buyers' preferences firsthand, but this information would be passed on by other Kuna traveling from the tourist areas and from Panama City. Women were also informed by intermediaries who had been briefed by store owners in Panama City as to what would sell. These two examples illustrate the range in knowledge producers have about consumers, their likes and dislikes, and how *molas* will be used once purchased.

Consumers also have varying amounts of information about *molas* and the social context within which they are produced. One tourist asked me where they (the Kuna) "really lived." She thought the island had been set up to show tourists how the Kuna used to live and that the Kuna changed their clothes at the end of the day and went home. Most tourists I spoke with were somewhat more informed. The point is that *molas* sold as souvenirs become detached from their original meaning and social context.

At the other extreme, art collectors who buy *molas* as investments are highly knowledgeable about the history of *mola* designs and the quality of *molas*. Both producers and consumers are affected by each other's levels of production knowledge. Some producers have used this to their benefit. For example, some Kuna women in the area of San Blas frequented by tourists use the buyers' lack of knowledge about what constitutes a high-quality *mola* to sell poor-quality *molas* at high prices.

The *mola* cooperative took another approach and in 1985 developed a new strategy for marketing high-quality, high-cost *molas* and at the same time reviving interest in "traditional" geometric *mola* designs both among the Kuna and abroad. A few of the better *mola* makers from one chapter of the cooperative started researching the "traditional" geometric designs that had been painted onto cloth or sewn into *molas* by their grandmothers and great-grandmothers. They sewed these designs into *mola* panels that, because they were "traditional" and of high quality, sold through the cooperative for fifty dollars, more than twice the price of other *mola* panels. The "authenticity" of these *molas*, in addition to the quality of stitching, was used as a main selling point. Tourists and merchants alike were educated about the history, social context, and meaning of these *molas*. The cooperative also used these *molas* to educate younger Kuna women about their own history.

As the local anthropologist, I was a source of production knowledge for both producer and consumer. As illustrated by the story about the snowmen, I was often questioned by producers about *mola* use in the United States. Similarly, tourists questioned me about the social context for *mola* use in San Blas. Occasionally, I was caught between a producer and a consumer. One Kuna woman tried to convince a somewhat leery tourist that she had made "by hand" several cloth sequined elephants. These elephants had been purchased in Panama City and were handmade in India, not San Blas. My help was elicited from both sides, placing me in a very awkward position. My Kuna friend called on me as a friend to help her convince the tourist to buy the elephant. The tourist wanted to know if elephants really lived in the jungles of San Blas and whether the woman had really made the elephant. I managed to satisfy both parties by answering truthfully that there were no elephants in San Blas and that the elephant was not made locally; however, if the tourist liked the elephant she should purchase it. I also explained why the Kuna woman was so desperate to sell the elephant. The tourist purchased the elephant. (This was the only time I encountered a Kuna woman inventing a story to convince a tourist to buy.)

Reflections

Class, gender, and ethnicity form an intricate tapestry defining who sells what to whom, where, and for how much. The division of labor by gender determines who can sell where and accounts, in part, for unequal access to income from *mola* sales. It is important to note, however, that, although gender clearly defines access to certain markets, socioeconomic differentiation among the Kuna cuts across gender lines. Furthermore, Kuna men and women both earn less than non-Kuna retail store owners and intermediaries who sell to stores in the United States, Europe, and Japan. Selling *molas* has not allowed Kuna merchants to purchase land or labor, or to acquire power locally or nationally. How producers' possibilities for selling their *molas* are affected by their local community's and household's incorporation into the global economy will be explored in chapters 8, 9, and 10, describing specific Kuna communities.

Although new social contexts for using *molas* have affected Kuna *mola* makers' relationship to their craft, this cannot be viewed as unidirectional. Producer and consumer knowledge about the production, exchange, and consumption of *molas* within specific historical and cultural contexts is a dynamic area within which conflicting and sometimes converging interests are defined and negotiated. *Mola* designs, colors, and shapes have all changed as a result of their commercialization. Graburn (1976:31) points out that the "impetus for innovations may come from inside or outside the Fourth World—as a result of artistic excitement, ethnic revitalization, or simply as an economic response to the *perceived* desires of the consumer."

Kuna *mola* makers not only have responded to the perceived de-

sires of the consumer but also have carefully observed consumer behavior and have attempted to shape that behavior. In some cases, the
Kuna have used their knowledge about consumers to their advantage. They have taught tourists and merchants about the social context and value of designs and in the process have developed products
with increased value on the market. Creating new designs and products is not always a creative process, however. Some "innovations"
have been externally imposed on impoverished *mola* makers who
are forced to sew almost anything that provides them with a source
of income.

   Appadurai (1986:13) has argued that things have a social life and
"can move in *and* out of the commodity state, that such movements
can be slow or fast, reversible or terminal, normative or deviant."
Molas are clearly simultaneously both in and out of the commodity
state. Most Kuna women sew *molas* for their own use as well as to
sell without ever wearing. The extent to which individual Kuna
women commoditize their *molas* depends on a series of interrelated
factors related to household subsistence production and migration.
Chapter 7 describes how a group of Kuna women have attempted to
equalize access to the market by organizing a *mola* cooperative.

7.
Kuna Women Organize

Wet and hungry we arrived at Tubuala, an island located in the eastern part of San Blas. It had rained much of our journey and our umbrellas and colorful sheets of plastic had done little to keep us dry. About twenty cooperative members from Tupile, six preschool children, and I had traveled in the cooperative's large dugout canoe with an outboard motor to Tubuala to give a ten-day skills-building seminar to cooperative members living in that area of San Blas. The Tubuala chapter of the cooperative was hosting the event and quickly showed us to the households where we would be staying. After drinking hot chocolate, bathing, hanging our hammocks, throwing the few clothes we had brought over a bamboo pole that had been cleared for us, and resting awhile, I and one of the cooperative leaders from Tupile followed our host from Tubuala to the *congreso*, where sixty-three women and three men from ten communities were gathered for the start of the seminar. The cooperative's female administrator and a male Kuna extension worker from the Ministerio de Desarrollo Agropecuario (MIDA) who had provided technical support to the cooperative for years had flown in from Panama City to attend.

Tubuala's *sakla* and Kawidi (one of Kuna Yala's three *caciques*) greeted us and hot drinks were passed around. The next ten days were spent together as a group, primarily in the large *congreso* house. The cooperative leaders talked to the group at length about the importance of the cooperative and about what did or did not sell. We divided into small groups and learned how to cut and sew *mola* animal pillows. Seminar leaders (all outstanding *mola* makers) worked with individuals to help them improve the quality of their stitching and designs. I observed, worked on a *mola*, and talked with different women about the commercialization of *molas* and the gender division of labor in their communities. The participants had been selected by their local chapters to attend

Mola cooperative members in front of the cooperative on Tupile

the seminar. Each of them was expected to hold a miniseminar when they returned to share what they had learned with cooperative members in their home community.

It rained for most of the ten days. We sat, sewed, joked, talked, and compared what we had been given to eat and drink in our host households. Our hosts, the cooperative members from Tubuala, served us a special meal of wild boar (smoked dry and then rehydrated) with *tule masi*. In the afternoons we walked around the island in small groups visiting different households. Every evening we all attended Tubuala's *congreso* and listened to the *sakla* chant and the *arkar* interpret. Seminar participants were as curious about my life as I was about theirs, and I spent many hours repeating details about my life. The women were particularly interested in craft production in the United States and in Guatemala and in my knowledge about issues related to women and development.[1]

The *mola* cooperative, organized in the 1960s to increase Kuna women's income-generating potential, has become a way for producers to gain some local control over the distribution of income from *mola* sales. While the Kuna have developed many projects designed to maintain local control over important economic resources such as land, urban housing, and the tourist trade, the *mola* cooperative is the only project in which women have taken exclusive leadership.

Early History

The *mola* cooperative, today known as Los Productores de Molas R.L., grew out of a project organized in 1967 by Peace Corps volunteers to teach women how to sew and market baby clothes. The goal of this project was to provide women with an income-generating activity. It was not very successful, however. Kuna women chiefly attributed the project's initial failure to the fact that in those days few Kuna babies wore clothes. Some of the women felt that they had no need for this type of sewing skill (i.e., using sewing machines). Furthermore, until then, sewing by machine was considered an activity done by men. Some women suggested that helping them to organize and to find better markets for their *molas* would be more useful. Several Kuna women pointed out that *mola* producers were receiving very low prices from intermediaries and that perhaps by organizing something could be done. Intermediaries, at that time, paid $2.50 to $3.00 per *mola* panel. These prices were so low that in 1974 the Congreso General Kuna mandated a minimum price of $4 per *mola* panel.

Responding to the Kuna women's suggestions, the Peace Corps volunteers turned their efforts toward organizing groups of women around *mola* production and marketing. Eight groups were formed. Peace Corps volunteers rented and staffed a storefront in Panama City where a variety of handmade items from Peace Corps projects all over Panama were sold. These goods, including *molas*, were flown to Washington, D.C., where they were sold through the Peace Corps offices (Alvarez 1969; Barahona 1979; Reynolds 1968). The Peace Corps also provided some working capital, supplies, and business expertise to the cooperative. In 1967, a precooperative was officially established so that members would qualify for national government supports such as cooperative education classes (Swain 1977:77). By this time, eight local chapters were in operation with a total of 350 members. Membership continued to grow.

Several years later, the Panamanian government asked the Peace Corps to leave Panama. When volunteers left, so did the resources they had offered to the cooperative, and membership decreased dramatically. For example, on one island membership dropped from 250 to 25. Still, a small group of women, who by then called themselves the "*mola* cooperative," struggled on. Overhead for the store in Panama City was more than the cooperative could manage. Thus, soon after the Peace Corps left, the cooperative moved its inventory to the Kuna administrator's home, from which it continued to sell and to export *molas.*

To the women who remained members, the cooperative represented something much more than easy access to cash. These women envisioned the cooperative as a vehicle through which to (1) participate in the planning and implementation of economic development projects locally and regionally; (2) contribute financially to the support of selected projects; and (3) represent women's special interests through formal participation in the all-male Congreso General Kuna.

The cooperative's primary obstacle then, as now, was lack of capital. Without capital, members had to wait until the *molas* were sold before producers could be paid. Women in other communities wanted to join the cooperative, but without funds cooperative leaders had no way to mobilize. They decided to seek full legal status as a cooperative in order to obtain loans. On October 31, 1974, the cooperative, now officially named Los Productores de Molas R.L., became one of three artisan cooperatives in the Republic of Panama to be officially licensed by the Autonomous Panamanian Institute of Cooperatives (IPACOOP), the department responsible for cooperatives nationwide. It also became the first officially recognized cooperative in the San Blas region. As stated in the bylaws, the producers' primary goal was to create a steady market for *molas*.

Technically, gaining legal status as a cooperative entitled the group to access to credit through banks and technical assistance from the Panamanian government. Unfortunately, a small women's handicrafts cooperative did not fit under any of the banks' lending categories, and the women were unable to secure any credit or loans. Cooperative leaders found out that funds might be available through the Inter-American Foundation (IAF) and decided to apply for a grant for expansion and improvement. The primary goal of the Inter-American Foundation is to support self-help economic development projects, initiated at the local level, in Latin America.

International Funding

Receipt of a $30,000 grant from the Inter-American Foundation in 1978 marked a turning point for the cooperative. The grant enabled the cooperative to (1) expand membership; (2) further diversify products sold by the cooperative; (3) lower production costs; (4) develop new educational and income-generating opportunities for members; and (5) increase women's participation in politics.

Expanded Membership

One of the goals of the *mola* cooperative was to provide equal market access to producers throughout the San Blas region. This was accomplished by expanding the number of local chapters. Five new local chapters were added to the original eight, and membership soared from 300 in 1977 to over 1,300 in 1981. By 1985, the *mola* cooperative had grown to include seventeen local chapters (sixteen in San Blas and one in Panama City) with a total membership of 1,496.

The cooperative used IAF funds to hold new-member workshops and to increase the pool of capital. New-member workshops were intended to assist a group of interested women on an island with no local chapter to become part of the cooperative. These gatherings focused on describing the principles behind, the benefits of, and the specific operational details of becoming working members of the cooperative. They were usually conducted by the cooperative's administrator, president, vice-president, and secretary and one or two Kuna men who had received formal training in running cooperatives in Panama City. Interested producers could sign up as members of the cooperative at the end of the workshop. The cooperative received requests to hold more new-member workshops than members had time or resources to conduct.

Part of the IAF grant was added to the cooperative's small pool of capital that was used to pay producers. Increasing the cooperative's operating capital meant that new local chapters could be added to the cooperative without requiring that producers be paid only after their *molas* sold. Since women depended on the income from the sale of their *molas*, the cooperative has tried to pay producers right away, on receipt of their *molas*.

Diversified Products

IAF funds allowed the cooperative to further diversify its products and to increase the number of members who knew how to sew these different items. In addition to *mola* panels, *molitas,* and patches, the cooperative now sells stuffed animal *molas* of varying sizes and shapes (toucans, fish, squirrels, elephants, etc.), *mola* pillows (round, square, and heart-shaped), shoulder bags, change purses, eyeglass cases, belts, Christmas stockings, and Christmas tree ornaments. Sewing machines were purchased with IAF money to finish new products such as *mola* handbags and pillows. Some of the cooperative's most highly skilled producers started sewing *molas* with "traditional" geometric designs. Samples of these beautiful, intricate, extremely high quality *molas* were prominently displayed in the cooperative's store in Panama City. These *molas* could be special ordered and cost around fifty dollars.

A regionwide education committee was formed on the island of Tupile in 1980 to organize and conduct product diversification workshops. The Tupile chapter of the cooperative was one of the first chapters to be organized, and its members sewed the widest variety of products. In contrast, members of some local chapters knew how to sew only *mola* panels, *molitas,* and patches. Furthermore, producers in the eastern region of San Blas, where women spent more time engaged in agricultural production, sewed lower-quality *molas* than did producers in western San Blas. Most producers in the west spent most of their time sewing *molas* and generally did not work in the fields.

Subregional workshops were held throughout the early 1980s to

Sewing *molas* with other members of the *mola* cooperative

teach members skills such as how to use patterns to cut the animal shapes, how to create interesting animal features (eyes, nose, feathers, claws, etc.), and, in general, how to improve the quality of their sewing. Education committee members volunteered their time to organize and lead these workshops. Representatives from local chapters came to the workshops and then were responsible for teaching members of their own chapters the skills they had learned. As in the new-member gatherings, the cooperative administrator and one of the two Kuna men who had studied the principles of cooperativism spent part of the product-diversification workshops reviewing the principles and organization of the cooperative. IAF funds were used to purchase a large dugout canoe and an outboard motor and to cover other transportation costs such as airfare and gasoline so that workshops could be held.

These workshops facilitated one of the cooperative's larger goals: to link goods produced by cooperative members to market demands. They provided opportunities for members who had direct experience with buyers in Panama City to share their observations about what did and did not sell. For example, a member of the education committee spent one month in Panama City learning about how the cooperative's retail store functioned and observing buyers' behavior.

She told women attending one workshop that tourists did not like bright pink or lime green, so they should not use these colors because the cooperative would be unable to sell their *molas* and everyone would suffer.

Lowered Production Costs

Bulk purchasing of cloth and thread with IAF funds lowered members' production costs and almost eliminated the need for cash to start a *mola*. Members could now acquire the cloth they needed to start a *molu* at their local chapters. In the past, they had to purchase cloth at the local stores. In 1981, for example, cloth cost from $2.50 to $2.80 per yard at local stores and thread cost $0.45 to $0.50 per spool. Cloth through the cooperative cost $1.25 per yard and thread cost $0.35. Furthermore, the cost of the cloth acquired through the cooperative was recorded and then deducted from the total price the member received for a finished *mola*. (Thread had to be paid for at the time of purchase.) A producer can now obtain cloth to start a *mola* through the cooperative even if she has no cash to purchase cloth. Bulk buying of cloth has reduced the cost of the raw materials needed to sew a *mola* by more than half.

When the cooperative started to buy cloth and thread in bulk, these supplies were purchased by the cooperative administrator and her assistants in Panama City and sent directly to each local chapter. In the early 1980s, central cloth and thread committees were organized to keep track of local chapters' inventories, to coordinate with cooperative workers in Panama City, and to distribute cloth and thread to local chapters throughout San Blas.

Purchase of the sewing machines for use in the local chapters allowed cooperative members to become involved in all aspects of production and also lowered production costs. Whereas finishing work for pillows and bags, for example, had been done by paid cooperative members in Panama City, much of this work could now be done in San Blas by unpaid cooperative members as a part of the production process. Women took turns contributing their labor, and while not all women knew how to operate a sewing machine, many were learning.

Increased Educational and Income-Generating Opportunities

Although activities in addition to the production and sale of *molas* were not planned or funded, the IAF grant stimulated many local chapters to become involved in such activities. These ranged from the bulk purchase and resale of food and clothing to savings and lending programs. Co-op–sponsored workshops provided women with opportunities to share ideas and experiences. Some co-op leaders arranged for informal internships in other communities to learn about how to organize other income-generating activities.

Local chapters have also increasingly supported co-op members' acquisition of literacy, accounting, and leadership skills since receipt of the IAF grant. For example, many chapters requested assistance with literacy skills from schoolteachers in their community as part of a campaign sponsored by the Ministry of Education to increase adult literacy skills. Some women were afraid to study by themselves but participated enthusiastically as part of a larger group of women. Other chapters have formed informal study groups to teach members accounting skills.

Local chapters also provided a source of volunteer community labor. They swept public paths in anticipation of celebrations or important gatherings, cooked, and served food and drink at special gatherings. Some chapters sponsored special feasts for all of the children in the community. Some of these activities will be described in greater detail in the discussion of the three field sites, particularly Tupile. Although these voluntary activities did not generate any income, the cooperative was increasingly viewed as contributing to the well-being of the community.

Increased Political Participation

The expansion and increased organization of the cooperative provided women with a vehicle for increased political participation. For example, in 1981 the president of the cooperative met with Kuna political leaders to ask them to pressure the national government to enforce the 1967 law that prohibits the importation of products that compete with Panamanian handicrafts. That same year, three representatives from the *mola* cooperative attended the Congreso General Kuna. They were the first women ever to attend the *congreso* officially, and because of their status as a recognized, regionwide organization, they had the right to speak. At this *congreso, La Carta Orgánica de San Blas,* a legal document that delineates the San Blas Kuna's political and social rights and describes their economic base, was being revised. *Mola* exports were not included in the 1945 *Carta Orgánica* as an economic resource. Cooperative representatives present at the meeting proposed that *molas* be added to the document as one of the region's most important resources. Consensus was reached on this point, and it was added to the document. The cooperative also donated five hundred dollars to the General Congress committee charged with defining and protecting the boundaries of the *comarca* of San Blas.

Many cooperative members also began to participate increasingly in their local *congresos*. In communities where women attended religious *congresos* during the day and men discussed social, political, and economic concerns in the evenings, cooperative leaders began occasionally to attend and speak at the evening meetings. Local *congresos* had previously involved both men and women for religious as well as political meetings. In 1985, many communities, including Mansucun, the village described in chapter 10, still brought men and women together for both types of *congreso*.

The Cooperative in 1985

By 1985, the cooperative was well established in the San Blas region, with an official membership of almost fifteen hundred. It was divided into seventeen local chapters, sixteen in San Blas and one in Panama City. All of the *molas* produced for the cooperative were sold through a small retail store located in the back room of a government building in Panama City. The store administrator, a Kuna woman, was responsible for exporting *molas*, tending the store in Panama City, promoting the cooperative both nationally and internationally, representing the cooperative at international artisan fairs, purchasing materials (cloth, thread, etc.) to send to the local chapters in San Blas, managing the cooperative's finances, and pricing *molas* sent from the local chapters. Two other Kuna women assisted the administrator. Each of the three women was paid a small salary out of the cooperative's general operating fund.

Cooperative leaders at the regional level volunteered their time. A regionwide president, vice-president, secretary, and treasurer were elected every two years by an executive committee comprising representatives (usually the president, vice-president, and secretary) from each local chapter. Like general congress leaders, these elected, unpaid leaders were from different communities. They met twice yearly with the cooperative's administrator and the leaders from each local chapter. Meeting sites were rotated among different communities. The Tupile chapter had regionwide administrative responsibilities for distributing and inventorying cloth supplies and for keeping detailed financial records.

Similar to the overall organizational structure, each local chapter had an elected president, vice-president, secretary, treasurer, and a number of committees. Local chapter leaders would occasionally travel to Panama City to learn more about cooperative operations there and to share their perspectives with the administrator and her assistants.

Most chapters divided members into smaller work groups. Each work group had one or more leaders. Although every chapter had a house, none was large enough to accommodate all the members at one time. Use of the cooperative building for cutting cloth and for sewing was usually rotated by work group. These groups might also be involved in a wide range of other income-generating activities, ranging from one-time activities such as selling rice and fish to buying and selling rice, plantains, or kerosene on an ongoing basis.

Membership in the cooperative is open to any *mola* producer. Membership requires the purchase of a five-dollar share, which is returned if the person decides to withdraw from the cooperative. Official counts of membership in the cooperative do not accurately represent the number of people actively involved, however. In 1985, the cooperative boasted a membership of 1,496 persons; however, it was common for one or two producers in a household to become official members while the other women "helped" them sew *molas* for sale through the cooperative. The member would cut cloth at the cooperative for two or three *molas* at a time. She would sew one *mola* and give the other two to female relatives to sew. In this way, the entire household benefited from the cooperative, but only one person was responsible for attending meetings (members were fined ten cents if absent).

Membership in the cooperative was passed on from a mother to a daughter as part of her inheritance. If a woman went for an extended period to Panama City, a daughter, granddaughter, or niece would take over her responsibilities for attending meetings and participating in other cooperative activities. Thus, although the cooperative talks about individual membership, it is more accurate to think of households as members.

Cooperative members receive most of the sale price of their *molas*. For example, a producer in the 1980s would earn $17.80 in cash for a *mola* selling for $20.00. Prices were determined for each *mola* by the administrator in Panama City. Criteria for pricing included fineness of stitching, use of color, and overall presentation of design. The producer received the final sale price minus the cost of the cloth

($1.25 for a large *mola*), administrative overhead costs ($0.80), and personal savings ($0.15).

Personal savings were deposited in an interest-drawing bank account in Panama City. Members might withdraw their savings at any time for personal use. Overhead income was used to pay the administrator and the other women who worked in the cooperative store. It was also used to pay for office supplies and gasoline for the cooperative's boat, which transported members to and from cooperative educational seminars. Leftover funds were used for outreach or helping new local chapters get started, or they went into the revolving fund for cloth or became part of the cooperative's general pool of capital.

Key Issues

The cooperative has faced five major issues as it has grown and developed: cooperative leadership; men's role in the cooperative; access to working capital; transportation; and competition from other *mola* producers and sellers.

Leadership

Who provides leadership for the cooperative has been an important ongoing issue. Most members think that a Kuna woman who wears *mola* should represent the cooperative. Reflecting this viewpoint, cooperative presidents were elected throughout the 1980s who were Kuna women who dressed in *mola,* spoke only Kuna, and resided in San Blas. Because of the language barrier, the cooperative presidents have mainly dedicated themselves to representing the cooperative within the San Blas region and to coordinating activities among the local chapters.

The administrator of the cooperative, whom I shall call Pilar, has a much more highly visible leadership role regionally, nationally, and internationally than the co-op's president. She wears *molas* only on special occasions and even then does not wear full Kuna dress. Nonetheless, she is highly regarded by most cooperative members and provides active leadership for the cooperative. Pilar's leadership role in the cooperative has not been controversial. Members recognize that it is in their best interests to have someone administer the cooperative who speaks Spanish fluently.

Throughout most of the 1980s, Pilar traveled extensively with other cooperative leaders throughout San Blas to speak to existing chapters as well as to women interested in organizing new chapters. They also led seminars, attended the cooperative leadership's biannual meetings, and, since 1981, have represented the cooperative at the Congreso General Kuna. Pilar was a key spokesperson and advocate for the cooperative with Kuna "traditional" political leaders in San Blas and legislative representatives (both Kuna and non-Kuna). She was also well known in the various government ministries responsible for craft production, promotion, and exportation.

Men's Role in the Cooperative

Early in the cooperative's history, conflict arose over whether or not to accept male *mola* producers (all *omekits*) into the cooperative. After much debate, they were allowed to become members. Most local chapters now have one or more male members, the largest number being four. In 1985, the *omekits* who were active in the cooperative were considered highly skilled *mola* makers.

Most of the *saklas* and local congresos, many comprising only men, have been supportive of the cooperative. Not all of the *saklas*, however, have been supportive of all of the cooperative's activities. For example, women from one community complained that their *sakla* did not always give them permission to attend cooperative meetings and workshops on other islands.[2] They said that the *sakla* was concerned that they might get into trouble. In that community, it was highly unusual for women to travel without their husbands or male relatives. Another local chapter resolved this same issue by inviting the *sakla* to accompany them to a workshop. Attending the workshop gave the *sakla* an opportunity to find out more about the cooperative and its activities. I spoke with the *sakla* during the workshop. He was very impressed with the cooperative and commented that the cooperative was following Kuna traditions and that from now on he would allow the women in his community to attend all cooperative events.

Not all conflicts were this easily resolved. A cooperative leader from Playón Chico told the following story:

> Some politicians [men] told us [the women] to leave the cooperative, saying that they could help us form our own cooperative with all of their political connections. So . . . the entire Playón Chico chapter withdrew its membership. The months went by and the men couldn't find an outlet for the *molas* in Panama City. The stores that had connections with the cooperative would not

buy from the men. Finally, we all asked to return to the cooperative. We were ashamed, but explained that it wasn't our fault . . .
the men had pressured us and promised things they couldn't
deliver.

Many members feel strongly that the cooperative should be led by
women at all levels. As a result, conflict has arisen in several local
chapters where Kuna men have taken on management functions
within the cooperative. For example, in one local chapter, a well-
meaning man who wanted to be supportive began "helping"
the women with their accounting. Before long, he was calling and
leading cooperative meetings. The women in the local chapter had
mixed feelings about his involvement because the elected leaders
wanted to run their own cooperative but were unsure of their leadership skills.

Access to Capital

Lack of capital was an obstacle from the cooperative's inception. Initially, the cooperative store functioned on a consignment basis. Because there was no capital, however, producers could not be paid until their *molas* were sold. The 1980 Inter-American Foundation grant
provided the cooperative with enough capital so that producers could
be paid immediately, regardless of whether their *molas* had been
sold. Each time a new local chapter was added, the overall pool of
capital became smaller relative to the overall number of members.
Lack of capital will probably continue to be a concern for the cooperative as long as it continues to expand.

Transportation

The availability or lack of funds is not the only reason producers
experienced delayed payments. Local chapters would wait until a
sufficient quantity (usually enough to fill one or two empty one-
hundred-pound sugar sacks) of *molas* were finished before sending
them to Panama City. Producers sometimes had to wait one or two
months before their *molas* were sent. Even when the sacks were full,
local chapters often waited to send them until someone they trusted
was traveling to the city.

Furthermore, the logistics of moving large sums of cash from Panama City to the islands were quite complex. Trusted friends and relatives hand-carried cash to the local chapters. Informal networks were

used to discover who was traveling to San Blas. Cooperative members, their relatives (male and female), local store owners, Kuna political leaders, and other friends of the cooperative were asked to take money to local chapters from Panama City. Communities that were inaccessible by plane experienced even longer waits before payment was received. Many producers, knowing that it might take several months before they were paid, would sew *molas* for other markets in addition to those produced for the cooperative, even though they received lower prices.

Competition

As mentioned previously, selling *molas* is one of the three primary sources of income for the San Blas region. The cooperative, although the largest and best-organized, was not the only group in 1985 producing and selling *molas*. For example, on one island a male entrepreneur organized a competing *mola* cooperative. He convinced the women on this island who had organized a local chapter of Los Productores de Molas R.L. to withdraw their membership and work for him. On another island, a woman organized a group that did piecework. This group also called itself a cooperative and tried, unsuccessfully, to open a store on the island of Carti-Sugtupu. The men and women who lived on Carti-Sugtupu did not want competition for *mola* sales to tourists from the piecework cooperative. The store was not approved.

When communities located in the third *corregimiento* started to open local chapters of the cooperative, conflict arose with the male Kuna intermediaries who bought *molas*. These men were all either store owners or itinerant traders. Cooperative leaders convinced these intermediaries that the cooperative would benefit them, too. Cooperative members would improve their skills and receive cash for the *molas* they sold through the cooperative. This cash would be spent at the stores, and the intermediaries would be relieved of having to go to Panama City to stand on the street corner and sell *molas*. Apparently, this argument made sense to the traders because they ceased to condemn the cooperative. By 1985, many traders had only good things to say about the cooperative.

Summary

Cooperative members, along with nonmembers who sell their *molas* through the cooperative, have improved their earnings from *mola* sales. The cooperative has accomplished this by (1) eliminating some of the intermediaries in the marketing chain, thereby increasing prices received by producers; (2) lowering producers' costs for cloth and thread by purchasing them wholesale; (3) raising *mola* prices; (4) diversifying their line of products; and (5) offering women the opportunity to improve the quality of their handiwork. Furthermore, the cooperative has provided most Kuna women with equal access to the market for *molas* in a region where earnings from *molas* are highly differentiated. The cooperative has encountered many of the same difficulties as other women's development organizations in Latin America.[5] How and why women have unequal access to the market for *molas* will be clearly described in chapters 8, 9, and 10.

8.
Tourism and *Molas* on Carti-Sugtupu

"Soar dummat taniki" (The big boat has arrived). It was a dark, moonless night, and I was crowded into an outhouse with several other women trying to see the ship. (Outhouses provide the best lookout points because they are built over the ocean and protrude past the jumble of houses.) All along the edge of the island the outhouses were packed with people looking at the glow of light moving steadily along the horizon toward the island. "Taniki, taniki" (It's coming, it's coming), people cried. We stood watching until a very large ocean liner came clearly into focus. Then we went back inside and sat talking and sewing *molas*. When the island's generator shut down (around 9:00 P.M.), someone lit a kerosene lamp and we continued to sew into the wee hours of the night.

By 8:30 A.M. the next morning, the main street of the island was festooned with *molas*. The Kuna women, themselves a colorful sight, sat waiting hopefully and expectantly for the tourists to arrive. Small children were dressed up ready to pose for pictures. I positioned myself near the narrow pathway that led from the dock to the main street and watched while three little girls were posed with pipes in hand and parakeets on their heads to encourage picture taking by the tourists (fifty cents a picture). The tourists arrived. Many of the women wore big, floppy hats; most of the men wore bermuda shorts. Most were elderly, a few walked with canes, and many had cameras or camcorders. The Kuna had effectively roped off the main street and the entrances to houses by hanging *molas* everywhere so the tourists wandered up and down looking at the items set out for sale: *molas*, necklaces made from local materials, carved wooden boats, shells, roughly carved Kuna dolls, and an odd assortment of things purchased by the

Selling *molas,* T-shirts, and other goods to tourists

Kuna in Panama City. Kuna children ran about begging money from the tourists. The older boys paddled out to the cruise ship and dove for money and fruit tossed overboard.

A shuttle boat continued to bring passengers to the island until about three in the afternoon. When the cruise liner left with its one thousand passengers, the outhouses were empty. We were all too tired to care. As I visited different households around the island, the general consensus was that this had been a boat full of "bad tourists." Some women had sold a *mola* or two, many had not sold a thing. No one in my household sewed *molas* that evening as we all went to sleep early.

Mandinga Bay, known locally as the Carti region, is located in the western third of San Blas in the first *corregimiento.* Geographically it is closer to Colón, Panama's free trade zone, than is the rest of the region (see map 2). Numerous tiny islands, both inhabited and uninhabited, are situated in this area. A road links Mandinga Bay to the Pan American highway and to the rest of Panama. Twenty-five kilometers are gravel-covered and passable in a four-wheel-drive vehicle. The remaining twenty-one kilometers are dirt and passable only to vehicles equipped with powerful winches (Chapin 1990:44). This forty-six-kilometer road is the only road in the entire region. So far, it has not been used to transport agricultural produce out of the region. Men in the Carti region are actively cultivating the areas bordering the road, however, in anticipation of future transport from their fields down to the water's edge. Either individually or collectively, these men are eager to claim this newly accessible land by clearing and planting it.

Tourism in San Blas is centered in the Carti region. Mandinga Bay provides a protected harbor and yet is deep enough to allow transatlantic cruise ships to enter. All hotels, with the exception of two small ones virtually unknown and unused by tourists, are located in this part of San Blas. The sale of *molas* to tourists and intermediaries has provided one of the primary sources of income for this area.

In 1985, the island community of Carti-Sugtupu had a population of 1,047: 297 men, 389 women, 193 boys, and 168 girls. In addition, 427 people from Carti-Sugtupu lived in Panama City, including 220 men, 90 women, 60 girls, and 57 boys. I do not know how many lived in Colón and Changuinola (a banana plantation where some Kuna men go to work). In 1985, there were 104 households on Carti-Sugtupu, with an average size of 8 persons. The smallest household comprised 2 adults; the largest, 27 men, women, and children. Twenty-six percent (n = 27) of the households had 2 to 5 persons residing there, 60 percent (n = 62) had 6 to 10 persons, 11 percent (n = 11) had 11 to 15 persons, and 3 percent (n = 3) had 16 to 27 persons. Over half of the households spanned three generations; a little under one-fourth, four generations; and the remainder, one or two generations. Thus, the average household spanned three generations with 8 persons in residence.

Households are defined here as "a group of affinally, consanguinally, and/or adoptively related individuals who eat together in a common kitchen for most meals" (Holloman 1969:135). For the purposes of this study, I divided households into three basic types: extended households with a senior couple, one of their married daughters, and her offspring; compounded extended households comprising two married daughters, their parents, partners, children, and sometimes children's children; and nuclear households comprising a couple and their offspring. The first two household types correspond to the "prototypical" matrilocal Kuna household commonly referred to in the literature (Stout 1947; Holloman 1969; Costello 1982).

Table 2. *Household types, by single mothers, on Carti-Sugtupu*
(n = 104)

	Nuclear Households		Extended Households		Compounded Households	
	%	No.	%	No.	%	No.
Single mothers	0	0	24	26	28	28
No single mothers	14	14	21	21	7	7
Total	14	14	45	47	35	35

Note: On Carti-Sugtupu, 7 percent (n = 7) of the households did not fit any of these patterns.

Extended, compounded, and nuclear households can be thought of as three distinct, but not necessarily sequential, stages of the domestic cycle. For example, extended households become compounded when more than one daughter marries and remains in her mother's household or when a daughter who has left to form her own independent household moves back with her children. Women usually return to their mother's households when their husbands migrate to the city, when there has been a marital fight, or when the marriage is dissolved. The move toward setting up independent nuclear households has been noted in several communities as a way for men to avoid working for their in-laws (Holloman 1976; Costello 1982).

The percentage of single mothers is higher in compounded than in extended households. Compounded households support widows, women who have separated from their partners, and women who have children whose biological father does not recognize or live with them and who have no other partner. On Carti-Sugtupu, about half of the households in 1985 were extended (45 percent, n = 48); 35 percent (n = 35) were compounded, extending over either three or four generations; and 14 percent (n = 14) were nuclear (see table 2). Single mothers resided in either compounded or extended households.

Carti-Sugtupu is situated in Mandinga Bay a little under one mile from the mainland shore.[1] The island is no more than one-half mile long and is about one-sixth mile wide. Oblong in shape, it has one straight, fairly narrow path down the middle lined by houses. Smaller paths extend out from this principal one. Often they are no more than spaces between the houses' cane walls and are only wide enough for one person to walk through at a time.

Houses are built right down to the water's edge. There are no empty house sites and, as is true on many other densely populated islands, the Kuna fill in the shallow areas surrounding the island with dead coral and sand to create additional space. *Ulus* are pulled up on logs behind the houses and out over the water. Wooden planks lead to smaller structures also built out over the water that serve as bath- and outhouses. Carti-Sugtupu has two docks used by larger boats and by visitors from other islands. The newest dock has two concrete outhouses with signs in English; these are used by tourists.

In the center of the island, tucked in amid cane houses, stands the primary and secondary school, a large, green, two-story concrete building. The *congreso* house, built with local materials, is located near the school. Other impressive concrete buildings include the health center, which serves most if not all of Mandinga Bay; a Catholic church, run by a Kuna priest; six stores, several of which sport signs in English for the tourists; a building that houses the electrical generator; offices and warehouse for the community-owned trade boat; two buildings that belong to local chapters of national political parties; and several private homes. Buildings constructed with local materials include the *congreso*, two other local chapters of national political parties, fourteen small stores, a community-owned hotel, and the vast majority of homes (see map 3).

Molas and the Tourist Trade

The development of the tourist trade and the shift from production of *molas* for personal use to that for sale are inextricably intertwined in the Mandinga Bay region. As described in chapter 5, the accessibility of the Carti region to tourists improved and numbers of tourists visiting the area increased greatly during the 1960s. Tourists in the 1960s were interested in buying *molas*. Initially, women sold their worn *mola* blouses; however, as households became more dependent on cash income, producers began to sew specifically for the market. By 1985, after increased *mola* commercialization, almost all (365 of 389) adult women residing on Carti-Sugtupu were sewing *molas* for sale. They also continued to sew *molas* for their personal use. The latter were usually of a higher quality than those made specifically for sale and might bring higher prices, depending on how worn they were. Production of *molas* for immediate or eventual sale came to be women's primary daily activity.

Although both Kuna and foreign intermediaries have bought and continue to buy *molas* on Carti-Sugtupu, compared to tourists they

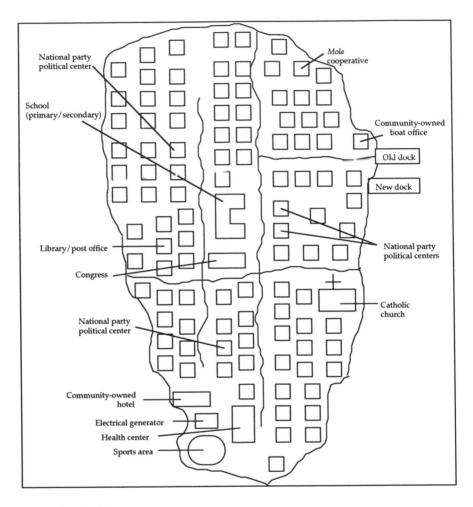

Map 3. Carti-Sugtupu

have purchased very few *molas*. Tourists pay higher prices than do intermediaries or even the *mola* cooperative. Information from my 1985 survey of ninety-two women residing in thirty-three households reveals that the overwhelming majority of women, some 87 percent (n = 80), sold their *molas* directly to tourists. The second most widely exploited option for marketing *molas* was the *mola* cooperative, in which 22 percent (n = 20) of the women were members. An additional 24 percent (n = 22) helped cooperative members sew *molas*, even though they themselves did not belong to the cooperative (see fig. 2). Another 8 percent (n = 7) reported traveling or send-

ing their *molas* with someone to Panama City to be sold, while
15 percent (n = 14) of the women traveled to Nalunega and Aquadup,
two nearby islands where cruise ships also stop, to sell their *molas*.
None of the women said that they traded or sold their *molas* in the
local stores or to traveling Kuna merchants. Nor did anyone sell *molas* to other Kuna women for their personal use; however, 26 percent
(n = 24) of the women bought *molas* from their relatives, friends, or
other women to resell to tourists. Four women actually traveled to
other islands to buy *molas*. Unlike on Mansucun and Tupile, tourists
were the principal buyers of *molas* on Carti-Sugtupu.

Cruise ships entered Mandinga Bay from September through June.
When a cruise ship anchored, about half a mile from the island, the
young men and boys from Carti-Sugtupu paddled rapidly out to meet
the boat and dove for coins thrown by tourists. Meanwhile, women
displayed their *molas,* festooning the main streets in anticipation of
the tourists' arrival. Women who came from surrounding islands to
sell their *molas* were charged a three-dollar fee by the community.

When tourists disembarked on the island, they found primarily
molas for sale. Quality and price varied tremendously, with a single
mola panel costing from five dollars to fifty dollars. Some panels
were taken from blouses that the owner had obviously put a lot of
care and time into; others were appliquéd "tourist *molas*," sometimes only partially finished. These *molas* were rapidly sewn the
night before a ship's arrival in the hope of gaining an additional sale.

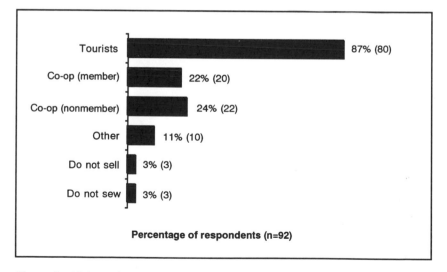

Figure 2. *Mola* marketing options in Carti-Sugtupu

In addition to single panels and whole blouses, there were also *mola* patches (one dollar) and other odd-sized tourist *molas* ranging from three dollars to five dollars in price. During 1984, one woman began appliquéing parrots and the words "San Blas" or sometimes "Kuna Yala" onto T-shirts. They sold so well that a year later it was rare to find a woman who was not making and selling these T-shirts. *Mola* bags, belts, and hats with "San Blas" embroidered on the front were other items that drew considerable attention.

Some non-*mola* items were also displayed for sale. Kuna men made necklaces from locally found shells and seeds, elaborate carved wooden boats, arrows, and painted balsa wood Kuna dolls. While many men and women strung necklaces, only a few men carved boats and dolls. The necklaces cost one dollar or two dollars, the dolls cost two dollars, and the average boat cost ten dollars. Kuna men and women purchased postcards, sequined elephants from India, and ivory necklaces in Panama City for resale to tourists; however, none of these purchased or handmade items sold as well as *molas*. For example, one man said that he had not sold a single boat over a six-month period.

In general, producers sold their own *molas*. As was noted previously, however, women with capital on Carti-Sugtupu bought *molas* from women in Carti-Sugtupu or from women on other islands who needed cash. These *molas* were stockpiled and resold, at a profit, during the tourist season. For example, small *mola* patches were purchased for twenty-five to seventy-five cents and resold for one dollar.

Women with capital who bought *molas* generally ran small stores. The story of how one woman found the money to buy *molas* from her friends for resale follows: Albertina's husband had a government job and received a salary of twenty dollars per month. Albertina borrowed money from her husband and opened a small store in the corner of their sleeping house. She sold an odd assortment of goods such as soap, thread, a few cans of food, salt, and matches. With her earnings, she purchased *molas* from friends who came to visit from other islands. One day she bought five *mola* panels for eight dollars apiece from three friends who needed cash immediately in order to buy supplies. She hoped to resell each of them for ten dollars.

Some women from Carti-Sugtupu who had relatives on the other two islands where cruise ships stop traveled there regularly to sell their *molas*. They paid men with outboard motors $2.50 to take them. These women paid a fee to the community on the island they were visiting in order to sell their *molas*. Women without relatives on these islands did not go. When asked why, they replied: "Where would I eat, drink, and rest?" Traveling to other islands, then, was an option exploited only by women with relatives whom they could visit. Women residing on islands where no cruise ship stopped had several options for selling *molas*. They could (1) travel to an island where a cruise ship had stopped; (2) sell at lower prices to the Kuna women on Carti-Sugtupu; (3) send *molas* with friends or relatives to Panama City; or (4) sell to buyers traveling to San Blas from the United States specifically to buy quantities of *molas*. These buyers, who generally owned or administered retail stores specializing in ethnic handicrafts, went to the various small island communities (including Carti-Sugtupu) to buy *molas*. Some bought only several hundred dollars' worth, while others spent one or two thousand dollars within a two- or three-day period.

The *Mola* Cooperative

After tourism, the *mola* cooperative provided the second most widely used option for selling *molas*. *Molas* were sent directly to Panama City for sale through the cooperative store and were not sold locally to tourists. This local chapter was organized in the late 1960s and was the only one in Mandinga Bay. In 1985, it had seventy-five members and provided an alternative to the tourist market for women residing on Carti-Sugtupu. The cooperative had not focused its organizing efforts in this region because many members from the rest of San Blas thought that the need was greater elsewhere.

Women from Carti-Sugtupu, and from other communities in the area, argued that the nature of tourism created an urgent need for a cooperative. Tourists could not be depended on to buy *molas*; thus, women were often left without cash. On one day in 1985, for example, eighteen of twenty-four women from Carti-Sugtupu sold no *molas* when a cruise ship entered the bay. The remaining six sold *molas* ranging in price from five dollars to twenty-five dollars. One woman described the situation in this way: "The boats only come every month or so. The tourists come to sightsee . . . they do not buy many *molas* and only pay twenty-five dollars for a very good *mola* . . . five dollars to ten dollars for a regular to poor one. Besides, when women do sell a *mola*, the money is all gone by the end of the day."

Active cooperative members were assured of a steady source of income. Also, the cooperative-sponsored savings plan provided women with a reserve of cash to use in case of emergency, illness, or death in their household. This was important during the tourist season as well as at other times. Apart from sewing *molas,* their principal activity as cooperative members was bulk buying of plantains and kerosene to resell.

Division of Labor by Gender

Producing *molas* for sale has changed how women spend their time. Before *molas* were commercialized, women went regularly to the mainland to fill water containers, wash clothes, catch crabs and river shrimp, pick fruit, collect coconuts, gather firewood, and sometimes to work with men planting, weeding, and harvesting crops. Women were also responsible for child care and household-related tasks such as processing, preparing, distributing, preserving, and storing food; washing dishes; and sweeping. Food processing included the following tasks: cleaning and smoking fish; pounding and winnowing rice; squeezing sugarcane; drying, shucking, and grinding corn (in metal meat grinders); drying, roasting, and grinding cacao; husking and grating coconuts; peeling plantains; and curing meat.

Today, because of commercialization, sewing *molas* is the chief activity engaged in by women and girls. Women rarely go to the river or anywhere else on the mainland. Although the younger women are still mostly responsible for household tasks, grandmothers often assume the major responsibility for tasks in the kitchen to free the younger women for sewing *molas.* Therefore, *mola* commercialization has changed the organization of women's labor among generations.

Since there is no aqueduct on Carti-Sugtupu, fetching water from the mainland river is a daily task.[2] Unlike the custom on other islands, where going after water is exclusively a women's activity, this task has been carried out by both men and women on Carti-Sugtupu. Since *molas* were commercialized, however, men have started providing most of the island's water. It is rare to see a man leave for the mainland without filling his canoe with empty water containers. The men explained that the river is far away and that women would have no time to sew *molas* if they went to the river daily. Some women were delighted to be relieved of this responsibility; others looked forward to their infrequent trips with great anticipation. Many grandmothers, used to spending time on the mainland, continued to go on a regular basis. Some of their granddaughters had been there so few times, however, that they did not know where the fields they would one day inherit were located.

My conversations with both men and women about women's participation in agricultural production suggested that women were no longer active. Men and women from other San Blas communities also had a similar perception. Survey data revealed that a substantial number of the women, however, representing both the older and the younger generations, continued to be active in tasks related to agriculture. Most cut plantains (90 percent, n = 60). Approximately one-third of the sixty-six women surveyed knew how to plant rice (36 percent, n = 24) and plantains (39 percent, n = 26) and how to fish (39 percent, n = 26), although only about half of these women had actually planted rice (n = 12) or plantains (n = 12) in the past year. Almost all the women who knew how to fish still went fishing (35 percent, n = 23). Over half of the women collected coconuts (59 percent, n = 39) and picked fruit (74 percent, n = 49). Thus, the perception that women did not engage in subsistence tasks or that only the oldest women participated would be incorrect.

In addition to the changes in how women have spent their time and organized their labor, the production of *molas* for sale has resulted in greater flexibility in the division of labor between men and women. Many husbands on Carti-Sugtupu have learned to cook, prepare hot drinks, and sweep, tasks that were performed exclusively by women before *molas* were commercialized. Men explained that their participation frees their wives for sewing *molas*. Older men still felt that these tasks were "women's work" and did not participate.

Men were still responsible for most agricultural subsistence production, including the following tasks: felling trees, planting, weeding, and harvesting. As was mentioned earlier, men provided most of the community's fresh water. Most of the younger women, when asked if they went to the fields to work, laughed and said that they never went to the mainland, because that was "men's" work. Many young women complained that, although their husbands worked, they did not work very hard. Older men also criticized the younger men, saying that they were lazy and should be out working in the fields or fishing. During the day it was a common sight to see young men hanging out on the island or to find them asleep in their hammocks. A noted exception were the young men who were active in Igligalu, an agricultural production *sociedad*.

Both men and women fished. In fact, Carti women were known throughout San Blas for their fishing skills. Women spoke enthusiastically of going fishing and regretted that they no longer had time to fish. Men caught most of the fish the community consumed.

To summarize, women were spending more time producing *molas* and less time going to the mainland or doing household tasks since the commercialization of *molas*. In many households, the oldest woman had taken over some of the daily work to free younger women's time for *mola* production. Before the arrival of a cruise ship, men also regularly participated in tasks formerly defined as "women's work" so that all of the women could dedicate their time to sewing *molas*. Women still participated, albeit minimally, in agricultural production and fishing.

Household Subsistence Strategies

The average household's diet in the 1980s was quite different from that of several decades earlier. Boiled plantains had become the staple of the Kuna diet. On Carti-Sugtupu, *tule masi*, the plantain-based main meal, is generally eaten between 11:00 A.M. and 4:00 P.M. Rice with canned fish or beans is an alternative meal on those days when the ingredients for *tule masi* cannot be found. If a household is short on cash, there may be no meal at all. Women complained that men no longer provided them with cocoa, corn, wild game, or even with sufficient fish or plantains. Although men were still primarily responsible for providing their households with subsistence foodstuffs from the jungle and the sea, food was often purchased.

Purchasing food for daily consumption had become the women's responsibility. This often entailed not only going to buy the plantains, rice, or fish but also providing the cash with which to make the purchase. One Kuna woman portrayed women's participation in household maintenance in this way: "we buy the plantains . . . our husbands work in the *monte* [jungle] . . . they have no money. Sometimes, they bring back coconuts, but only a few. We are the ones who earn the cash and buy the food." This complaint was widely heard.

Interviews I conducted to better understand household subsistence strategies gave substance to women's complaints. Female heads of thirty-three households were asked what crops the men in their household had planted. Three households had no crops at all. Over half had planted rice (n = 19) or corn (n = 21), while about two-thirds were growing yucca (n = 23) and sugarcane (n = 25). The sugarcane was used primarily for special occasions, however, and not for daily use. Purchased sugar fulfilled daily needs.

I used the purchase of plantains and fish as indicators of dependence on cash income. Nearly all households I interviewed (91 percent, n = 29) had planted at least some plantains. They were not producing well because of a blight, however, so all but two households reported buying at least some plantains. Fully 60 percent (n = 19) of the households sampled bought all of the plantains they consumed, 25 percent (n = 8) purchased approximately half, while 9 percent (n = 3) were occasional buyers. While Mansucun and Tupile residents continued to be mostly self-sufficient, poorer soil combined with a plantain blight required Carti-Sugtupu residents to import most of their plantains.[3] Most of the plantains were produced by Kuna subsistence farmers living in the eastern region of San Blas.

During 1984–1985, the blight was so severe in the Carti region that almost all plantains consumed on Carti-Sugtupu had to be imported. Other crops such as yucca and rice were not affected. Plantains were purchased by the Kuna trade boats in Colón and in the eastern region of San Blas. Those coming from Colón were grown in Changuinola, a banana-producing region in Panama owned by the United Fruit Company. On Carti-Sugtupu, plantains were purchased in bulk from the trade boats, often in advance, and were then resold. The *mola* cooperative and other *sociedades* were the organizations primarily involved in purchasing and selling plantains. Women with cash bought plantains in bulk for their own households. Purchasing plantains was a daily task for women in households without a stockpile of plantains.

Mandinga Bay is the area of San Blas where fish is most abundant and easily accessible; however, 41 percent (n = 13) of the households sampled purchased fish on a daily basis. A total of 16 percent (n = 5) bought fish half of the time and 25 percent (n = 8) purchased it every now and then. On Carti-Sugtupu, this meant that fresh fish was purchased about once a week on days when the household had run out or when it was more convenient to buy fish rather than to go fishing. Only six households of those interviewed never purchased fish. Wild game did not provide a major addition to the diet. Men complained that the area was overhunted so that game was scarce.

By 1985, women were cultivating social networks in order to ensure that they would know when an *ulu* with fish had arrived. There never seemed to be enough fish to go around. Whenever fish was for sale, word spread like wildfire. Women and girls would grab their enameled or plastic basins and dash to the *ulu,* shouting out orders and waving dollar bills clenched tightly in their fists. Fish approximately ten inches long sold three for a dollar. In contrast, women whose husbands were members of fishing *sociedades* were advised when the catch came in. They walked calmly, already assured of their portion of fish, and stood quietly with the rest of the women while the fish was carefully counted and distributed. The association, however, did not fish daily.

Women from Carti-Sugtupu also purchased fish more often than did women from Mansucun and Tupile. Unlike the situation with plantains, however, this practice cannot be explained by ecological factors. Fish is most abundant in the Carti region, where numerous coral reefs provide excellent habitats for fish and safe, calm waters for the fishermen. One partial explanation relates to women's participation in fishing. Women from Carti-Sugtupu no longer fished as regularly as they used to, nor did they contribute gathered foods to the diet. Since men had not increased their fishing activities, women now purchased fish with money from their *mola* sales.[4] Women never did fish much in Tupile, while in Mansucun women continued to fish in the river.

Households on Carti-Sugtupu imported house-building materials, no longer abundant in the area surrounding Mandinga Bay, from the eastern region of San Blas. It cost $200 to $300 to roof a medium-sized house. Two men calculated that the total cost of purchasing labor and materials for a medium-sized house on Carti-Sugtupu was $400. On Tupile, the cost of thatching a medium-sized house was estimated between $50 and $100. Trees used to make *ulus* (canoes) were also no longer abundant and were purchased either from the eastern region or from the Colombian traders. A rough-hewn, medium-sized *ulu* cost $250, a finished one, $350.

On Carti-Sugtupu, 34 percent (n = 11) of the households interviewed reported *mola* sales to be their primary source of income. Income from wages or pensions was relied on by 13 percent (n = 4), while 9 percent (n = 3) depended on income from stores and other activities. Only 6 percent (n = 2) of those interviewed reported remittances as the primary source of income and none as a secondary source. Fully 38 percent (n = 13) could not choose one source of income as more important than another; they relied on a combination of income-generating activities. Nonetheless, these data become especially interesting when compared with data from the other two communities.

When asked specifically about remittances, 55 percent (n = 18) responded that they received cash, food, or other items such as clothes and school supplies from kin living outside San Blas. Of those who received remittances, nearly all received cash (n = 15) or foodstuffs (n = 12) on a monthly basis. Five households received fifteen dollars or less; another five, sixteen dollars to thirty dollars; three, thirty-one dollars to fifty dollars; and two, over fifty dollars per month.

A household census revealed that 46 percent (n = 48) of Carti-Sugtupu households had one or more single mother. The number of single mothers living in a particular household ranged from one to three. Eighty-six (22 percent) of 389 adult women with children had no partner. The single women were either widowed (n = 32), divorced (n = 27), had husbands who were living and working elsewhere (n = 25), or had children (not recognized by their biological father) but no partner (n = 14). Women who lived with a partner and had children by other men were not included in these calculations.

It was fairly common for children resulting from affairs to live with the mother and her husband. These children usually had their biological father's last name. In some households supporting single mothers, no men were present. In others, the senior man worked alone to provide for his daughters and their children, or worked with a son-in-law or a grandson-in-law. In either case, providing sufficient food for a large household with so few hands to work was difficult, if not impossible. This, combined with the plantain blight and women's decreased participation in agricultural production, had created a situation where households were no longer able to produce enough basic foodstuffs.

Whether or not women had to provide for their children varied by household type. Compounded households were more likely to have single mothers present than were extended households. Almost all compounded households had one or more single mothers, while this was the case for only slightly over half of the extended households and none of the nuclear households. Only one father lived by himself with his children. In general, when a man's partner died, he either remained with his in-laws or moved with (sometimes without) his children back to his mother's house.

Case Studies

This section presents ethnographic descriptions of men's and women's productive and reproductive roles and household headship in specific Kuna households. Special attention is given to female-supported households. Household headship is a complex concept and needs careful attention. Mencher and Okongwu (1993:3) have identified four major aspects of headship: "1) authority or power, 2) decision-making, 3) sources of economic support, and in some instances 4) control over and possession of children in case of divorce or death." Different household members, even those living elsewhere, may perform some of these functions. Each of the following two chapters will also present household case studies. A discussion of household headship and a comparison of the three communities will follow the case studies presented in chapter 10.

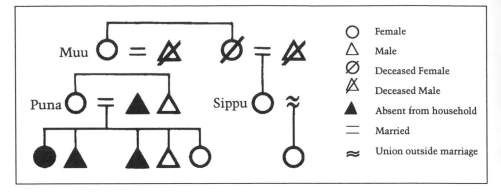

Figure 3. Puna's household

Puna's Household

I watch as a needle is carefully threaded and the first stitch taken. The room is packed and everyone's eyes are glued to the small television screen. We are watching an eye surgeon perform an operation. Muu, the grandmother, tells the children to get out of my hammock. They stay, I pull one onto my lap, arrange the other two at my side, and although I am exhausted, take out my notebook and start to write.

Puna and Sippu are the female heads of this somewhat unusual compounded household (see fig. 3). They are cousins. Sippu has a three-year-old daughter. The child's biological father lives in another San Blas community and does not recognize the girl as his. Puna's husband works in Panama City. Three of their five children, two boys and a girl, live with him and go to high school. Puna's two small children, her sickly mother, and her unmarried brother, who has a bad back and cannot work, complete the household. They all live in two very small, poorly built houses. The house that serves as a kitchen leaks badly when it rains. When all of the hammocks are lowered for the night, they touch each other and there is barely room to move. Tonight, half a dozen men and boys are crowded into the back of the house, and women from neighboring houses keep dropping by to show Puna the *molas* they are sewing and to watch how the surgeon sews. One of Sippu's friends stops by to buy a white T-shirt. Sippu has an arrangement with a female friend in Panama City (also Kuna) to send her T-shirts in exchange for *molas*. She then sells these T-shirts, purchased for two dollars apiece, for three dollars to other women who appliqué birds and the words "San Blas" or "Kuna Yala" and sell them to tourists for ten dollars. Sippu's friend comments that they sell better than *molas* and are a lot less work. After the woman leaves, Sippu digs deep into her bag of cloth scraps and pulls out a small wad of bills. She laughs and tells me that her bag of cloth is a bank, but not to tell. When I ask her what she plans to use the money for, she tells me she is saving up in order to hold a three-day hair-cutting ceremony for her young daughter.

This household depends almost entirely on the sale of *molas* for cash. Puna and Sippu take turns buying sugar, kerosene, plantains, fish, and other needed items for the household. They make household-related decisions jointly, although each woman manages her own money. Puna's husband works in Panama City to support their three older children's studies. There is no extra income to send home. Indeed, Puna sends them money whenever she can. Before leaving, her husband made arrangements to lend his *ulu* to a male friend in exchange for providing Puna's household with fish, firewood, and water. If the friend goes fishing and catches more than his household needs, Puna receives fish. Even with this arrangement, Puna and Sippu buy fish regularly. They also purchase all the plantains, yucca, and rice consumed by the household.

Puna and Sippu spend the major portion of every day sewing *molas*. They stop only long enough to cook a meal, wash some clothes, attend to one of their children, or go to the *mola* cooperative. They are both active cooperative members and both women wear *molas*. Sippu has a gift for drawing *mola* designs. Many women ask her to copy designs for them or to create a new design. She gives of her talent and time freely. Sippu likes to fish but never has time to go. Neither woman goes to the mainland much anymore. Puna used to go with her husband from time to time. Now there is no *ulu* to take.

Puna calls me into the kitchen and hands me a cup of highly sweetened coffee. The fire is out, the coffee is cold, and there is almost no *tule masi* from our main meal left. Puna invites me to sit down to share what is left with the children. I thank her and pretend that I am not hungry.

Arminta and Kilu's Household

The sun is barely up when I enter Arminta's large, spacious kitchen. She is alone, sitting on a low hand-carved seat fanning the fire. We exchange greetings and she hands me a cup of hot chocolate thickened with ripe plantains. Arminta has already started heating water in her enormous cauldron (approximately 3 feet in diameter and 1½ feet high) so it will be ready when her husband and the rest of the men in her household return with fish, plantains, and yucca for the main meal. She has a household of twenty to feed and plans to make enough food so there will be leftovers for a light evening meal. We sit for a long while discussing (in Kuna) men's work and women's work. She is as curious about the division of labor in my household in the United States as I am about hers. Arminta explains to me that she is the female household head (*akkweti*) and coordinates the household's female labor. She decides what the household needs, purchases necessary goods, and manages income from her husband's coconut groves as well as her own earnings from coconut and *mola* sales. If Kilu, her husband, needs money, he must ask her for it. Arminta does most of the cooking and food preparation in order to free her two daughters and six granddaughters (two married with children of their own) for sewing *molas.*

When we have exhausted this topic, she suggests that I go over to their sleeping house and sew my *mola* with her daughters. Arminta scolds me, "You will never finish your *mola* if all you do is write in that notebook!"

Kilu and his sons-in-law have built two medium-sized sleeping houses. Rodolfina calls to me as I leave the kitchen: "Tage Nagagiri-yai tage . . . mormake!" (Come Nagagiriyai, come sew *molas!*) The room is filled with women of all ages sewing *molas.* The older boys have accompanied their fathers fishing or to the jungle; the younger boys and girls (under five years of age) play in and around the house; the babies are nestled in their mothers' hammocks watching them sew or are nursing. Everyone wants to see my *mola.* It gets passed around and carefully inspected. They agree that my stitching is quite good but that the colors I have chosen are rather unusual and that there is a lot of empty space left to fill. Someone asks me if everybody in the United States can sew *molas.* I assure her that they cannot. Another woman asks why I do not have any children. This question starts a discussion (familiar to me) about with which of the Kuna men I should "buy children." Sexual innuendos, both verbal and nonverbal, start to fly and the adult women, myself included, double over with laughter.

Women in this household sell their *molas* primarily to tourists. Two women are members of the *mola* cooperative, and one also goes weekly to sell *molas* on the two other islands where cruise ships stop. These women often take their female relatives' *molas* along to sell. Each *mola* producer receives and controls the cash from the sale of her handiwork. The married women spend their earnings primarily on clothes for themselves and for their children and on school supplies. They also buy supplies to contribute to the household. For

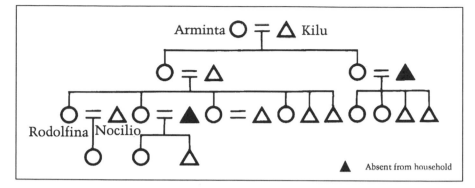

Figure 4. Arminta and Kilu's household

example, if the household is running low on sugar, several women might confer and decide to contribute toward a large sack (approximately 100 pounds), which costs twenty-five dollars and lasts a household of twenty less than one month. If *mola* sales have been good for a particular woman, she will usually treat the household to a meal of rice and canned fish. Throughout the San Blas region, women seem especially to enjoy buying rice, cooking a large meal, and then sharing it with as many people as possible.

Kilu coordinates the labor of Nocilio and the other men and boys (see fig. 4). The men fish and cultivate rice, corn, yucca, plantains, coconuts, and sugarcane. They also gather a wide variety of tropical fruits, including mangoes, oranges, and limes. The two men marked as absent on figure 4 work outside of San Blas, one in Changuinola, a banana plantation, the other in Panama City. Only one of the two men sends money back to help his wife and children. This husband also has sent a kerosene stove and a tape deck. His wife, daughter, and wife's two sisters bake bread to sell almost daily. It is considered a serious business. Other household members who want to eat bread have to purchase it.

Arminta and Kilu still control all of the household's coconut plantations. Some day these plantations will be inherited by their children. Still, all assume that all income from coconut sales will be spent on commodities for the household (e.g., salt, coffee, sugar, and kerosene). In this household, men provide most of the food for the daily meal. Because of the blight, however, they purchase most of the plantains consumed and other household necessities with income from *mola* and coconut sales and with cash sent by the two men working outside of San Blas.

Summary

Mola commercialization in Carti-Sugtupu had become extensive by 1985. Most women produced *molas* specifically for sale. These *molas* were sold primarily to tourists at an average cost of twenty dollars per panel or through the *mola* cooperative. A few women with capital bought *molas* from other women and resold them at a profit to tourists. *Molas* were not traded in the stores for merchandise. By sending *molas* to Panama City to be exported, the small Carti-Sugtupu chapter of the *mola* cooperative provided an important alternative source of income, given the seasonal nature of tourism. The cooperative on Carti-Sugtupu comprised mostly women highly dependent on *mola* sales for daily survival.

Mola commercialization on Carti-Sugtupu has had a tremendous impact on women's daily activities. Whereas women previously went to the mainland regularly to fetch water, harvest fruit, and assist with agricultural activities, in 1985 they spent the major portion of their time on the island sewing *molas*. This was especially true for younger women. The division of labor by gender had also begun to change as a result of *mola* commercialization. Recognizing the importance of income from *mola* sales, in 1985 men were participating in tasks considered "women's work," such as cooking and sweeping, to free their wives for sewing *molas*.

Men's and women's control over resources differed, depending on the type of income and the age of the couple. Women controlled their own income from coconut and *mola* sales. They also managed their husbands' earnings from selling coconuts. Men earning salaries managed their own funds, as did women. Senior women (*akkwetis*) were still responsible for distributing agricultural produce and fish provided by men.

At the time under consideration, almost all households on Carti-Sugtupu relied on a combination of subsistence agriculture and cash-generating activities. In contrast with Mansucun and Tupile, however, most households regularly purchased plantains and fish, the two dietary staples. Households on Carti-Sugtupu depended heavily on tourism and the sale of *molas* for survival. The degree of dependence on *mola* sales varied somewhat among households, but the need for cash to purchase imported plantains and other staples was pervasive. Compounded households had a much higher percentage of single mothers and were more dependent on *mola* sales than were extended or nuclear households.

No longer self-sufficient, the island of Carti-Sugtupu has come to be intricately connected with and dependent on the international market for subsistence foodstuffs and other goods. Carti-Sugtupu is similar to the majority of other communities in Mandinga Bay, where agricultural production is low, tourism is prevalent, and *molas* are commercialized to a great extent. Chapter 9 presents Tupile, an island community where, as on Carti-Sugtupu, women spend most of their time producing *molas* for export to the United States, Europe, and Japan.

9.

The *Mola* Cooperative On Tupile

Eight women, ranging in age from fourteen to forty-five, sit hunched over on low wooden benches or in hammocks sewing *molas*. A tape deck playing popular Latin music sits on a nearby table and a Coleman lantern hangs overhead. It is pitch black outside and the wind is howling around the house. Several small children are sleeping in the hammocks. I ask one of the women to tell me why being a member of the *mola* cooperative is important to her. Kuna women tend to be long-winded, so I shall share only part of what she told me:

> Without the cooperative I didn't have money to buy cloth to make *molas* and couldn't buy anything for my children. Also, sometimes *molas* didn't sell so well outside the cooperative. This cooperative helps us a lot. We save money so that if a member gets sick or something happens and she doesn't have any money the cooperative can help. We bought twenty sacks of sugar and twenty sacks of rice to distribute on credit to all of the co-op members. If one day a member doesn't have anything to eat or drink she can come get food and cloth at the cooperative and pay back what she owes when she finishes her *mola*. The members say the cooperative is good for their families, and me . . . I love the cooperative very much.

The island community of Tupile is situated in the middle of the San Blas region. It lies within the political boundaries of Corregimiento Two, which extends from Tigre Island to Ustupu. This area includes four small coastal and nine island communities. Populated islands in this area lie far apart and are often separated by stretches of open sea. Most are sheltered from the sea by barrier reefs, however, which provide good, protected fishing. Before 1882, the inhabitants of Tupile, Playón Chico, and Aligandi (the communities on either side of Tupile) resided on the smaller islands of Nutup and Monotup and in the coastal community of Kwibgandi. In 1882, a tidal wave caused all three populations to move inland along the banks of the River Wanukandi. An epidemic around the turn of the century caused a subsequent move to the islands of Aligandi, Tupile, and Playón Chico. The distance between these communities is approximately an hour's travel by outboard motor. A long stretch of coast unprotected from the open sea separates Tupile from Aligandi. During the windy season, the undulating sea is filled with huge white-capped waves, making travel between the two islands extremely dangerous, if not impossible.

Molas have been commercialized to a much greater extent in this area than farther east, where Mansucun is located. Five out of six of the largest communities in this area (including the two most populated communities in all of San Blas) have active local chapters of the *mola* cooperative. *Molas* are only rarely traded for goods in the local stores, and intermediaries must travel to communities where there is no cooperative to buy *molas*.[1] Many merchants are no longer active in the *mola* trade. Tupile is similar to the other communities in Corregimiento Two in terms of (a) geographic location, (b) division of labor by gender, and (c) lack of tourism (as compared to the Mandinga Bay region).

Travel to and from Panama City is facilitated by landing strips located either on the mainland near several of the larger communities or on the island itself. Tupile's "airport," located on the mainland, is actually no more than a grassy runway and a small, empty concrete house that shelters passengers and baggage when it rains. One commercial plane usually lands daily, bringing with it passengers, cargo, and newspapers. A private plane lands once a week to buy lobster and octopus and often to leave merchandise, including eggs, chickens, baked goods from Panama City, and other assorted items. Travel also takes place within the region by sea. The Tupile community collectively owns a trade boat.

Tupile is an elongated island one-third of a mile long and one-sixth of a mile wide (Holloman 1969) (map 4). In 1984, Tupile's population numbered 1,231, residing in 130 households. The majority of these households (59 percent, n = 77) spanned three generations; 17 percent (n = 22), four generations; 22 percent (n = 28), two generations; and only 2 percent (n = 3), one generation. A total of 17 percent (n = 22) of the households had 2 to 5 persons residing there; 45 percent (n = 58) had 6 to 10 persons; 29 percent (n = 38) had 11 to 15 persons; and 9 percent (n = 12) had 16 to 27 persons.

In 1985, most of Tupile's households were either extended (39 per-

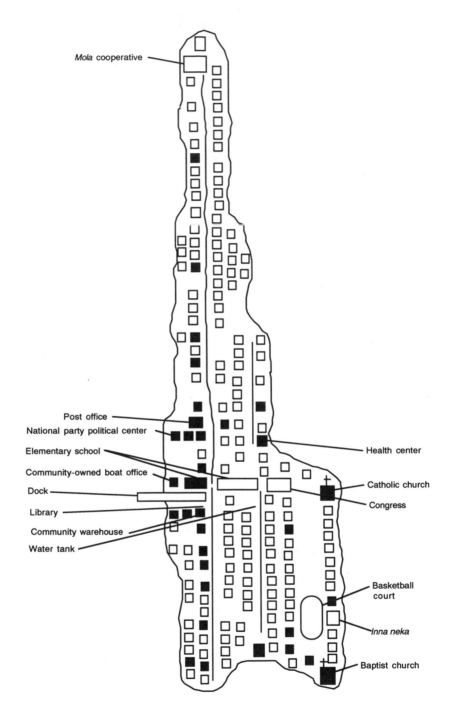

Mola cooperative

Post office
National party political center
Elementary school
Community-owned boat office
Dock
Library
Community warehouse
Water tank

Health center

Catholic church
Congress

Basketball
court

Inna neka

Baptist church

Map 4. Tupile

Table 3. *Household types, by single mothers, on Tupile (n = 130)*

	Nuclear Households		Extended Households		Compounded Households	
	%	No.	%	No.	%	No.
Single mothers	1	1	31	40	23	30
No single mothers	15	20	8	10	17	22
Total	16	21	39	50	40	52

Note: On Tupile, 5 percent (n = 6) of the households did not fit any of these patterns.

cent) or compounded (40 percent); fewer were nuclear (16 percent) (table 3). Over half of Tupile's households included at least one single mother. Out of a total population of 413 adult women, 179 were single mothers, 29 were widowed, 41 were separated (divorced), 31 had children but no partners, and 29 had partners who were absent from the household. These women lived primarily in compounded households.

The island is located approximately one-half mile from the mouth of a mainland freshwater river. Shallow coral reefs surround the island, protecting it from the open sea. Even so, the island's mainland side is calmer and is preferred for beaching *ulus*. The cement dock is also located on this side. A cluster of cement buildings lines the path to the dock. These buildings include the library, the community-run warehouse, the office for the community-owned boat, and, at the end of the path, the elementary school. The *inna neka* (*inna* house), basketball court, health center, and two churches (one Catholic, one Baptist) are located at one end of the island, while the *mola* cooperative is at the other end (see map 4). Mixed in among the houses are twenty-two stores (thirteen medium to large and nine small) ranging in size from a large room in a two-story concrete building to a tiny sectioned-off area of someone's cane-walled, thatched-roof house. Unlike many other islands, Tupile has a straight, wide sandy path extending from one end of the island to the other lengthwise.

Mola Commercialization and the Cooperative

Very few women from Tupile sold their *molas* commercially before the *mola* cooperative was organized in the late 1960s. During the

Out for a stroll on the island's main pathway

early 1960s, local stores began to accept *molas* in exchange for merchandise. *Mola* panels had a trade or cash value of between $2.00 and $2.50. Several woman recalled that this price did not even cover the cost of the cloth and thread used. For this reason, women traded their *molas* only when they had no coconuts to exchange or cash to pay for needed storebought goods. Some women took their *molas*, or sent them with relatives, to be sold in Panama City; however, this did not happen on a regular basis.

As was discussed in chapter 4, a number of factors in the 1960s created conditions that increased the need for cash income. In Tupile, women were faced with a dilemma: on the one hand, they needed cash; on the other hand, the only cash-generating activity available to them did not generate much, if any, profit. The *mola* cooperative was organized to confront and improve these exploitative marketing arrangements.

Mola production was women's principal income-generating activity in the community of Tupile by the 1980s. Only girls under eight years old and very old women who had lost their sight or who suffered from rheumatism never sewed *molas*. The amount of time dedicated to *mola* production varied. Older women spent more time on household tasks to free younger women's days for *mola* production. Women with full-time jobs sewed *molas* only in the evenings and on weekends. In contrast, pregnant women, who are supposed to stay inside the house, spent all day and evening sewing. Most women combined *mola* production with child care, other household-related tasks, and any *sociedad* or cooperative activities in which they were involved.

A number of options existed in Tupile during the 1980s for marketing *molas*, though most were sold through the *mola* cooperative. In addition to the cooperative, some twenty-five women were involved in sewing piecework and another thirty in a *mola* marketing project sponsored by the Catholic church. There were also several foreign intermediaries who visited the island and bought *molas* on a semiregular basis. The account to follow describes each of the marketing options then available to Tupile producers.

Most of the women's income-generating activities in Tupile, and especially *mola* production and sales, were organized through the *mola* cooperative. Fully 64 percent (n = 83) of Tupile's 130 households were represented by one or more of the cooperative's 161 members; however, official membership did not represent the extent of participation in the cooperative. As was explained previously, it was common practice for nonmembers to help members sew *molas*. In Tupile, the cooperative had been so successful that local intermediaries had gone out of business (see fig. 5). Sales had risen from $10,000 to over $30,000 within a six-year period.

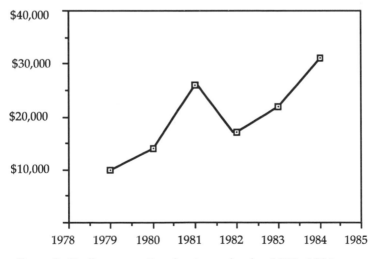

Figure 5. Tupile cooperative chapter *mola* sales, 1979–1984

Housed in a two-story concrete house located at one end of the island, in 1985 the cooperative was the finest-looking building on the island of Tupile and perhaps even in the entire region. It was painted yellow and green and was decorated with pink seashells and round rocks painted black. A balcony extended around the second floor, and wooden shutters secured the numerous windows when the cooperative was closed.

The Tupile chapter was divided into four production groups, each with an organizer. These leaders were responsible for keeping records, for organizing additional income-generating activities, for encouraging production, and for overseeing the quality of the *molas* produced. Each group was responsible for distributing and recording the distribution of cloth to its members. During their work time, producers might cut cloth for *molas* they planned to sew. Leadership positions were voluntary.

Groups rotated in their use of the cooperative building. One group came in the morning, another in the afternoon. Attendance was not required, but in general women looked forward to spending part of the day there, for it was a time for socializing as well as sewing. Friends stopped by each other's houses on the way to the cooperative. Once there, they sat, often quietly for long periods, sewing. Small children ran around, in and out of the building, playing. The silence was occasionally broken by loud, boisterous laughter, when someone inevitably told a joke or launched into a lengthy account of an event. In the evenings, the building was often open for whoever wanted to stop by and sew, socialize, or work on a special project. Evening use of the building required some planning since there was no electricity and one, preferably two, Coleman-type pressure lamps had to be borrowed and kerosene purchased, about one dollar's worth of kerosene per lamp.

Each subgroup was involved in a wide range of income-generating activities, including bingo, numbers raffles, pig raising, savings and lending programs, and selling rice, sugar, and children's clothes. Group decisions were made by consensus. Once an activity was agreed on, members were expected to contribute their time to the project voluntarily. If resources were needed, members were also required to collaborate. Usually this involved sewing an extra, small *mola* to donate to the project.

Profits from group enterprises were kept in small padlocked wooden boxes. One woman stored the box while two others served as keepers of the keys. All three had to be present when the box was opened. Cash was lent from these boxes to individuals or small busi-

Cooperative members dividing up rice purchased in bulk

nesses at 15 percent interest compounded bimonthly. Profits were either used to finance additional projects or were distributed among members of the group at Christmas. Women considered providing a hot drink and a piece of bread or a meal for all the island's children a very satisfying way to spend their collective earnings.

Besides engaging in cash-generating activities, these groups cooperated with the island as a whole by providing an organized and willing body of labor. For example, the week before a major celebration, the cooperative decided that it would be responsible for keeping the island's public spaces swept clean before, during, and after the celebration. The four work groups took turns sweeping.

Although the majority of women produced and sold *molas* through the *mola* cooperative, some women sewed piecework for a fashion designer in Panama City. This designer (a Panamanian woman) sent cut pockets, collars, sleeves, and other items to Tupile through a Kuna woman from Tupile who was living in Panama City. As was indicated in chapter 6, the colors and designs for those items were all specified.

A group of twenty-five women sewed piecework. They had an elected president and sometimes referred to their group as the "other cooperative," even though the group was part of a piecework production system and was not a cooperative. Membership in the two groups overlapped somewhat. Women who sewed piecework thought that they were getting higher prices than those paid by the cooperative; however, they were never sure how much they would be paid for any given item and had no way of negotiating or setting the price. One woman from the *mola* cooperative pointed out that the piecework *molas* had intricate and tedious patterns that took a great deal of time to sew. Even if the price was slightly higher than for a cooperative *mola*, it would take substantially longer to produce them.

In addition to the *mola* cooperative and the piecework group, a *mola* marketing project was organized in 1983 by the Catholic church. Requests for *molas* from the United States, Germany, and Australia were divided up among the priests working in San Blas. The priests then bought *molas* from their parishioners. In 1983, there were only four orders; one of these was for 236 *molas*, another for 100. These orders were divided among eight islands. On Tupile a group of thirty-one women participated in the project.

Occasionally, buyers from the United States came to Tupile to purchase *molas*. Two buyers were well known to women on the island. One woman came once a year and purchased two thousand dollars' worth of *molas* each visit. Tourists were an extremely rare sight, though an occasional yacht sometimes sailed as far as Tupile. Navigational charts either did not exist or were unavailable to the public for the waters east of Playón Chico. This meant that only the adventurous attempted to navigate the potentially treacherous reefs to reach Tupile or the other communities farther east. These tourists or, rather, traveler-adventurers, were usually on low budgets and bought very few, if any, *molas*. Travelers on one yacht traded items such as fishing line, hotel soaps, free samples of shampoo and cream, cloth, a grinder, and other miscellaneous objects for *molas*.

Division of Labor by Gender

On Tupile, like on Carti-Sugtupu, *mola* commercialization has had a tremendous impact on the way women spend their time and organize their work. Unlike the situation on Carti-Sugtupu, however, there has been little impact on the division of tasks between men and women on Tupile. Over the past thirty years, there have been major changes in Tupile women's daily activities. These changes have resulted primarily from the construction of an aqueduct and from the commercialization of *molas*. The shift from producing sugarcane to purchasing white sugar has also had implications for how women spend their time.

Before an aqueduct was constructed in the 1970s, women traveled daily to the mainland freshwater rivers to fetch water for cooking, washing, and bathing. This task took several hours. Women went alone, with their husbands, or with other women. In households with only one small *ulu*, some women left for the river at 3:00 or 4:00 A.M., returning by 6:00 A.M. so that their husbands or fathers would have transportation to get to their fields. Girls as young as ten years of age were sometimes sent by themselves when the weather was calm. In the windy season, women from several households would often pool their resources and hire a man with a motorized *ulu* to take them to the river to get water.

Trips to the river were a time for socializing, washing clothes, gathering firewood, harvesting fruit, and hunting for crabs and river shrimp in addition to the primary task of procuring water. Some women accompanied their husbands for the entire day, often bringing along children of various ages. Sometimes, the women and children helped collect coconuts and fruit and weeded and harvested other crops.

Old women talked enthusiastically about how strong they were and how hard they had worked when young or middle-aged. They talked proudly of harvesting and carrying heavy loads of plantains and of hunting river shrimp, crab, and fish with their bare hands. They spoke of their skill with their *ulus* and of sailing alone in strong winds. They still saw themselves as highly skilled and independent women, limited only by their aging bodies. Many grandmothers continued to go to the mainland. At least two groups went on a weekly basis to clean the cemetery. Other grandmothers, often to the chagrin of grandchildren, who felt they should not go off by themselves, went alone to the jungle to search for fruit or crabs. Middle-aged and elderly men painted a similar picture of their mothers, grandmothers, and aunts. They spoke in glowing terms and rather nostalgically of women's physical strength.

Although going to the river was in part a social occasion, it was still hard work. When women heard about aqueducts on other islands, they began to lobby in Tupile's *congreso* for an aqueduct to bring fresh water to Tupile from the mainland river. Once the aqueduct was approved by the island's *congreso*, they worked with the men on its construction. The aqueduct was constructed of plastic pipes extending from a clear-running stream, located about a forty-five-minute walk from the mainland coast, to the island of Tupile. The pipes were sunk under the sea between the coast and the island. The aqueduct was constructed to function by gravity and no pumps, generators, or other machinery was used. Tupile also had a cement water tower through which water passed before running through the system of pipes on the island that extended to each household. Every household then had a spigot. Women's newly freed time was turned to *mola* production.

Once *molas* were commercialized, women rarely went to the river, and their participation in agricultural activities has markedly decreased. A 1985 survey of 171 women showed that very few participated in agricultural activities. One-third said they cut plantains (35 percent, n = 60), roughly one-quarter of the women reported collecting coconuts (29 percent, n = 49); even fewer indicated that they picked fruit (14 percent, n = 24).[2] Very few women knew how to plant rice (4 percent, n = 7) or plantains (5 percent, n = 9) or how to fish (8 percent, n = 13), and even fewer had actually done so within the past year.

"Women's work" on Tupile included processing, cooking, preserving, and storing food, sweeping, washing clothes, caring for children, and sewing *molas*. Most women spent the bulk of their day sewing *molas*. Many women sewed in the evenings and a few sewed well into the night. When the planting began and men had little time to devote to fishing, women hunted for little red island crabs, sea barnacles, and, occasionally, *salu* (river snails) to supplement the diet. Women also liked to go net fishing for *sigabula* (tiny fish) along the mainland coast. None of these activities, however, were carried out on any regular basis. Women viewed them as special outings in search of delicacies.

Women reorganized the division of labor among themselves to facilitate *mola* production. In many households, grandmothers had taken over most of the food preparation and preservation as well as a substantial amount of the child care. Since these tasks were often repetitive and each required many hours of labor, these women were busy from sunup to sundown. They explained that they took on the extra work so that their daughters and granddaughters would have time to sew. One of the implications of this new organization of labor at the household level was that some young women did not know, and were not learning how, to cook. In most households, each woman was still responsible for washing her own clothes as well as those of her husband and children. Sometimes, however, one sister washed the other's clothes so that she could work on a *mola*. This reorganization of household-related tasks among women occurred particularly in households that depended heavily on the sale of *molas* to meet subsistence needs.

With the exception of *omekits*, men were ridiculed if seen doing "women's work," tasks such as cooking, beverage preparation, and sweeping. One cooperative member's husband did not mind helping in the house and kitchen. He was also active in caring for their two small children. He drew the line, however, at sweeping or washing dishes, activities that take place in public view. This man confided to me that a few men helped their wives but, like himself, kept a very low profile.

Two non-*omekit* males swept openly in public view. One was an older man who liked to see things clean and did not pay any attention to what people said. He was accepted as an exception and was not ridiculed. The other man was paid to be the caretaker of the grade school. Sweeping the classrooms and courtyard was part of his job. He used a tall, storebought broom, thus distinguishing himself from women, who sweep bent over using locally gathered jungle plants as brooms.

In summary, *mola* commercialization combined with the construction of an aqueduct markedly changed women's participation in agricultural activities. By 1985, women rarely went to the mainland. Instead, they spent most of their time sewing *molas*. The division of labor by gender had not changed, although women had reorganized their responsibilities within households.

Household Subsistence Strategies

Subsistence agriculture, fishing, hunting, and gathering provided the bulk of household foodstuffs for Tupile households. Coconuts were still traded for goods with the Colombians in 1985; however, neither coconuts nor *molas* were exchanged in local stores. While Tupile used to have an abundance of food, by this time, many households were purchasing both fish and plantains.

Nonetheless, on Tupile, subsistence agriculture and fishing still contributed most of the food consumed by households. Almost all (91 percent, n = 30) of the thirty-three households interviewed were growing plantains. Nearly three-fourths had planted both rice (67 percent, n = 22) and corn (79 percent, n = 26); however, only about one-third were growing yucca (39 percent, n = 13) and one-quarter, sugarcane (24 percent, n = 8). Three households had no crops at all.

In contrast with those on Carti-Sugtupu, most Tupile households (61 percent, n = 20) produced sufficient plantains to meet their needs. Only one household (3 percent) purchased all the plantains they consumed, three (9 percent of the sample) bought half, and nine (27 percent) purchased plantains "every once in a while." "Every once in a while" in Tupile meant that when cutting plantains was not possible because of illness or bad weather, households would buy enough plantains to tide them over for a day or two. Sometimes Colombian schooners brought small quantities with them from islands farther east, and occasionally neighbors or friends had a surplus they were willing to sell. If no one had extra plantains they were willing to sell, households bought rice, if they had resources, or went hungry.

Tupile households purchased less fish than households on Carti-Sugtupu. While 57 percent (n = 19) of the Tupile households sampled "never" bought fish, another quarter (24 percent, n = 8) purchased fish "every once in a while" (for the same reasons they bought plantains). Only two households (6 percent) reported buying all of the fish they consumed, while an additional three (12 percent) bought fish every other day. Tupile men complained that game was scarce; however, three days rarely went by without some man bringing back a deer, rabbit, wild boar, or other animal to the island. In fact, two men hunted on a regular basis and sold the game they killed. Tupile women made it their business to know when something good to eat was being cooked in another kitchen. If it was the kitchen of a relative or close friend, they would stop by and more often than not be invited to eat.

Before *molas* were commercialized, Tupile households depended primarily on the sale of coconuts to provide them with cash income. Coconuts were also traded at the local stores for merchandise. By 1985, although coconuts were still an important source of cash and continued to be exchanged with Colombian traders, *molas* had become the most important source of income for many households. Fully 33 percent (n = 11) of the households reported the sale of *molas* to be their primary source of income; 18 percent (n = 6) reported wages; 15 percent (n = 5), the coconut sales; and 15 percent (n = 5), remittances from relatives. The remaining 18 percent (n = 6) of households depended primarily on income from stores and from diving.

Remittances from relatives living outside of San Blas were received by 67 percent (n = 22) of the households. Of these, just above half (36 percent of all households, n = 12) received cash on a monthly basis, while nearly one-fourth (21 percent, n = 7) were also sent foodstuffs. Five households received fifteen dollars or less; another six, sixteen dollars to thirty dollars; one, thirty-one dollars to fifty dollars; and three, over fifty dollars per month. Six households reported that the amount of cash sent varied greatly; relatives sent what they could, whenever possible.

Subsistence agriculture, fishing, hunting, and gathering had provided the bulk of foodstuffs for households in the past. When asked what the diet was like twenty-five years ago, people described a varied and abundant array of foods including, among other things, locally grown yucca, yams, cocoa, rice, and corn, in addition to plantains, the staple. Wild game also supplemented the diet, as did fish. Hot drinks were sweetened with sugarcane grown by the men on the mainland and processed every few days by the women. Kitchens were regularly filled with piles of overripe plantains, and neighbors were called over to drink *madun,* a favorite hot drink made from ripe plantains (sometimes cocoa is added). Food was almost always left over from the day before to be eaten at breakfast. In addition to foodstuffs, there was an abundance of cane, vine, and thatch, materials used in house construction, and a special kind of large tree used for making *ulus* could still be found in the jungle. Corners of houses used to be piled high with coconuts, which were traded or sold in order to purchase trade goods.

A large percentage of women from Tupile were single mothers and received no support from their children's biological fathers. Out of a sample of 171 adult women, 117 (68 percent) had partners. Ninety-two of these women lived with their husbands, while 24 had partners who were living and working elsewhere. These men helped to support their households. None of the 54 women without partners received support for themselves or their children, however.

Case Studies

Ethnographic descriptions of two households follow. Pseudonyms have been used and care has been taken to ensure that the actual households described cannot be identified.

Muu and Tada's Household

It is still dark outside. Muu (the grandmother) slips out of her hammock and goes out back to bathe. She passes through the sleeping house, across the island's main path, and into her kitchen wearing only an old *saburrette* wrapped around her waist. By the time I get up, bathe, and go into the kitchen, Muu has the fire going and is busy sweeping the floor. Tada (the grandfather) and Rogelio (their son-in-law) soon join us. Muu tells Tada that she needs firewood and that their sack of sugar is running low. They confer and decide that it would be good to buy fish today so that both Rogelio and Tada can go harvest coconuts and cut firewood. Tada and Rogelio drink the hot chocolate that Muu has prepared, take a gourd with hot chocolate for later, and head toward their *ulu*. Eliana and Luisa, Muu's two married daughters, are out back washing clothes. They stop what they are doing to help Muu and Tada put the *ulu* into the water. By this time, the sun is almost up and so we awaken the household's seven children, bathe them, dress the older ones for school, and give them all hot chocolate to drink.

Several years ago, Muu and Tada lived with two unmarried daughters, a married daughter (Eliana), Eliana's husband, Rogelio, and their two children. Luisa, another daughter, lived with her husband, Pedro, and her five children on a nearby island. Pedro got involved with another woman, so Luisa took her children and returned to her parents' household on Tupile. An unmarried daughter was sent to Panama City to study and to help yet another of Muu's married daughters care for small children. (See fig. 6 for household composition after changes occurred.)

Before Luisa and her children moved in, Tada and his son-in-law provided sufficient plantains and fish to meet the household's daily needs. Coconuts were sold or traded with the Colombian traders for

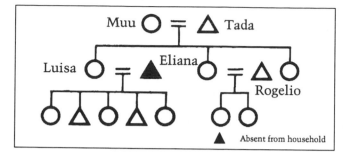

Figure 6. Muu and Tada's household

cocoa, sugar, soap, and other goods the household could not produce. Tada's credit with the traders was good, so he could make large purchases, such as a hammock, a metal storage bin, or a large metal pot, simply by making a down payment of coconuts.

When Luisa and her children moved in, the household started buying fish and plantains several times a week. Some of Tada's plantains are a two-hour walk from the river; although they are producing well, he and his son-in-law cannot carry back enough to meet the expanded household's needs. Luisa's husband, a schoolteacher who earns about three hundred dollars per month, sends her money for the children monthly.

Muu manages the household. Like most women her age, she keeps her husband's money (from selling coconuts) in addition to her own. Tada once commented: "If I had money in my pocket it would just fall out and get lost . . . then I would have nothing. If I need something I just ask my wife." Muu earns money from the coconut groves that she inherited from her parents and occasionally from selling *molas* to one of the foreign intermediaries who come to the island.

Luisa and Eliana both sew *molas* for sale, and Eliana is an active member of the cooperative. Like her mother, Eliana manages her husband's income from his coconut groves along with her own. Neither of them has yet received the bulk of their inheritances, but each has been given the rights to harvest certain groves by their parents. Although Muu and Tada cover most of the daily household expenses, Eliana depends on her *mola* income to buy school clothes and supplies for her two children and clothing for herself. She is also trying to save enough money so that she and her eldest daughter can wear *mola*. The money Luisa receives from her husband allows her to buy what she needs for her children. If he were ever to stop sending money, she too would be completely dependent on *mola* sales. Both women use their *mola* income to buy fish and other goods for the household on a regular basis. Without this income, they would often go hungry.

Well past noon, Tada and Rogelio return from the mainland. We all go to meet them and help unload their *ulu*. Muu sends Eliana and me to sell the coconuts to a Colombian canoe that arrived at Tupile's dock earlier that morning and to buy some fish from the fishing collective. When we return, the sun is no longer overhead. Eliana gives Muu the leftover money from the coconut sales, which she stashes away, and we are called to eat.

Fully 23 percent of Tupile's households are similar to Muu and Tada's in that they support women without partners but with children. Most women are not as fortunate as Luisa to have financial support from a former partner.

Sia's Household

It is raining for the third day in a row. I decide to visit my friend Antonia's household and ask Eliana if she wants to join me. We wait for a pause in the downpour and make a dash for Antonia's house. Antonia's mother, Sia, her two older sisters, and her *omekit* brother are all sitting in the kitchen sewing *molas*. Antonia brings us some hot chocolate. I start asking questions about how they make ends meet and am delighted when Sia begins to talk about her *omekit* son. She says that women consider themselves very lucky to have such a son. These sons help their mothers with the housework, they sew *molas* for their mothers and sisters, and they contribute income from *mola* sales to the household. She explains that without her son's help they would have a very difficult time supporting themselves. All of her daughters' husbands have gone to the city in search of work. They do not send back much money, and her husband is growing old and cannot keep up with all of the agricultural work needed to feed the twelve children that live in their household.

Sia and her husband, Elardo, live in a compounded, three-generation household with Sia's ailing father and their eight children (see fig. 7). In 1985, 52 of 130 Tupile households were compounded and, like Sia's household, many (23 percent, n = 30) had one or more single mothers.

This household depends primarily on the sale of *molas* for survival. Sia and her daughters all sew *molas* for sale through the *mola* cooperative. One daughter, Antonia, is very active, as is Julio, one of her sons. The other four women, ranging in age from thirteen to fifty,

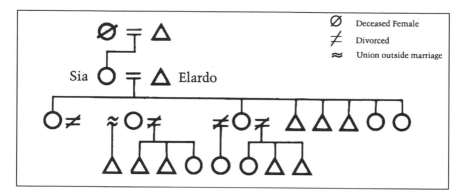

Figure 7. Sia's household

help sew the two cooperative members' *molas*. Sia attends to most of the household tasks so that the younger women may have the entire day to sew. Sia's daughters buy all of the household staples, including cocoa, rice, sugar, kerosene, and fish. The household often drinks watered-down hot chocolate in order to save money. Sometimes it is not much more than sweetened hot water. They eat only once a day, and some days there is nothing at all to eat.

Elardo provides plantains for the household but does not plant any other crops. One of his sons fishes and occasionally helps him in the fields. He has no sons-in-law to help him, and his other son spends all of his time sewing *molas* and working on projects through the *mola* cooperative. Elardo earns very little money from selling coconuts. His groves are not producing well, and he cannot depend on this income as he used to. The household is highly dependent on *mola* income for survival. Much of the food they consume is purchased with money from *mola* sales.

Summary

Mola commercialization in Tupile was extensive in the 1980s. Although women continued to produce *molas* to wear, almost all the women also produced specifically for the market. Although initially women traded their *molas* in the local stores, by the 1980s, they sold the *molas* almost exclusively through the cooperative. Producers received an average price of ten dollars per panel and twelve dollars for a large-sized animal-shaped pillow. Well over half of Tupile's households had at least one member of the cooperative; many had more. Local merchants had been completely eliminated from the *mola* trade. Piecework production was minimal, with the overwhelming majority of women preferring to work through the cooperative.

This local chapter of the *mola* cooperative was very active. In addition to *mola* production and marketing-related activities, members had developed other income-generating activities and collective projects such as the bulk buying of food. Initial capital for these activities was acquired by pooling earnings from *mola* sales. Here *mola* commercialization was viewed as a means by which to develop locally sustainable projects not dependent on the international market.

As in Carti-Sugtupu, *mola* commercialization in Tupile had a major impact on the way women spent their time. In 1985, sewing *molas* was the primary daily activity for most women. In some households, women reorganized the distribution of household tasks among themselves to facilitate *mola* production. Older women took over their daughters' and granddaughters' responsibilities so that these young women could dedicate themselves more fully to sewing *molas*. The division of labor between the sexes remained unchanged, even though *molas* were produced extensively for sale.

As in Carti-Sugtupu, agricultural produce and fish continued to be managed by the *akkweti* in Tupile and were considered resources for household use. Men's and women's control over cash differed according to source of income. Women managed their husbands' income from coconut sales as well as their own for purposes of household maintenance. They also controlled their earnings from *mola* sales. Men kept their income from lobster sales for personal use.

Mola sales were an important source of cash for most of Tupile's households. The income was especially crucial for single mothers whose partners were gone and did not help to support their children. Decreased subsistence production resulting from men's migration to Panama's urban centers made those left behind dependent on imported foods purchased with cash from *mola* sales. Women's low participation in agricultural activities made them even more dependent on cash.

Tupile households relied on a combination of subsistence agricultural production, fishing, hunting and gathering, and cash-generating activities. Overall, households were considerably less dependent on the purchase of fish and plantains than were those in Carti-Sugtupu. As in Carti-Sugtupu, however, compounded households had a much higher percentage of single mothers than did nuclear or extended households and were more dependent on *mola* sales than were the other two types.

Tupile is similar to many other San Blas island communities with active local chapters of the *mola* cooperative. In 1985, the Tupile chapter was considered one of the most successful chapters in that intermediaries were no longer involved in the *mola* trade. Other chapters looked to the Tupile chapter for leadership in their own struggles to improve women's income-generating potential. Chapter 10 presents Mansucun, a mainland community where women continue to barter their *molas* for goods in local stores.

10.
Molas and Middlemen in Mansucun: A Discussion of Female-supported Households

As night falls, one of the few kerosene pressure lamps in town is lit. In its steady glow, I can see the interior of the store. A few canned goods, deodorant, soap, flashlight batteries, cloth, thread, and a few other goods dot the shelves. A small selection of children's clothing hangs on a line strung from the ceiling. On the floor, large square tin boxes hold sugar, rice, and, when available, flour. The corners are all filled with coconuts, piled up as high as they will go without crashing down into the tiny path cleared in their midst. Mansucun's community-owned trade boat is being repaired and no Colombian canoe has entered the village for several months. The coconut traders want to increase their prices, so they are holding out. The store is almost out of kerosene, and most of the lamps (tin cans with wicks) lit nightly in sleeping houses to deter vampire bats are unlit. Dark shadowy figures are streaming toward the *congreso;* the sky is full of stars.

In many ways, life in Mansucun in the 1980s was similar to that of the coastal Kuna communities around the turn of the century (described in chapter 4). Men and women both participated in agricultural activities. Subsistence-based agriculture, fishing, and hunting were mainstays of life, supplemented by the coconut trade.

In 1985, Mansucun's women did trade their used *molas* for goods in local stores, but *mola* commercialization was much less extensive in this area than in the rest of San Blas. As a result, less cash circulated. At that time, Mansucun had a recently organized chapter of the *mola* co-op, one of seven local chapters in Corregimiento Three. Plans were in process to organize new local chapters in two additional communities where large groups of women were eager to join the cooperative. Tourism was almost nonexistent and there were no hotels. Yachts occasionally sailed over from a resort island situated off the coast of Colombia, but they were an infrequent sight and generally returned the same day. Agricultural production was comparatively high, and surplus plantains and avocados were sometimes shipped for sale to other parts of San Blas.

Mansucun is located in the easternmost third of San Blas, several hours by motorboat from the Colombian border. This area, known as the third *corregimiento*, includes six small coastal mainland and seven island communities. The seven communities are located on five islands. On at least one of these two islands, the population has split into two administratively separate communities. There is no physical distinction between the two, and neighbors may belong to different villages (Howe 1982b). Geographically, much of the coastline is rocky. Few barrier reefs protect the coast from the sea, and, generally, islands located here are an hour or two apart. Thus, for many communities, sea trade is cut off during the windy season, when waves are high and travel is difficult. Fish are also less abundant here than to the west. Unlike the rest of Panama, most of Corregimiento Three has not been charted by cartographers. Detailed navigational maps exist for the rest of the coast, yet there is no map for this area.

Mansucun is similar to the other communities in Corregimiento Three in terms of (a) geographical location, (b) division of labor by gender (women participate in many agricultural tasks), and (c) lack of tourism. It is also similar to the other eleven small coastal communities located in the rest of San Blas in terms of (a) size, (b) dependence on itinerant traders for goods, and (c) importance of intermediaries in the *mola* trade.

Molas have been commercialized to a greater extent on the larger island communities in Corregimiento Three, where both intermediaries and the *mola* cooperative have been active. In contrast with Mansucun, where the cooperative is not very active, conflicts have arisen between *mola* producers and intermediaries in these communities.

Unlike the rest of the small coastal communities in San Blas, Mansucun has a landing strip. A twin-propeller plane, ranging in size from eight to sixteen seats, flies by daily but does not always land. If someone wishes to travel, Mansucun's airport attendant waves a white flag as the plane goes by. If there is room for passengers, the plane lands; otherwise, it returns for them the next day. Some merchandise is brought by travelers to the community, but most arrives

Table 4. *Household types, by single mothers, on Mansucun*
(n = 61)

	Nuclear Households		Extended Households		Compounded Households	
	%	No.	%	No.	%	No.
Single mothers	7	4	23	14	23	14
No single mothers	26	16	10	6	6	4
Total	33	20	33	20	29	18

Note: On Mansucun, 5 percent (n = 3) of the households did not fit any of these patterns.

on the community-owned trade boat. Mansucun is also the only small coastal community to own a trade boat.

Mansucun is a small community with a total population in 1985 of 424 individuals living in 61 households. The households ranged in size from 2 to 27 persons. Thirty-six percent of the households had 2 to 5 persons residing there, 54 percent had 6 to 10 persons, 18 percent had 11 to 15 persons, and 2 percent had 16 to 27 persons. Most households spanned either two or three generations, with an average of 8 persons in residence.

In 1985, one-third (n = 20) of Mansucun's households were extended and spanned three generations. Others were compounded households (n = 18), comprising several nuclear family units living together in one household. One-third (n = 20) were nuclear. Only three households did not fit into one of these basic household types. Fully half of Mansucun's households supported at least one single mother. Most of these women with children but no partner lived in either extended or compounded households. Few nuclear households had single mothers (see table 4).

As I approached from the sea, Mansucun appeared as a blur of thatch-roofed houses against a backdrop of tall coconut palms and jungle green. A closer look revealed a cement dock jutting out into the water and houses built right down to the water's edge. The community-owned trade boat was often moored at the dock, unloading merchandise or, more often than not, waiting to be repaired. Some *ulus* were tied to or pulled up onto logs at the water's edge. Many households preferred to beach their *ulus* at the mouth of an inland river located about a twenty-minute walk down the coast.

Commerce in Mansucun was centered in the area near the dock in three stores and a small bread-baking enterprise. The *congreso* house was also situated in this area. A wide, straight, clean-swept, sandy path extended the length of the community. At one end of town there was a four-room elementary school, a library, a Baptist church, the *mola* cooperative house, and a large open space used for playing soccer and basketball (see map 5). The house-lined main path extended from this point, parallel to the sea, and disappeared into the underbrush on the edge of a mangrove swamp. The *chicha* house was located at this end of the community. The swamp was an ideal breeding ground for mosquitoes and a tiny flying, biting insect. Although malaria seemed to be under control (houses are sprayed and blood samples are checked yearly), people were still afraid of the disease. Unlike residents in Tupile and Carti-Sugtupu, people in Mansucun often cracked jokes about dying from mosquito bites.

A coconut grove extended behind the last row of houses. This grove collectively belonged to Mansucun women. Three community wells were located in this grove, with an old *ulu* set up beside one well for washing clothes. Many small trails extended beyond the grove into the jungle, where most people went to relieve themselves. One trail turned into a larger well-used path, lined with graceful coconut trees and lush jungle grasses. This path led along the coast to the river and to Navagandi, another coastal community.

Kuna canoes along the San Blas coast

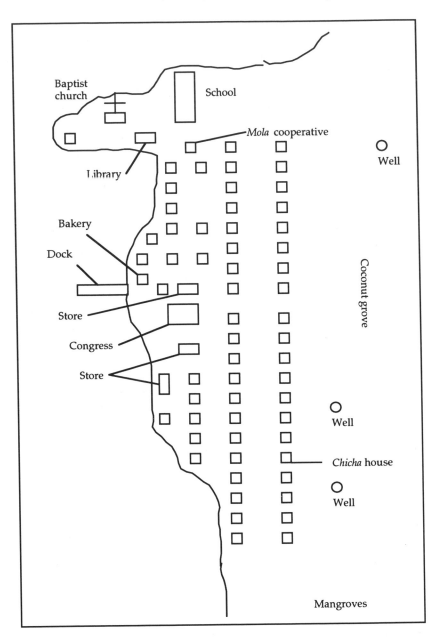

Map 5. Mansucun

The Commercialization of *Molas* through Middlemen

As was true in most San Blas communities, when *molas* first began to be commercialized in Mansucun, women traded their *molas* for merchandise available in local stores or carried by itinerant traders. Unlike the situation in communities within the tourist region or in those like Tupile, where the *mola* cooperative had monopolized the market for *molas,* this pattern of exchange has continued to the present in Mansucun. Although in Mansucun *molas* were still produced primarily for personal use, this practice began to change with the organization of a local chapter of the *mola* cooperative in the early 1980s.

In 1985, production of *molas* specifically for sale was still low; however, most women in Mansucun sold their used *mola* blouses. Responses from 66 of 146 adult women revealed that 89 percent (n = 59) sewed *molas* that they later sold, 8 percent (n = 5) sewed only for their personal use, and 3 percent (n = 2) did not sew at all. Women generally sewed blouses to wear that, once worn and faded, they traded or sold. Most of the women's time was spent planting, harvesting, processing food, and in general carrying out a wide array of agricultural and household-related tasks. *Molas* were sewn in the late afternoons when the day's work was done and in the evenings during the community *congreso,* which began when the sun went down and lasted for three to five hours. In contrast to women on Carti-Sugtupu and Tupile, Mansucun's women were required to attend the nightly *congreso* meetings along with the men. Attendance was taken and absent men and women were fined.

Mansucun's women sold or traded their *molas* in local stores or with Kuna traders from larger islands (see fig. 8). Local merchants and itinerant traders paid an average of three dollars per *mola* panel, depending on the quality of the design and stitching. These *molas* were usually traded for rice or cloth. Alternatively, women sent *molas* to Panama City through the cooperative or through personal networks. A few *molas* were sold to the occasional tourist.

The *mola* cooperative had thirty-eight members representing thirty, or just half, of Mansucun's households. Since 1983, a dozen women had canceled their membership because it was taking a long time (one to three months) for them to receive cash. Often, members did not receive their money for several months after the *molas* had been sent to Panama City to be sold through the cooperative store.

This local chapter limited its activities to *mola* production. Furthermore, it produced only *mola* panels and not the wide array of other items made by many other cooperative chapters. Cooperative

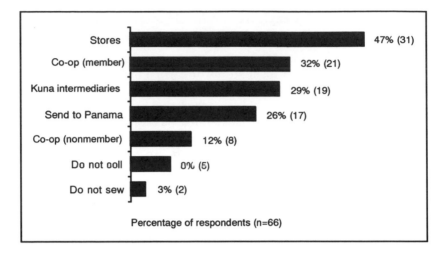

Figure 8. *Mola* marketing options in Mansucun

members would have liked to send representatives to Tupile, where the cooperative had been very active, to get ideas for other cash-generating activities; however, the women were not sure that they would have time to organize additional activities even if they were able to learn from the Tupile chapter. They also wanted the cooperative's educational committee to plan a workshop in their community to teach them accounting skills and how to improve and diversify their products.

Although producers received higher prices for their *molas* through the cooperative, organizational problems had prevented these women from taking over *mola* marketing by eliminating male Kuna intermediaries. As was mentioned before, their payments were often delayed, as was the arrival of cloth from Panama City. This situation was further complicated by cooperative members' lack of accounting and record-keeping skills. Community support for the cooperative had been minimal. For example, cooperative members had had a difficult time receiving permission from the *congreso* to attend cooperative-sponsored workshops where they could learn additional skills. These workshops would have required women to travel to other San Blas communities.

Some women sent their *molas* to Panama City with family members or friends. For example, three store owners often traveled to the city to buy merchandise. In addition to bringing the *molas* that had been traded for goods in their stores, they took a small quantity of their wives' female relatives' *molas* and sometimes those of close friends to be sold in Panama City. The makers of these *molas* received whatever the *mola* sold for, usually around ten dollars. Mansucun's women were much less likely to travel to Panama City than were women from the other two communities.

Until 1977, Mansucun's women were prohibited by the local *congreso* from traveling to Panama City. In that year, a man requested that his wife be allowed to accompany him to the city. He was denied permission but helped his wife escape. Several months later, they returned home and were fined by the *congreso* for disobeying community rules. The couple refused to pay the fine, arguing that women should be allowed to travel, too. After much discussion, the fine was lifted and the rule prohibiting women from traveling was changed. Still, Mansucun's women tended not to travel as much as those from the other two communities I studied.

Women's final possibility for marketing their *molas* was to travel to a tourist resort island just over the Colombian border. This trip required an outboard motor and took a minimum of five hours. During the windy season, December through May, the sea is so choppy and the waves so large that this trip is impossible by canoe and is dangerous even in a large vessel. On very rare occasions and only in good weather, a yacht may travel up the coast as far as Mansucun. In 1985, such tourists were known to pay as much as twenty dollars for a *mola*, but tourism was not a steady outlet for *molas*.

When sewing *molas*, Mansucun's women often talked about eating rice. Rice cooked in coconut milk was considered a special dish. It provided a change from the daily diet of plantains and fish, though elderly men and women generally preferred plantains and considered rice an inferior food and not very filling. Rice was almost always served on festive occasions, during funerals, and to guests. Kuna women, particularly the younger ones, yearned to eat rice. One young woman owned only two *mola* blouses because she exchanged a worn *mola* for rice every time she finished a new one.

In general, the quality of *molas* in Mansucun was well below that of *molas* in Carti-Sugtupu and Tupile. In part, this can be explained by the fact that the *molas* were sewn mostly at night under inadequate light. Most women agreed that it is much harder to sew intricate designs and to keep stitches small without good light. Also, because of the extremely low prices received for their work, some women there would quickly stitch together *molas* specifically to trade. Women often used the sturdy cloth from their husbands' torn or worn-out pants as backing for the *molas* they wore when working.

Table 5. *Average household production and sale of molas in 1980, by community*

	Average molas produced per household	Average molas sold per household	Average household income from molas
Carti-Sugtupu	105	54	$1,080
Tupile	61	50	$600
Mansucun	16	5	$25

Notes: Averages of *molas* produced and sold were calculated from data collected in the *Cuarto censo agropecuario 17 al 24 de mayo de 1981.*

Average household income was calculated by using approximate usual prices received for *mola* panels in each community ($20 at Carti-Sugtupu; $12 at Tupile; $5 at Mansucun).

These *molas* tended to be rugged, less intricate, and less likely to wear out or rip when the women engaged in hard physical labor. Finer *molas* were sewn to wear to the *congreso* in the evening or on special occasions. Still, intermediaries often paid women the same prices for good and poorer quality *molas.*

Kuna male intermediaries controlled *mola* marketing in Mansucun in the 1980s. The *mola* cooperative had not succeeded in challenging this role. In Mansucun, relations of production were similar to those described for the entire region in the 1950s, when *molas* were just beginning to be commercialized (see chapter 5).

Mola commercialization has resulted in unequal distribution of resources among women residing in different communities. This can be explained in part by producers' different access to markets. While *mola* commercialization has been linked with the tourist trade on Carti-Sugtupu from the beginning, this has not been the case for the other two communities, where tourism is practically nonexistent. Tourists have paid the highest prices for *molas* while Kuna intermediaries have paid the lowest. The implications of these differences for *mola* production and for household income are highlighted in table 5. Women from Carti-Sugtupu sold about half of the *molas* they produced and earned the highest amount of income. Tupile's women sewed fewer *molas* but sold most of what they produced. Yet, for an almost equal number of *molas* sold they earned only a little more than half of what Carti-Sugtupu households earned. The average number of *molas* produced per household on Mansucun was manifestly the lowest, as was the number of *molas* sold. Furthermore, average household income from *mola* sales in Mansucun was exceedingly low.

Division of Labor by Gender

Mola commercialization had not affected either the division of labor or women's daily activities in Mansucun in 1985, as it had in the other two communities. Women of all ages still regularly went to the jungle and to the river. It was rare to find women at home during the day. Some houses were entirely empty, while in others a young girl was left behind to care for the babies. Although men had primary responsibility for subsistence agricultural production and fishing, interviews revealed that women also participated in many of these activities. Some women assisted with the planting, weeding, and harvesting of rice, corn, and coconuts.[1] Most women collected coconuts, cut plantains, and gathered fruit; most cut, gathered, and carried firewood (*sappan*); and most fished in the river and stalked land crabs and river shrimp.

According to the 1985 survey data, most women indicated that they collected coconuts (92 percent, n = 61), picked fruit (92 percent, n = 61), and cut plantains (83 percent, n = 55). Over half of the women said they fished (61 percent, n = 40). Only three women (5 percent), however, indicated that they knew how to plant and harvest rice or plant plantains and had actually done so within the past year.

In addition to performing activities related to agriculture, Mansucun's women were responsible for a variety of household tasks. They washed clothes and dishes, swept the house and surrounding paths, and bathed children. They were responsible for food distribution, processing, preparation, and preservation and for carrying water for cooking, bathing, and sometimes for washing clothes. The water was fetched from the village well located at the edge of the jungle. In general, this last task fell to the young women and teenaged girls. A woman or girl working alone made as many as twenty-five such trips daily, though usually a younger sister or other female relative helped her. Men did not assist with any of these activities.

Household Subsistence Strategies

In Mansucun, households still produced sufficient foodstuffs to meet most of their daily needs. Selling or trading coconuts and *molas* was the primary means households had for acquiring consumer goods. Most households, however, did not depend on *mola* sales for daily survival. The barter system, no longer prevalent on most islands in the western part of San Blas, was still very much alive in Mansucun. Coconuts were traded for daily purchases in local stores of items such as sugar, salt, cocoa, and kerosene. Coconuts were also exchanged with Colombian traders for hammocks, plastic sandals, children's clothes, plastic buckets, and other items. *Molas* were traded for *saburrettes, musues,* cloth, and sometimes other goods.

Agricultural production was higher in Mansucun than in the other two communities I studied. Interviews with thirty-three *akkwetis* in 1985 revealed that almost all households grew plantains (n = 32) and corn (n = 29), two-thirds grew yucca and sugarcane (n = 20), and about one-third planted rice (n = 13). Only one household planted no crops at all; this household purchased all of its food.

In Mansucun, most of the thirty-three households (65 percent, n = 20) produced sufficient plantains to meet their own needs and did not buy plantains at all. Only three households (10 percent) indicated that they purchased "all" the plantains they consumed; another two (7 percent) bought about half, and six (19 percent) purchased plantains every once in a while.

About half (48 percent, n = 15) of Mansucun's households responded that they never purchased fish. Only two households (7 percent) indicated that they bought fish every day. The rest (n = 14) purchased fish every once in a while. In Mansucun fresh fish was not available for daily purchase. Occasionally, a collective group of fishermen who owned a large net would catch more than their members' households needed. This excess was then sold. Otherwise, canned tuna and sardines, which were about four times the price of fresh fish, were the only fish available on a regular basis.

In Mansucun, coconuts and *molas* were identified as important sources of income for their households by those I interviewed. Fully twenty of these households (60 percent) considered coconuts to be their most important source of income. Eight *akkwetis* did not think any one income source was more important than another. In sharp contrast with the two communities already described, only one person from Mansucun stated that the sale of *molas* was the household's most important income-generating activity. Income from a store (n = 2), wages (n = 1), and remittances (n = 1) were rated as the primary sources of cash for four other households.

Mansucun's residents received relatively few remittances of cash or food from relatives in Panama City or elsewhere. Fewer than one-quarter (18 percent, n = 6) of the thirty-three households interviewed reported receiving remittances in 1985. Of these, three received cash

Returning home after harvesting coconuts

on a monthly basis, two received both cash and food, and one received only food. Of the five households sent cash, two received less than fifteen dollars, two received between sixteen and thirty dollars, and one received fifty dollars per month.

Although *molas* were considered important sources of income, households did not depend on their sale to meet their most basic needs. As was discussed earlier in the chapter, *mola* production specifically for sale was low. Households received few remittances and in general were not greatly dependent on the cash economy. Mansucun, though connected to the international economy through the trade of coconuts and *molas*, was still primarily subsistence-based.

Case Studies
Bunguaru's Household

Bunguaru, her children, and I have spent the morning harvesting coconuts from the *finca* her father left her when he died. When we get to the river, we drop our loads and all jump into the cool water. The crabs that live in the river's banks are startled by all the commotion and skitter into their holes. The heat of the day is washed away and we splash each other, talk, and joke. Bunguaru lives with her three

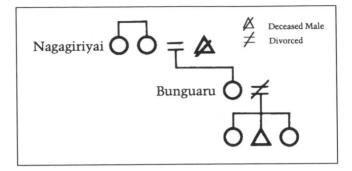

Figure 9. Bunguaru's household

small children, her mother, and her mother's sister Nagagiriyai. Bunguaru's husband left her about two years ago, Nagagiriyai is unmarried, and Bunguaru's mother's husband died four years ago (fig. 9).

This three-generation almost all-female household depends on a combination of subsistence agriculture and income from the sale of coconuts and *molas*. Bunguaru and her mother plant and harvest plantains, collect coconuts, and provide the household with firewood and water. They also fish and stalk crabs. Bunguaru and her mother are members of the *mola* cooperative and sew *molas* whenever they are not out in the jungle or washing clothes. Income from *mola* sales is used to buy household and personal necessities. Nagagiriyai is not well; her eyesight is bad and she cannot sew *molas* or help with most of the daily tasks. She and her sister, however, have small coconut groves that they inherited from their father. Bunguaru also has a small grove. Coconuts from these groves are traded for sugar, salt, kerosene, and cloth. This household has few consumer goods and often goes hungry. Trading *molas* and coconuts provides this nearly all-female household with consumer goods. Fish and plantains are not purchased. For this group of women, losing their husbands has not made them dependent on purchased foodstuffs. Although they sometimes go hungry, in general they are able to make ends meet.

Albertina's Household

Albertina is fanning the fire, and her fourteen-year-old daughter Lucia is lying in her hammock trying to nurse and comfort her crying baby. The rest of the household is out in the jungle, harvesting coconuts, collecting firewood, picking fruit, and stalking land crabs. Albertina and her husband, Danilo, live with their children and grandchildren in a compounded household (fig. 10). Albertina's eldest daughter, Edelmira, has two children. She lent one girl to some neighbors who were childless; the other girl lives with her. Edelmira's husband is a health worker on a nearby island. He comes home once or twice a month to visit, and although he receives a salary, he does not contribute to daily household expenses. Instead, he has bought furniture (a wardrobe, a bed, and a chair) and a tape deck and hopes to set up an independent household as soon as he can save enough money to buy a house site on the island where he works.

Overall, the household produces sufficient food to meet its needs. Antonio, Danilo's young son-in-law (age fifteen), does most of the fishing. His fishing skills are not very good, and as a result, the household does not eat much fish. He is skilled at stalking land crabs with a harpoon, however. With the help of the women, Danilo and Antonio have planted plantains, rice, corn, yucca, and sugarcane, among other things. This household never buys plantains or fresh fish. Sometimes on rainy days, when Antonio does not go fishing, they buy canned sardines.

Coconut sales provide most of the household's cash income, supplemented occasionally by *mola* sales. Albertina and her two daughters accompany Danilo to their coconut groves about twice a week. The youngest daughter (age fourteen) stays at home with her newborn and the other young children. They collect an average of about one hundred coconuts per week, which are traded for needed goods at local stores or with Colombian traders.

Mola sales are not vital to this household's daily subsistence. All the women sew *molas* in the late afternoons and evenings when no other task is pressing, but only for their own use. Two of Albertina's daughters sew nightly when they attend the *congreso*. Albertina does not go because she is tending the new mother and child. Edelmira is a member of the *mola* cooperative and sews some *molas* specifically for sale. She receives higher prices for her *molas* there than by trad-

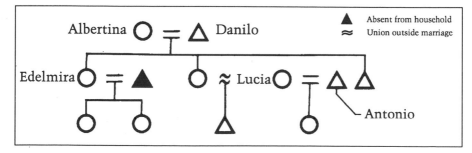

Figure 10. Albertina's household

ing them at the store; however, she does not like waiting several months before receiving cash through the cooperative so she still trades some of her *molas* at the store. She buys school supplies and clothing for her two children in addition to clothing for herself with her income from *molas*.

This compounded household does not depend on income from *mola* sales to meet its daily needs, even though there are many women and children and few contributing men living there. Subsistence agriculture and the coconut trade provide for the household's needs.

Summary

Overall, the extent of *mola* commercialization in Mansucun was minimal in 1985, especially when compared to that in Carti-Sugtupu and Tupile, where *molas* have been commercialized to a much greater extent. Few women produced *molas* specifically for sale, though most traded their used *molas* for cloth and other goods at local stores, receiving only three dollars per panel. Production for sale was stimulated by the recently organized *mola* cooperative, where women received higher prices for their *molas*. Delays in distributing profits, however, made it difficult for women to count on this income. Tourism was virtually nonexistent.

Mola commercialization had little impact on the division of labor by gender or on the way women spent their time. Women still actively participated in agricultural tasks and sewed *molas* only in the late afternoons and evenings. Agricultural produce, fish, and coconuts continued to be managed by the household *akkweti* as household resources. Income from selling *molas*, lobsters, remittances, or earnings from wage labor were viewed as personal and not as household resources. Women controlled their earnings from *mola* sales as well as income from coconuts, while men kept their income from lobster sales and from wage labor.

Mansucun's households produced most, if not all, of the food they consumed. As a result, households were not dependent on the cash economy for most of their basic needs. In general, households did not purchase fish or plantains, the two staples of the Kuna diet. A closer look at individual households revealed that, although single mothers depended more on *mola* sales than did other women, they still produced much of their own food and were less dependent on cash than were the single mothers described in earlier chapters. In Mansucun we begin to see patterns that, in the other communities, where *mo-*

Table 6. *Reasons for single motherhood, by community*

Woman's Status	Carti-Sugtupu		Tupile		Mansucun	
	%	No.	%	No.	%	No.
Divorced	7	27	10	43	5	7
Dead	8	32	7	28	16	24
Absent	6	25	7	29	13	19
No partner	4	14	7	30	2	3
Living with a partner	75	291	69	288	64	93
All women	100	389	100	418	100	146

las have been commercialized to a greater extent, serve as the basis for differential access to resources and quality of life among women.

Female-Supported Households

The number of households solely or largely supported by women is growing worldwide. This is certainly true in San Blas. Kuna women become single mothers in several ways: divorce or separation, death of partner, absence of partner due to wage labor migration, or no partner (biological father does not recognize or take responsibility for a child and the woman has not found another partner). One-quarter of the women on Carti-Sugtupu and fully one-third of the women on Tupile and Mansucun were living as single mothers (table 6).

Male mortality rates appear to be significantly higher in Mansucun than in the other two communities. Malaria was much more prevalent in Mansucun in the 1980s, but one would think that this disease would affect men and women equally. The number of women divorced and living without a partner on Mansucun was lower than in the other two communities. This can be explained, in part, by the Mansucun *congreso's* willingness to intervene in marital relations. Almost twice as many Mansucun women's partners were absent as in the other two communities, however.

What the categories of divorce and separation and absent partners mean within the current context of San Blas needs further explanation. Divorce or separation of couples married in the Kuna style can be initiated by either partner. A man can "separate" from his wife by packing up his hammock, clothes, and tools and returning to his mother's household. When a women wants her husband to leave, she simply places his belongings outside the door. Couples may separate for short or long periods or permanently. The *congreso* need not be notified, though if there has been a fight, as there often is, the couple may be called into the *congreso* for mediation. Guilty parties are usually fined. Since marriages are easily formed and dissolved, a couple's status may be somewhat ambiguous to others in the community and even to the couple themselves.

Migration to Panama City blurs the distinction between "separated" women and those whose partners are working for extended periods in Panama City or Changuinola. In some cases, neither partner is sure whether he or she is still married and just living apart for a period of time or is actually separated. For example, Isabel and Jaime and their newborn son lived in Isabel's mother's household. One year after the child's birth, Jaime went to work in Panama City. For a while he sent money every couple of months. Then it came less frequently and eventually only at Christmas. Isabel learned from female friends living in Panama City that he had found another woman. Eight years later, Jaime came back to visit. He claimed that they were still husband and wife and wanted Isabel to move with him to Panama City. She chose not to go. Jaime left, promising to visit her regularly and to send money. Nine months later Isabel gave birth to a second child. Like Isabel, mothers living apart from their partner often receive no support from their children's father(s).[2]

Approximately half of the households in each of the three communities I studied were supported by mothers living without partners. Similar patterns of household composition were found among the three communities. As shown in table 7, very few of these women lived in nuclear households; most lived in extended or compounded households. Close to 80 percent of compounded households had one or more single mothers, while only a little more than half of extended households could be characterized in this way. Mansucun had a somewhat higher percentage of single mothers living in extended households (70 percent). On Tupile and Carti-Sugtupu, where women participated little in agricultural production, I found no female-headed nuclear households. In Mansucun, however, where women produced some of their own food, women lived alone with their children in four households.

How important *mola* sales were within the overall context of household maintenance strategies varied with the dependence of particular households on cash income for purchasing foodstuffs. This varied not only among the three communities but also from among households supporting and supported by single mothers. Carti-

Table 7. *Household types, with and without single mothers, by community*

	Nuclear Households		Extended Households		Compounded Households	
	%	No.	%	No.	%	No.
Carti-Sugtupu (n = 104)						
Single mothers	0	0	54	26	80	28
No single mothers	100	14	46	21	20	7
Total	100	14	100	47	100	35
Tupile (n = 130)						
Single mothers	5	1	58	40	80	30
No single mothers	95	20	42	10˙	20	22
Total	100	21	100	50	100	52
Mansucun (n = 61)						
Single mothers	20	4	70	14	78	14
No single mothers	80	16	30	6	22	4
Total	100	20	100	20	100	18

Notes: On Carti-Sugtupu, 7 percent (n = 7) of the households did not fit any of these patterns. For Tupile (n = 6) and Mansucun (n = 3), 5 percent of the households did not fit into these categories.

Sugtupu was the most dependent on purchase of foodstuffs, Tupile less so, and Mansucun the least. Most Carti-Sugtupu households bought plantains daily, in contrast with the situation in Mansucun and Tupile, where very few households purchased them on a regular basis. Poorer soil combined with a plantain blight required Carti-Sugtupu's residents to import most of their plantains, while Mansucun and Tupile residents continued to be mostly self-sufficient.

Women from Carti-Sugtupu also purchased fish more often than did women from the other two communities. Unlike the situation with plantains, however, this practice cannot be explained by ecological factors. Fish is most abundant in the Carti region, where numerous coral reefs provide excellent habitats for fish and safe, calm waters for the fishermen. One partial explanation relates to women's participation in fishing. Women from Carti-Sugtupu no longer fished as regularly as they used to, nor did they contribute gathered foods to the diet. Since men had not increased their fishing activities, women now purchased fish with money from their *mola* sales. Women never did fish much in Tupile, while in Mansucun women continued to fish in the river.

Household case studies revealed that, despite differences among the three communities, similar factors determined the extent to which a particular household depended on *mola* sales to meet daily needs. These factors were men's overall capability to provide basic foodstuffs, the availability of other sources of income, and the number of single mothers with children to support.

Households where single mothers resided with their children were generally more dependent on *mola* sales than were other households. The case studies of households in Carti-Sugtupu, Tupile, and Mansucun reveal some important differences between households where single mothers resided and those where women had partners to help them provide for their children. Due to the absence of men's labor, hunger was more prevalent in households where single mothers resided; however, in Mansucun, women's continued participation in agricultural production prevented them from becoming dependent on income from *mola* sales, even when their partners were absent. Cash earned from *molas* sometimes supported household members living in Panama City as well as those in San Blas. Some women regularly sent cash to their children who were studying in Panama City. Determining the extent to which households in Panama City are supported with income from *mola* sales is a task that is left for future researchers.

Matrifocal households in San Blas remain flexible units, expanding and contracting with labor migration, economic hardship, divorce, death, and abandonment of women with children. During times of economic hardship or household unrest, women and their children often return to their mothers' households (see the description of Tada and Muu's household in chapter 9).

As was described in chapter 8, four aspects of headship are important to examine: "1) authority or power, 2) decision-making, 3) sources of economic support, and in some instances 4) control over and possession of children in case of divorce or death" (Mencher and Okongwu 1993:3). Different household members, even those living elsewhere, may perform these functions. I offer the following preliminary observations about household headship among the Kuna, based on case study material. I hope that these observations will serve as a stimulus and starting point for further study.

Authority/or Power

In San Blas, household members' authority or power is subject to the consensually run community *congreso*. Kuna households and their members are not isolated units. The *congreso* regulates travel, mediates inter- and intrahousehold disputes, organizes community projects and the labor they require, stipulates food contributions each household must make to support various types of community-wide celebrations and events, and publicly shames or fines people who do not behave appropriately (Howe 1986b). Women's and *ome-kits'* travel is more restricted than is men's, especially outside of the San Blas region, although both men and women must request travel permits in order to leave whatever community they are living in or visiting (Stier 1983; Howe 1986b). Members of the *mola* cooperative who initially had difficulty receiving permission to travel to participate in cooperative functions are now readily given permission in most communities.

Travel aside, men and women are generally fined equally for inappropriate behavior. For example, on one island adulterers were each fined fifty dollars payable to the community chest for their transgressions. Nonetheless, Kuna men perceive Kuna women as quarrelsome and in need of being controlled; women do not accept this definition of themselves passively (Howe 1986b:230–232).

Within Kuna households, primary authority or power is shared, usually by the senior male and female in the household. Although no systematic data have been collected, this pattern appears to be changing among younger couples, who choose to live in nuclear households. Household heads are given the Kuna titles *akkweti* and *ibedi*. Authority is handed to the next generation when the elder(s) become too infirm to participate in the household's economic activities. At the community level, some islands have established a "retirement age" when adults are no longer expected to participate in community work parties. Women complain that some young men, especially those who have spent a lot of time in Panama City, do not respect their female partner's authority.

Decision Making and Sources of Economic Support

Kuna women are increasingly providing essential income to maintain their households. The extent to which women support their households depends on household organization and the number of contributing men relative to the number of women and children.

Who makes decisions about labor and the utilization and distribution of resources varies with different economic activities. In multigenerational households, the senior man usually makes decisions about and controls the agricultural and wage labor of his sons-in-law and his unmarried male offspring still living in the household. The senior woman tells her partner what the household needs, organizes the women's and girls' labor, and in general controls the distribution of resources brought into the household by her husband or noncash resources brought by her sons-in-law (fish, agricultural produce).

Women individually control their own income from *mola* sales. Who controls and makes decisions about men's income varies. In the early 1980s, women complained that, unlike with income from agricultural produce, meat, fish, or the sale of coconuts, they often did not have a say in how income from diving or from wage labor was spent (one important exception was remittances). Some men bought beer, cigarettes, and consumer goods that had no general household use. Women living in merchant households had varying degrees of control over and input into decisions related to cash resources.

Whether men's earnings were considered for household or for individual use affected how dependent women were on cash from *mola* sales. Among the older generation, women generally kept their husbands' earnings. They could draw on this money to purchase needed household items. Husband and wife conferred about large expenditures. Coconuts were considered a "household" resource.

Access to and distribution of income has been changing among younger couples, however. Defined by generation and type of income-generating activity, this phenomenon has not been limited to any particular island. In several case studies, younger men controlled their own earnings and used them for mostly personal and not household expenses. These men's wives were much more dependent on their own income-generating ability, since they could no longer count on money for household expenses from their partners. Income from diving or wage labor was more likely to be used by men for individual purchases than was income from coconuts. Coconuts were often traded by women so they could acquire needed household items directly.

Women's access to resources provided by men (food, coconuts, and cash) to use for household subsistence needs varied not by community of residence, or by domestic organization, but rather by type of income-generating activity and by generation. Thus, within a particular household, women might have access to and control over certain resources and not others. With the new emphasis on purchased foodstuffs, women not only had less food to distribute, they also had increased responsibility for earning the income with which to buy it. Thus, gender has played an important role in determining women's access to resources by defining appropriate activities for men and women.

11.
Insights from San Blas: Crafts, Gender, and the Global Economy

Mola commercialization is part of a larger process through which the San Blas region has become increasingly articulated with the international economy. The Kuna now depend on the export of goods and labor to generate income to purchase imported goods.

Mola commercialization has resulted from and contributed to the increasing dependency of the San Blas Kuna on the cash economy. The shift from a primarily subsistence-based to a mixed cash economy occurred initially through the commercialization of coconuts and the migration of Kuna men to the cities in search of wage labor. Subsistence agricultural production in many households and communities declined dramatically as a result of these social changes, and an increasing number of Kuna women have become single mothers either temporarily, because their partners were working outside of San Blas, or permanently, as a result of divorce or abandonment. With the decline in male subsistence agricultural production, many women began to sell their *molas* in order to purchase foodstuffs. In sharp contrast with many regions of the world, where women have remained in the subsistence sector and men have moved into the cash economy, Kuna women have directly entered the cash economy first through coconut cash cropping and subsequently through *mola* commercialization. In the 1970s and the 1980s, *mola* sales represented one of the three primary sources of income for the entire San Blas region.

The San Blas Kuna have become increasingly drawn into the global capitalist economy through the commercialization of *molas*. *Mola* production, exchange, and circulation vary widely throughout the region and have contributed to social differentiation based, in part, on gender. Overall, instead of being a "cohesive force" for maintaining an egalitarian distribution of resources within the region (Hirschfeld

1976; Swain 1982), *mola* commercialization has furthered regional differentiation among women and between the genders. The efforts of the *mola* cooperative to counteract this trend have been only partially successful. To ensure a more equitable distribution of resources from *mola* sales throughout the region, the cooperative would need (1) more working capital; (2) recognition by and support from the Congreso General Kuna and local *congresos* as the principal marketer of *molas* for the entire region; (3) and permission from Carti-Sugtupu and the other islands where cruise ships stop to allow the cooperative to open stores and encourage or require tourists to buy *molas* through the cooperative.

Gender, Class, and Ethnicity

Class relations, ethnic identity, and gender interweave to define resource distribution, in this case, capital from *mola* commercialization. Merchants in Panama City, the United States, Europe, and Japan earn the greatest profits from *mola* sales; producers—Kuna women and *omekits*—generally earn the least.[1] Kuna men, and on Carti-Sugtupu a few women, serve as intermediaries. The capital they earn through *mola* sales has furthered socioeconomic differentiation within San Blas and has contributed to incipient class formation at the local level. As was discussed in chapter 6, when a wider-angle lens encompassing the entire chain from producer to consumer is used to view class relations, class interests both coincide and conflict across ethnic and gender boundaries.

Among the San Blas Kuna, consolidation of wealth does not appear to have occurred, nor has accumulation of capital by merchant households translated into increased power or the ability to appropriate labor. Since land in San Blas cannot be bought or sold, Kuna merchants have invested their earnings, accumulated in part from *mola* sales, in their businesses, have purchased consumer goods, or have sent their children to Panama City to study (many nonmerchant households also send their children to study). Whether the next generation will stay in Panama City to work and, if so, what types of jobs they will be able to procure has yet to be seen. In the 1980s, *mola* commercialization did not enable Kuna men or women to join Panama's wealthy elite or even the middle class. Whether capital from *mola* commercialization and other business ventures will be accumulated and consolidated across generations or will be redistributed, resulting in continued egalitarian relations as suggested in the literature on the Kuna, is a question still to be answered.

Many Kuna communities are collectivizing capital to purchase and operate community-owned trade boats, warehouses, and stores. The regionwide *mola* cooperative also represents such an effort. The effect of these efforts is to both mediate and create subregional differences in the distribution of wealth. Therefore, even as the Kuna are increasingly swept into the global capitalist economy, communities, some more than others, are maintaining to a greater or lesser extent egalitarian relations within their communities with respect to economic resources.

Mola commercialization has resulted in the partial commoditization of ethnicity.[2] As was discussed in chapter 5, national strategies for promoting tourism in the 1960s to the 1980s focused on the packaging of "exotic Indian cultures." In the 1990s, the emphasis has shifted to ecotourism. This study lends credence to the idea that it is critical to link the role of ethnicity to its specific historical context. Unlike other indigenous groups in Panama (the Guaymi and the Emberá), the Kuna, because of their past experiences with collective forms of social organization and negotiating to protect their collective interests, have been able to use the "packaging of ethnicity" to their benefit (Bourgois 1988).

For indigenous women and men like the Kuna, commercialization of their crafts (often clothing) is tied to the commoditization of their ethnic identity. This has certainly been true for the Zapotec and the Nahua of Mexico (Stephen 1991*b*), the Taquileños of Peru (Healey and Zorn 1982–1983), and the Otavaleños of Ecuador (Collier 1949; Salomon 1973; Stephen 1991*b*).[3] What this study clearly shows is that international politics, the nature and extent of tourism, migration, subsistence production, local connections to national and international markets, and changing patterns of consumption may all affect craft commercialization, leaving producers vulnerable to forces largely outside their control. In San Blas, local-level factors affecting Kuna women's vulnerability include household composition, their status as single mothers, and the extent to which they and their households are dependent on income from *mola* sales for survival.

Further study of changes in ethnic craft consumption in the United States, Europe, and Japan and their effects on craft production and commercialization would contribute to our understanding of craft commoditization. Such a study would also provide information useful to policymakers and planners.

Some indigenous groups have benefited, at least in part, from the export of their crafts (Stephen 1991*b*; Healey and Zorn 1983; Salomon 1973). Similar features, such as preservation of a significant land base, commercial production for sale since the seventeenth or eighteenth century, a "history of locally controlling marketing and distribution through local and regional networks," and "noncapitalist institutions of exchange, such as reciprocal goods and labor exchanges," have created conditions favorable to self-managed development (Stephen 1991 b: 124).

Craft commercialization has affected men and women in different ways. For example, the Taquileños of Peru have stimulated and gained a high degree of local-level control over tourism to their isolated island. This has been accomplished by (1) purchasing collectively owned and operated boats to bring tourists to the island, (2) creating an islandwide store for craft sales, (3) developing a cultural museum, and (4) organizing home-stay visits for tourists. Like the Kuna, the Taquileños have received funds from the Inter-American Foundation. Taquileña women, however, have not benefited from craft commercialization in their community. Men's crafts are more popular and profitable, and women's participation in productive activities has been displaced. Relative to men, women have not benefited economically from the rise in tourism. They are excluded from the decision-making committees that manage the island's collective enterprises (Healey and Zorn 1982–1983).

Similarly, the effects of cloth commercialization on Baule women living in the Ivory Coast have been mostly negative (Etienne 1980). In the past, Baule men and women both participated in the production of cloth and controlled different aspects of cloth production and circulation, which were tied into control over land for subsistence agricultural production. With commercialization of the cloth, women lost their control over cloth and their access to land. Formerly egalitarian relations between men and women became asymmetrical.

Gender has defined roles for both producers and sellers among the lacemakers of Narsapur, India (Mies 1982). Socially constructed expectations dictating that women should remain in their homes and not "work" has allowed women there to make lace (making lace at home was not viewed as work) and prevented women from becoming involved in marketing their products. As a result, male intermediaries became wealthy while female lacemakers remained poor.

The increased commercialization of Mexican Zapotec weavings in the 1970s created a merchant class that purchased labor and employed weavers in workshops and through piecework production systems. Class relations among men and women developed even as the ideology of egalitarian relations within the community continued. In this community, the extent to which women benefited depended on their class position. Although men and women received the same wages for work done, women continued to perform all of the unpaid household labor in addition to weaving (Stephen 1991a:154–155).

In San Pedro Sacatepéquez, Guatemala, the female-dominated industry of weaving *huipiles,* first on backstrap looms and subsequently on footlooms, for sale to other indigenous women in Guatemala declined rapidly when the value of the Quetzal fell. *Huipiles* became too expensive for local women to purchase, and many women started wearing western dress. Since then, the male-dominated manufacture of yardgoods has completely replaced women's weaving (Ehlers 1990). Men weave and women sew the cloth into garments. Although women "help" their husbands, men control the profits from cloth and clothing sales.

Compared to the effects of craft commercialization on women relative to men, detailed in the studies just described, Kuna women have done quite well for themselves. They have (1) become active in marketing their *molas* (primarily but not exclusively through the *mola* cooperative), (2) retained their access to and control over land and over many other important economic resources, (3) entered regional and national politics and economic development planning processes, (4) learned business skills that have allowed them to join men in small and collective business ventures or to create their own income-generating opportunities, and (5) controlled the income from the sale of *molas* and, in many cases, men's income from other sources as well. The *mola* cooperative, supported by the already-existing egalitarian relations between men and women, played a major role in ensuring that women reaped some of the benefits from *mola* commercialization and learned skills that will expand their possibilities for income generation.

Artisan Petty-Commodity Production

Craft commercialization continues to flourish even as capitalism evolves. Clearly, Marx's prediction that it would disappear has not come true. Like what has been found in the urban informal sector (Benería and Roldán 1987), precapitalist and capitalist relations coexist among rural craft producers. Cook and Binford (1990:1) write: "The mainstream view in political economy has been that the historic role of capitalist producers is to extend the market exchange process to land and labor power by replacing (often forcibly) kinship- and community-based social relations with qualitatively new sets of social relations based on private proprietorship of the means of production."

In recent decades, capitalist and precapitalist relations of produc-

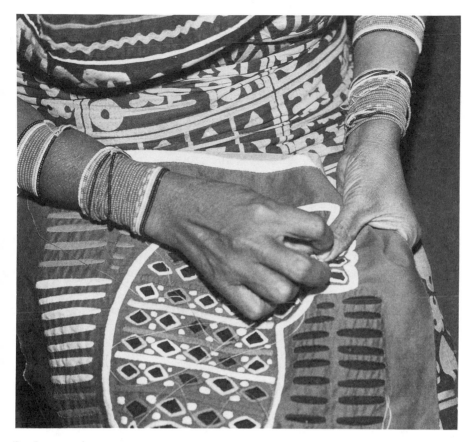

Sewing a *mola*

tion have coexisted in San Blas. Which predominates is historically specific. Kinship and community-based relations continue to exist and in some ways have been strengthened. Before the 1960s, craft production had, for the most part, retained precapitalist relations of production, exchange, and circulation. This situation changed dramatically during the 1960s, the 1970s, and the 1980s, when *mola* makers began to be affected by external market forces. Still, throughout these three decades, piecework production remained low. The nature and extent of piecework production appears to be changing rapidly in the 1990s due to the dramatic decline in tourism and a new fad among Panama's elite to wear pieces of *mola* incorporated into high fashion clothing. Piecework production is on the rise and patterns of *mola* consumption are changing. Given the Kuna's history, it seems probable that the *mola* cooperative or some other Kuna group (either already established or newly formed) will organize to meet these new challenges. How politics, class interests, ethnicity, and gender are embedded in this newly emerging social context is an area for future study.

Producers' and consumers' knowledge about the production, exchange, and consumption of *molas* within specific historical and cultural contexts is a dynamic area within which conflicting and sometimes converging interests are defined and negotiated. Rather than conceptualizing commoditization as a linear sequence from nonalienation to increasing alienation of the producer from that which is produced, commoditization is better thought of as a process in which there is room for negotiation among producers and consumers. As was shown in chapter 6, producers' and consumers' knowledge about each other's use of *molas* was often used as a locus for negotiation and control over price, design, and sales. How gender-related patterns of consumption are embedded in the organization of production is an area of research that deserves greater attention.

International and Local Gender-based Divisions of Labor

Historically, the division of labor by gender among the Kuna has been flexible and has changed in response to economic change; however, homogeneous definitions of the socially constructed gender-based division of labor within the region cannot be assumed. What is considered men's or women's work changes over time, across generations within a fixed point in time, and among different Kuna communities. Differences among the three communities studied in San Blas can be explained by the variations in how different Kuna communities have been incorporated into the global economy. Deere and León de Leal's investigation (1981) of three regions in Peru characterized by noncapitalist, predominantly capitalist, and advanced capitalist relations of production, respectively, argued that region, task, the manner in which wage labor is appropriated, and the class position of individual households all affect the rigidity of the division of labor along gender lines. My research suggests that these factors also operate within regions and among households within specific communities.

In 1985, the relationship between *mola* makers' productive and socially reproductive work varied among households and was related, again, to their dependence on income from *mola* sales. The most profound changes in the division of labor in San Blas occurred not between the sexes but among women of different generations. In Carti-Sugtupu and Tupile, the communities where *mola* commercialization was greatest, the senior woman of the household took over many of the younger women's social reproductive activities so the latter could sew *molas* for sale. Similar to the argument that women's subsistence labor subsidizes capitalist development by allowing wage earners to earn low pay and still subsist and reproduce the labor force, the low prices received by *mola* producers are "subsidized" by other women's labor and, in some cases, by men's subsistence activities.

Because *molas* are produced at home, there is still a tendency in the literature on the Kuna, as well as on the part of economic development planners in Panama, to view *mola* production as a leisure activity (Sherzer and Sherzer 1976). While this may be an accurate perception for women living in households that do not depend on income from *mola* sales, it is a misperception for women or households that do depend on this money for survival.

Studies on the newly emerging international division of labor by gender point out that local economies are linked to and are part of the global economy. Craft production contrasts starkly with other industries that have been studied. Most industries have moved from the industrialized north to the south, where labor is cheaper and non-unionized. The impact on women in places in Latin America, Asia, and the Caribbean where industry has relocated has been mixed (Fernández-Kelly 1983; Nash and Fernández-Kelly 1983; Nash and Safa 1986). In contrast, the commercialization of indigenous people's crafts, especially women's clothing, is embedded in local ethnic identities packaged for consumption (Stephen 1991a, 1991b; Healey and Zorn 1983; Tice 1989b).

Kuna *mola* makers have been linked to the global economy and the "formal sector" in limited and historically specific ways. First, an exploitation of their designs has been introduced in the form of production in Asian factories (probably by women) at lower cost. Kuna women's creativity is exploited and their "exotic" ethnic identity is commoditized to sell mass-produced items with *mola* designs in Panama City. Second, Kuna women are increasingly linked to the formal sector through recently expanded piecework production for the high-fashion clothing industry. This has been linked to changes in the ideology of consumption among the Panamanian elite.

Unlike homeworkers in Mexico City's informal sector producing for a domestic market (Benería and Roldán 1987) or the export-oriented footloose factories (Nash and Fernández-Kelly 1983), *mola* producers are export-oriented as well as producing for their own use. *Mola* commercialization, however, is still characterized by the same unequal relations of exchange between industrialized countries and the "Third World." Like the *maquiladoras* and homeworkers in Mexico, indigenous craft producers are highly vulnerable to external forces. Possibilities for organizing, however, seem to result in fewer negative consequences for craft producers. This is possible, in part, because of the uniqueness of each ethnic craft. Production of handmade objects requiring special skills to produce is not easily relocated.

Collective efforts of a number of indigenous groups have used the capital from craft sales to improve their quality of life. These groups have shown resilience and creativity at the local level in the face of national and international forces that often exploit and impoverish local regions.

This study of craft commercialization in a rural area of Panama is relevant to our understanding of social changes occurring at present in the United States. Rural women in parts of the United States are increasingly turning to the production and sale of crafts as a means of supporting their households. Craft sales supplement declining incomes for some households, while for others they provide the sole source of household income. In southwestern rural Washington State, for example, with the decline of the logging industry and the "technicalization" and automation of pulp plants, increasing numbers of men are unable to support their households. The divorce rate is rapidly rising and increasing numbers of women are left on their own to support their households. Employment opportunities for women are meager at best, and women increasingly are turning to craft commercialization to support their households financially. In the 1960s, craft commercialization was used as an economic development strategy for impoverished regions of Kentucky and North Carolina (Barker 1991). Craft sales remain an important source of income for many households. In the late 1980s in Nebraska, for example, many women whose households could no longer support themselves by farming and those who had suffered foreclosures on their farms were starting to produce crafts for sale. Many of these women's husbands were migrating to urban centers in search of employment. Some of these women were commoditizing their local identities in much the same way that ethnicity has been commoditized for the Kuna. Stores stress that their goods are made in a particular locale, whether a town or a state. Michigan now has a chain of stores called Michigania that exclusively carry handmade products "made in Michigan."

Clearly, there are some similarities among women living in rural areas of the United States and those in rural Latin America; however, there is also great potential for conflict over access to markets. How this will unfold if craft production and sales become a major focus of rural economic development in the United States is to be seen. Research needs to be done on how class interests converge and come into conflict across national borders.[4] The intersection of gender, class, and ethnicity across national borders is a rich area for future study. Specifically, how "Fourth World crafts" are integrated into and come into conflict with the market for handmade objects in the "industrialized" world is an area that needs further exploration. It is important, however, not to analytically dichotomize north/south as developed/underdeveloped, for Native Americans living in the industrial north also produce "Fourth World crafts." It is also critical to develop linkages between future social science research efforts and local, national, and international economic development planning processes. Many indigenous groups are increasingly challenging researchers to become more involved in the practical implications of their results. This raises ethical issues about the role of research and of the researcher that must also be addressed.

Policy Implications

Whether craft commercialization is a sustainable income-generating strategy for impoverished indigenous women living in rural areas depends on historically changing external forces such as tourism, political and economic circumstances, and changing national and global patterns of craft consumption. Thus, it is important to recognize that craft markets are historically specific and that they change. Policy planners and program implementors must pay as much attention to trends in craft consumption, both locally and globally, as they do to production and marketing strategies.

As was discussed earlier in this chapter, craft commercialization must be linked to national-level plans for stimulating tourism and must include marketing strategies that are not tourist-dependent. Most important, craft commercialization efforts and planning must be integrated into wider, long-term, sustainable economic development strategies. The Kuna are a good model for how people at the grass-roots level can develop income-generating strategies that increase local control over economic resources. While not all of their efforts have been successful, they are moving in the right direction.

Alone, the commercialization of crafts may not provide impoverished women with a sustainable stable income. As the Kuna have shown, however, craft commercialization can be used to help women develop and finance collective means for obtaining credit, access to foodstuffs and other commodities, language and business skills, and leverage for participating in regional and national economic planning processes. Thus, in areas like San Blas, where women already produce crafts, the commercialization of artisan goods may be used as a stepping-stone toward gaining local control over important economic resources and providing for women's increased participation in planning processes affecting their lives.

Producers often have differential access to markets for selling their crafts. Marketing opportunities can be equalized through production and marketing cooperatives. These cooperatives appear to be especially successful where collaborative forms of socially organized labor already exist. Cooperatives can facilitate women's inclusion in wider economic development planning processes and can increase the prices received by producers. Practical issues include access to credit, promotion and marketing strategies, technical support, and education for craft cooperatives.

The commercialization of crafts can, but does not have to, lead to the alienation of producers from their craft (e.g., *mola* producers sewing items that have meaning for the end user, but not for themselves). Tourism and other forms of marketing that contextualize the craft within the wider social setting of its production can enrich and benefit both producer and buyer. Knowledge about the production and use of *molas* has been employed by Kuna women as a locus for negotiating and manipulating control over the production and marketing of *molas*. As was discussed earlier, educating buyers is also one way that producers can affirm their ethnicity in a positive way and retain control over the production of their craft (i.e., in decisions about shapes, colors, sizes, and designs). Similarly, producers need more information about their markets. Foundations and economic development agencies could support producers' participation in international craft fairs, where they would have the opportunity to better understand their markets as well as to bypass local intermediaries.

Cooperative members in San Blas were eager for information about how other craft cooperatives function and about issues related to women and economic development. Foundations or economic development agencies could facilitate the information-sharing process in two ways: (1) contract with anthropologists or other social scientists working on issues related to women and development to serve as consultants to women's cooperatives; and (2) provide funds for women to visit cooperatives in other countries. The *mola* cooperative's model of providing internships for women in communities without a local chapter could be extended throughout Central America.

It seems likely that, as structural adjustment policies tighten the economic belts of countries in Latin America, rural households in the United States lose their former livelihoods, and footloose factories sprint around the world in search of greater profits, leaving unemployed workers behind, an increasing number of households worldwide will fall back on the commercialization of crafts for survival. Carefully thought out policies could stimulate the development of craft commercialization strategies that lead to increased control over economic resources at the local level, new cross-cultural sensitivity between producers and consumers, and sustainable economic development strategies.

Appendix: Methodology

Gaining Entry

In Panama, official permission to engage in field research must be jointly obtained from the Instituto Nacional de Cultura (INAC) and from the Patrimonio Histórico. The Patrimonio Histórico is the national-level organization responsible for coordinating all social science research undertaken in Panama. I signed legal contracts in 1981 and again in 1984 that stipulated my rights and responsibilities as an investigator. These documents granted me official permission to do research in San Blas. Although signing a contract with the Patrimonio Histórico is legally required and technically grants one permission to pursue research, it does not in any way guarantee acceptance by the Kuna of San Blas.

San Blas is not easily accessible to researchers. Permission from local community *congresos* must be obtained on all but a few islands to spend even one night there. Non-Kuna researchers and entrepreneurs engaged in activities objectionable to one or more communities have been asked and sometimes forced to leave the region. For example, two anthropologists who were taping Kuna religious chants had their tapes confiscated and were asked to leave the island of Ustupu in 1984.

In 1981, I obtained initial permission from the all-male local *congreso* to stay on Tupile. They wanted to know why this was an important study; exactly what I would be doing; specifically, how I could contribute to the community on a day-to-day basis; whether I would respect their traditions and laws or was out to change them; and whether I would publish my research and if so, in what languages.

Several people said that they wanted my research to be relevant to the social and economic problems they faced daily and did not want me to "steal" their traditions. From what I can gather, this fear seems to be based on accounts of what other indigenous groups have experienced with anthropologists and a critique of an anthropology that concerns itself with "traditions" to the exclusion of pressing socioeconomic and political concerns that impinge on and sometimes threaten to destroy the very lifestyles and, in some cases, peoples that the anthropologist is studying (Davis 1977). Although some anthropologists have studied Kuna "traditions," such as their chants (Young and Howe 1976; Chapin 1970) and lullabies (McCosker 1976), all of these researchers have been very careful to provide the appropriate Kuna organizations copies of their research in addition to participating in collective work parties held during the times they were conducting their studies. While in San Blas, I heard many individuals praising and appreciating the careful research done by these scholars.

My research was approved in a general way, though the men explained that, since my study concerned women, and they could not speak for the women, I would have to discuss my study with members of the *mola* cooperative. The cooperative would have final say over whether I could do the research. After a lengthy discussion at a general meeting of the *mola* cooperative, my study was wholeheartedly approved; the women agreed to collaborate in every way possible.

In 1984, I was again given permission by the *congreso* to stay and by the *mola* cooperative to carry out the research. Once approved by the *congreso* on Tupile and by the *mola* cooperative, I had no trouble being accepted into other Kuna communities, and never again was my research discussed at such length in another *congreso*. News travels fast in San Blas, so I quickly became identified with both the community of Tupile and the *mola* cooperative.

In the mid-1980s, official steps were being taken to ensure that research carried out in San Blas was beneficial to the Kuna as well as to the researcher. Kuna leaders, educators, and social scientists, among others, were all concerned with the nature of research that was conducted in San Blas (see Chapin 1991; Tice 1989b). Special concern was expressed about the appropriateness of research that records customs and traditions but does little to address the profound socioeconomic and political problems facing the Kuna people today.

The Congreso General Kuna passed a resolution in the early 1980s stating that all field research to be conducted among the Kuna must be cleared through the Centro de Investigaciones Kunas (CIK). The center also promotes and supports studies by Kuna researchers; another important function is to link practicing professionals working on issues facing San Blas with those involved in research. The center facilitates dialogue among academicians and practitioners and serves as an information clearinghouse. My research was discussed thoroughly and approved by the center's members. I continued to be actively involved with this organization throughout my stay in Panama.

At the local level, individual communities were requesting collaboration from researchers ranging from informal arrangements to teach English or to participate in community work projects to formal requests for copies of tapes, photographs, and written materials. I contributed to each community I stayed in by (1) participating in community work projects, (2) working with the *mola* cooperative, and (3) sharing my research findings. Community work projects, for example, usually involved preparing, cooking, and serving food for the entire community. This meant peeling, cutting, and roasting plantains, deboning dried fish and wild boar, tending fires, stirring large cauldrons of food over blazing hot fires for hours at a time, serving food and drink, washing dishes, and sweeping the public areas of the island.

National-Level Data Collection

The initial phase of my research took place in Panama City, where I spent two months investigating archival materials, interviewing key informants, and studying Kuna. The purposes of this phase were (1) to collect general background information about the San Blas region and (2) to describe, analyze, and better understand the organization of the market for *mola* sales both nationally and internationally. I investigated library resources located at the Smithsonian Institute of Tropical Research, the Panama Canal Commission, the Museo del Hombre Panameño, and the Universidad Nacional de Panamá. I collected statistical data pertaining to the San Blas region and to the commercialization of *molas* from census data archived in the Controlaría General de la República de Panamá.

I obtained historical information about national government involvement in promoting and marketing *molas* and other handicrafts through interviews with key personnel in ministries concerned with tourism: Instituto Panameño de Turismo (IPAT), Ministerio de Desarrollo Agropecuario (MIDA), Instituto Panameño Autónomo Cooperativo (IPACOOP), Ministerio de Comercio y Pequeñas Industrias, and Artesanías Nacionales. I also consulted current and historical documents in each of these ministries as well as documents in the national archives.

In the private sector, I conducted systematic interviews with seven store owners and five fashion designers, all located in Panama City, who used *molas* in producing clothing. I collected information about the organization of marketing for *molas* in order to understand the role of retailers, intermediaries, and fashion designers in *mola* commercialization. These data also illuminated relations between the San Blas region, Panama City, and the United States with regard to the production and marketing of *molas*. In the United States, I also identified the types of places where *molas* are sold or exhibited. These included import-export companies, retail stores, galleries, museums, marketing fairs, street fairs, and flea markets. In some cases, it was possible for me to visit these places and to talk with people who were responsible for acquiring or selling the *molas*. These data provided a larger context within which to understand external factors pertaining to the commercialization of *molas*. They also offered opportunities to cross-check local-level perceptions of the international market. I also spoke with buyers of *molas* in the United States, though not in any systematic fashion.

In Panama City, I identified and visited places where *molas* were sold. These places included street corners, grocery stores, stores specializing in handicrafts, pharmacies, and the *mola* cooperative. I also attended artisan fairs. In each place where producers or Kuna intermediaries were selling *molas* directly to consumers, I observed the type, quality, and price of items being sold. I spoke with producers, intermediaries, and consumers concerning their role in the *mola* marketing network. I questioned consumers about how they planned to use the *molas* they had purchased.

The Kuna I learned during my first stay in San Blas (1981) was supplemented by six weeks of class and private lessons at the University of Panama in Panama City. My professor, a linguist specializing in the Kuna language, was himself Kuna. Approximately 75 percent of my research in San Blas was conducted in Kuna. The remainder of the time I used Spanish, a language in which I was fluent before arriving in San Blas.

Language acquisition was essential to the study, since the overwhelming majority of Kuna women spoke very little, if any, Spanish. Even young girls just out of grade school, where they supposedly learned Spanish, were reluctant to speak it. Kuna men were more likely to speak Spanish, though many older men were monolingual. Some elderly men spoke fluent Kuna and broken English that they had learned working on U.S. ships in the early 1900s or in the Canal Zone. Children rarely spoke much Spanish. Women who could have served as interpreters were difficult to find and were often unable to interpret because of other commitments. All in all, the most dependable way to ensure communication was to learn Kuna.

Defining the extent of my ability to speak Kuna will point out both the strengths of and the limitations on types of information available to me. My fluency in Kuna is limited primarily to talking about daily activities and about topics related to my research. My comprehension of conversations discussing abstract concepts is limited, as is my ability to follow discussions in large meetings, where language flows quickly and goes on for hours. Whenever possible, I arranged for an interpreter during meetings. When speaking at length in a meeting, I usually spoke in Spanish, with someone translating into Kuna. I was always encouraged in the *congreso* and cooperative meetings at the very least to begin what I wanted to say in Kuna.

Regional-Level Data Collection

At the regional level, I interviewed political and administrative leaders about the economic development of San Blas and the role of *mola* commercialization in that process. I also thoroughly researched current files and other relevant archives located in the regional governor's office. I visited thirty-four of the fifty-four San Blas communities at least once, my stays ranging from half an hour to ten days. During these visits, I asked women and, in some cases, men where women in their community sold *molas* and about the division of labor by gender. I made these trips sometimes in the company of respected Kuna political leaders and at other times with *mola* cooperative members. Traveling in the company of people highly respected throughout the region provided me with easy access and entry into all of the communities I visited.

I also visited all thirteen of the local cooperative chapters at least once. I interviewed leaders and other cooperative members concerning the cooperative's role in their community; I reviewed written documents and records. Since cooperative documents were not kept in a centralized location, these trips proved invaluable. I was able to compare, contrast, and place in perspective my three field sites. In addition, I located important cooperative documents and records in individual homes and in chapters of the cooperative throughout the San Blas region and in Panama City. Cooperative leaders invited me to accompany them on their travels to attend and to participate in meetings and events in other communities. I attended two regional cooperative workshops, involving participants from a wide range of communities. These workshops presented opportunities for me to talk at length with women from all over the region.

Local-Level Data Collection

I spent eleven months living in Tupile, Carti-Sugtupu, and Mansucun. I spent six months on Tupile, where I developed survey instruments and other methods for collecting data. It took less time to collect comparable information on the other two field sites. I spent three months on Carti-Sugtupu and another six weeks in the community of Mansucun. I spent six weeks visiting other San Blas communities for purposes of comparison.

Understanding the impact of *mola* commercialization on households was my primary focus for research at the local level. Intensive participant observation complemented information from a household census and two other survey instruments. I generated quantitative data through a household census, a survey of household survival strategies, and a survey of the Kuna women's participation in the commercialization of *molas*. I collected similar information in each community for purposes of comparison.

I completed a community household census at each of the three field sites (Mansucun, n = 61; Tupile, n = 130; Carti-Sugtupu, n = 104). In accordance with Holloman's observations (1969:135), I defined a household as "a group of affinally, consanguinally, and/or adoptively related individuals who eat together in a common kitchen for most meals." Thus a single "household" might include several sleeping houses with a shared kitchen.

In addition, a stratified sample of thirty-three households was selected for each field site. The sample comprised different types of households (compounded, extended, and nuclear) with and without single mothers residing there. I interviewed (usually in Kuna) the female head of each household in the sample concerning her household's survival strategies. I used a separate interview schedule with the adult women residing in the sample households. I asked these women about their participation in *mola* production and sales and in agricultural activities. I also elicited other basic demographic information.

I developed the questions asked on these interview schedules in consultation with two Kuna social scientists, who helped to ensure that the questions were relevant and would elicit accurate responses. For example, I wanted to know how many *molas* women sewed or sold over a year's time. I quickly discovered, however, that women who produced *molas* for sale did not remember how many they had sewn or how much money they had earned even over the past month, much less over the past year. A Kuna linguist assisted with translation of the questions from Spanish to Kuna.

Overall, participant observation was relatively easy in San Blas and provided a wealth of information about daily life. Houses are located close together, some so close that a person can just pass between the outside walls separating two houses. Loosely spaced cane walls make it possible to sit inside during the day and still see everyone who passes by on the path outside. Doors to kitchens and sleeping houses are open during the day, and it is considered perfectly acceptable to stick your head inside or even to enter and sit down without being invited. On Carti-Sugtupu electric lights make it possible to see into houses at night without actually going inside. Tupile and Mansucun, however, do not have electricity.

Most of women's daily activities take place within the community. Many activities, such as washing clothes and dishes, bathing children, sweeping, and going to the store, take place outside of their houses. I participated in these activities in the households where I lived and also, as is customary among Kuna women, when I went visiting. Women enjoyed watching my often-awkward attempts to carry out the activities that they performed with such ease. They took great delight in showing me how to do a wide variety of tasks. Some of the tasks in which I participated were smoking fish, peeling plantains, grating coconuts, fanning the fire, carrying supplies from the *ulu* to the kitchen, going to the store, and sewing *molas*. I also went with other women to visit the sick and to clean the cemetery.

My opportunities for actually observing men's activities were limited to those that took place on the island or, in the case of Mansucun, within the community. I was not able to accompany men fishing or to their fields. Most of the men, with the exception of school-age boys, male teachers, and grandfathers too old to work, spent the major portion of their day fishing or working their fields on the mainland. Women on Tupile and Carti-Sugtupu were all too busy sewing *molas* to accompany me to the mainland. On occasion, I attended the all-male nightly *congreso* meetings on Carti-Sugtupu and on Tupile either alone or in the company of a female friend. More often, however, I joined the women and children in their evening visits to family and friends. Between visits we would circle by the *congreso* to see if there was anything of interest being discussed. Sometimes, the *congreso* house would be surrounded by women peering in, listening, and carrying on their own discussion. When we got bored listening to the men's talk, we left. In Mansucun, where both men and women participated in the nightly *congreso*, I went every

evening. Most information about men's activities was gleaned sec-
ondhand, however, from men when they returned from their day's
activities.

Information about *omekits* was difficult to obtain. When I asked
non-*omekit* males questions, they usually told me about their observations of (non-Kuna) homosexuals in Panama City. These were always negative. Although I knew four *omekits* quite well, they were
reluctant to answer my questions and usually changed the subject.
Kuna women answered some of my questions and in general were
more forthcoming with information.

Secrecy surrounding information about gender crossing has been
encountered elsewhere in North America. Derogatory attitudes of
Spaniards and missionaries forced *berdache* to give up their public
roles (Williams 1986). It is likely that Latin homophobia and missionaries have had a similar effect on the Kuna's willingness to discuss gender crossing. Accessibility of both the type and the quality
of information to an anthropologist depends on one's age, sex, and
marital status, personal life circumstances, how one is introduced
into the social setting, where one lives, and, of course, the social organization and customs of the place where the study takes place.
Other factors enter in as well, but I would like to focus briefly on
where I lived and ate and how this affected this study.

Because I was interested in the relationship between household
subsistence and *mola* sales, it was important to be as closely involved in daily life as possible. On Tupile I lived in an extended three-
generation household. My hammock hung in the sleeping house
alongside everyone else's. I had a pole suspended by two vines from
the ceiling to throw my clothes over and a small, low table for my
notebooks and other belongings. I ate whatever and whenever the
rest of the household ate and participated fully in daily household tasks such as grating coconut, cleaning fish, peeling plantains,
sweeping, and washing clothes.

On Carti-Sugtupu, *mola* cooperative members hosted my first two
week-long visits. I hung my hammock in one member's house, while
other members took turns inviting me to their houses to eat. This
system was well enough coordinated so that I always ate at least once
a day. Some days, however, I ate two, three, and four times in a row.
Once, I ate six meals. By my third trip to the island, I had settled into
one particular household, where I slept and ate whenever traveling
to Carti-Sugtupu. Invitations to eat continued to be extended to me
by my friends in the cooperative, so that I had the opportunity of
getting to know seven households quite intimately.

On Mansucun I stayed in a cooperative member's household, again slinging my hammock up alongside everyone else's. In Mansucun I ate my daily meal in the household where I slept. We only ate one meal per day, drinking highly sweetened hot chocolate throughout the day to stave off hunger.

Because I was a woman alone with cash but no male labor to contribute, my position in the households where I stayed was that of a wage-earning daughter. Like the Kuna women who were in my position, I purchased rice, sacks of sugar, cocoa, and fish. Through these experiences, I gained a great deal of firsthand information about the inner workings of household subsistence patterns. Living in San Blas without a male partner allowed me to share on a very personal level my hopes, fears, and dreams for the future with Kuna women in the same position. Many older women sat me down along with their daughters and gave us advice about men, about children, about being a woman, and about survival.

Notes

1. Introduction

1. I had hoped to have Kuna women's voices more fully present in this book. When I was in San Blas, however, many Kuna were very touchy about foreigners recording or photographing them. Some Kuna did not want their "traditions stolen" and used to further academic careers with no thought to returning something of use to their communities. During the time I was there, one anthropologist, who used a tape recorder without asking permission, was escorted to the airport and asked never to return to San Blas. The tape recorder and all of his field notes were confiscated. Similarly, two male missionaries who were caught taking photographs of the women at the river had their cameras and an outboard motor confiscated. Needless to say, I was very cautious.

2. Theoretical Framework

1. Unlike in much of the rest of Latin America, exploitation in Panama was based not on the extraction of labor and raw materials but rather on transportation and the circulation of capital (see Manduly 1980).

2. See Benería and Roldán (1987), Cook and Binford (1990), and Feldman (1991) for excellent discussions of the literature on the informal sector and on petty-commodity production.

3. García Canclini (1982) is one of the few studies to focus on crafts consumption. It has recently been translated into English (1993).

4. Some very interesting work on the relationship of changing consumer demands to the production and circulation of goods is currently in progress. See Roseberry (1992) and Schneider (1992).

5. The International Women's Tribune Center (IWTC) in New York City and the Office of Women at Michigan State University publish very useful newsletters. MSU's is called *Women in International Development Newsletter*. The Association for Women in Development (AWID) holds annual conferences and is also a useful way to network. There are many additional research and information centers throughout the world.

6. Mies's work on the lacemakers of Narsapur (1982) is one of the few books on crafts production to offer policy recommendations. Her study was prepared for the International Labour Office within the framework of the

World Employment Programme. This book also discusses policy implications in chapter 11.

7. One notable exception is Gamio de Alba's (1957) efforts to describe indigenous women's lives throughout Panama.

3. Traveling to San Blas

1. PEMASKY is a nongovernmental Kuna development project designed to conserve and protect the natural resources of the region. It has created a natural reserve with facilities for biologists and other scientists to come and study the surrounding rain forest. It is hoped that the project will discourage encroaching *colonos* (landless, non-Kuna Panamanian peasants) from entering the Kuna territory and destroying the delicate ecology of the rain forest so vital to the rapidly changing Kuna way of life (see Breslin and Chapin 1984; Chapin 1990).

Another concern of the project is to retain control over the only road that connects the San Blas coast with the Pan American Highway and the rest of Panama. Under construction since 1975, the road is passable only in the dry season and then only in a four-wheel-drive vehicle. At the time I was there, only the Panamanian military and vehicles with written permission from the PEMASKY office in Panama City were allowed to pass beyond the PEMASKY outpost located at the point where the road intersects Kuna lands. No public transportation yet exists, nor are there roads along the coast.

2. See Sherzer (1983) for more information on Kuna speech patterns.

3. The Kuna most commonly call plantains *mas* or *masi*. See Howe (1975) for a detailed description of the different kinds of bananas the Kuna plant. This is also a wonderful resource for information about Kuna agricultural practices.

4. Fashions in nose rings have changed considerably over the years. In 1947, women of all ages wore their nose rings hanging down to their upper lips (Stout 1947).

5. Howe (1986b) provides a wonderfully detailed description of these Kuna gatherings.

4. Political Economy of San Blas

1. The shift to the islands has been gradual. For example, the Tupile community moved in the 1880s, although another community did not move until the 1930s. Twelve communities are still situated on the mainland.

2. Panama is unusual in that the government has for the most part negotiated with the indigenous populations instead of violently repressing them (see Howe 1986a). Other indigenous peoples in Latin America have not been so fortunate (Davis 1977; Menchú 1984). Also see Holloman (1975) for a discussion of Kuna ethnic boundaries.

3. See Herlihy (1989) for historical background of the *comarca* concept and for information about *comarcas* for other indigenous groups in Panama.

4. In 1985, conflict between brothers and sisters over land use and inheritance was a growing concern. Unclaimed land may be three to four hours' walk away, and a number of young men were very displeased that their sisters had inherited the closer fields. Women argued that these men still had access to their wives' land and should not complain. Several women interviewed in 1985 said that their brothers had usurped their claims to land.

5. In 1985, community enterprises in the villages where I worked included airport transportation services, a community savings and loan bank (comprising a wooden box), a hotel, and a warehouse, to mention a few.

6. In 1985, if a woman inherited membership in a (formerly) all-male *sociedad* from her father, her husband or unmarried son could work in her stead. A brother might also help out, though this was not the case for the women I spoke with in 1985. Women without male relatives to work for them either hired labor or lost their access to the harvest and ultimately to membership in the group. In the mainland community of Mansucun, women who had inherited their fathers' rights to the Mansucun men's coconut grove were allowed to weed and harvest only if they had no male relative who could do this for them. Women had argued long and hard in the *congreso* for the right to work. Mansucun's women had their own coconut grove, which they exploited.

7. When I was in San Blas, older Kuna men often spoke to me in broken English and asked me if I had ever been to Japan or the Rockefeller Center in New York City, as they had. These grandfathers had learned English as young men during their travels. Some spoke only Kuna and English.

8. Girls were not provided these early educational opportunities. In the 1980s, both Kuna girls and boys were sent to school. See Swain (1982: 112–113) for an interesting discussion of young Kuna girls' and boys' aspirations on the island of Aligandi. Girls selected primarily classic western, nurturing female occupations, such as teaching, nursing, and secretarial work. More girls than boys, however, aspired to attend the university.

9. Women whose husbands dive are envied by others because they eat a lot of fish; larger fish can be speared than are generally caught with line and hook. One grandmother who had few men in her household and was constantly running out of fish decided to improve her situation by buying a spear gun. The spear gun was lent out daily to different divers who provided the old woman with fish.

10. Howe (personal communication) observed on Niatup that some households hire workers either locally or from another island to help them. Sometimes these workers will board with a household for a period of months. I did not observe this in any of the three communities I studied.

5. *Mola* Commercialization

1. Some additional information about these plants can be found in Duke (1968).

2. After I explained to the *congreso* on Tupile that I wanted to study the

commercialization of *molas* and that I was myself an artist, the *sakla* and the *arkar* decided to name me Nagagiriyai.

3. In 1985, Kuna women sewed many of these same designs onto the blouses they wore and the *molas* they exported. Men also continued to produce many of the same designs and handcrafted objects; however, men's crafts were for household use and had not been commercialized.

4. My interviews with older Kuna men and women from two different islands in 1984 confirmed Howe's observation.

5. Hirschfeld (1977:163) notes that, although *molas* mark Kuna ethnic identity, that they are "completely dependent on trade goods . . . and are made to be worn and eventually sold to Westerners" creates ambiguity.

6. Census data can provide rough indications of the extent of *mola* commercialization; however, they are not very accurate. Kuna women I interviewed did not easily remember how many *molas* they had sewn or sold in the past month, much less in the past year. Their husbands and male relatives, when asked by census takers to estimate *mola* production for their entire household, would have known even less. Furthermore, there had been rumors of the government's imposing a tax on *mola* sales, so it is highly likely that households underreported *mola* sales.

7. IPAT, "Estadísticas sobre el turismo. Total de visitantes ingresados a Panamá, por el Aeropuerto Internacional Omar Torrijos y la Frontera de Paso Canoa, de enero a diciembre" (n.d.).

8. A man from Carti-Sugtupu had befriended the general while working on the U.S. military base in the old Canal Zone and had given him *molas* as gifts. Kuna men working on the army bases often gave *molas* to military personnel as a gesture of friendship. In return the Kuna sometimes received favors or gifts of outdated military supplies. In a similar vein, one man from Carti-Sugtupu became friends with a cruise ship's captain. He gave *molas* to the captain, who in turn gave him several dozen old medicine cabinets, two auditorium seats, and some pieces of plywood.

9. See John Canaday, "*Molas* from the San Blas Islands" (*New York Times*, December 30, 1968), and "Get a *Mola* before Sewing Machines Do" (*Miami News*, July 4, 1969: section D).

6. *Mola* Production, Exchange, and Use

1. During the course of my research, I found a copy of the law and the cooperative's administrator went to speak with Panama's vice-president as she had promised. Although the vice-president was sympathetic to her concerns, as far as we know no actions were taken to enforce the law.

2. How *molas* are made has been described elsewhere (Sherzer and Sherzer 1976:30; Salvador 1976b; Parker and Parker 1977).

3. On the island of Tupile, the *omekits* I knew attended and sewed *molas* at the *congresos* held for women only. They also sometimes attended the men's *congreso*, but did not sew *molas*.

4. Sherzer and Sherzer (1976) distinguish between three types of *molas*:

(1) geometrical, abstract designs; (2) *molas* representing elements of Kuna life; and (3) *molas* incorporating elements of the non-Kuna western world. I would change the third category to read elements of the western world that are now part of the Kuna world and add a fourth category for *molas* that combine the second and third categories. It is important to remember that the Kuna are highly connected to the western world and that definitions of "Kuna traditional life" are historically rooted and changing. For a different way of categorizing *mola* designs, see Salvador (1976a).

5. In general, Kuna women tend to speak less Spanish than do Kuna men. Although both boys and girls learn Spanish in school, unless they go to Panama City for further education or to work, they tend to forget what they have learned. Individuals who work in the Canal Zone, Panama City, or elsewhere in Panama such as Changuinola usually learn Spanish and sometimes English (Sherzer 1983:23). In my experience, the Kuna women who spoke Spanish, with a few exceptions, did not speak very well. They were painfully aware of this fact and were embarrassed to speak in Spanish with me. In Mandinga Bay, the area of San Blas frequented by tourists, many Kuna women knew enough English words to sell their *molas*: "ten dollar," "twenty dollar," "you like . . . you buy?"

7. Kuna Women Organize

1. I lived and studied weaving production in a women's weaving cooperative in the highlands of Guatemala for over a year (1975–1976 and 1980).

2. Both Kuna men and women must request and receive permission from the *sakla* to visit other communities.

3. See Yudelman's study (1987) of five women's development organizations in Latin America.

8. Tourism and *Molas* on Carti-Sugtupu

1. Carti-Sugtupu is one of four small populated islands located very close to one another. It takes from fifteen to thirty minutes' paddling to reach the other three islands. They are reached by outboard motor in five to ten minutes. Administratively, each island is separate, though they often cooperate as the need arises.

2. Although I visited the river in 1981, I was unable to do so on my subsequent stay (1984–1985) because two young male Mormon missionaries living in a community near Carti-Sugtupu had gone to the river, hidden in the jungle, and taken photographs of the Kuna women bathing. The Mormons were discovered, and a *congreso* with representatives from four communities was called to decide how to punish them. The *congreso* decided that their outboard motor and their cameras would be confiscated for community use and that no foreigners (i.e., non-Kuna) would be allowed to go to the river. Any Kuna transporting or accompanying a foreigner to the river would be fined fifty dollars. I requested special permission from the *congreso*

on Carti-Sugtupu, pointing out that I was a woman, needed to bathe and wash my clothes, and should be allowed to go to the river. My request was denied. In this case, my status as an "outsider" was stronger than my identity as a woman.

3. Many women from Carti-Sugtupu felt that this was only a partial explanation. They thought that their fathers, husbands, and other male relatives were not as hard-working as the men from Tupile and other islands farther east. Some women complained that men now depended on them to earn cash by selling *molas* and had become lazy. My own observations partially supported theirs. Strong, healthy men representing a wide range of ages could often be found relaxing in their hammocks on bright, sunny days. Many men (all ages) also worked very hard, however, leaving the island before dawn and not returning until late afternoon.

4. Although women never provided the bulk of fish for their households, it seems that men did not increase their fishing activities when women stopped fishing. The women explained that they did not have time to go fishing; they were too busy sewing *molas*. Others pointed out that they no longer had an *ulu*. Most of the large trees that *ulus* had been made from had been cut down, so that now the *ulus* had to be purchased. Many households could now afford only one *ulu*, and these were ordinarily used by the men. Because women were now buying fish, some men dedicated themselves to fishing for sale on a regular basis. The women living in these men's households did not purchase fish.

9. The *Mola* Cooperative on Tupile

1. Tourists visit this area infrequently. In 1985, there was a small hotel and restaurant (Hotel Anai) run collectively by a Kuna *sociedad* on the island of Aligandi (see Holloman 1969:214; Swain 1977:76). Aligandi residents often ate in the restaurant.

2. I observed that, for the most part, picking fruit was still considered "women's work," although men also returned to the island with fruit. During mango season, women went as often as they could to gather mangoes. My observations do not agree with the survey results.

10. *Molas* and Middlemen in Mansucun: A Discussion of Female-supported Households

1. Annual planting and harvesting activities were not going on while I was in Mansucun, so I did not have the opportunity to observe these first-hand. Stier's work diaries for 41 women and 124 men in a nearby community show that women spent 10 days harvesting corn over a six-month period compared to men's 165 days. Her data also show that women were active in harvesting bananas and coconuts (Stier 1979:312).

2. Although more research needs to be done, it is my sense that Kuna men generally do not set up second households with other women in Panama

City. Housing in the city is expensive and difficult to find. Men often live together, with their sons and daughters, or with relatives.

11. Insights from San Blas: Crafts, Gender, and the Global Economy

1. There are some women and *omekits* in the region who are known by buyers for *molas* of outstanding quality. These producers may command up to one hundred dollars for a *mola*. Although they receive higher prices, their *molas* are usually exquisitely detailed and take longer to sew than the average *mola*.

2. Some items, such as *mola* bikinis, do not depend on the commoditization of ethnicity at all. Some buyers do not even know that bikinis are made from *molas*.

3. Stephen (1991b:125) has argued that, for Zapotec weavers, the complex relationship between ethnic identity and the production of indigenous crafts for tourist and export markets suggests that "local indigenous identity has been maintained not only through a process of historical opposition but also through an indirect process of opposition where today communities consciously redefine their ethnicity as an alternative to the commoditized version of their ethnic identity."

4. In Ann Arbor, Michigan, home to one of the country's largest art fairs and to a smaller weekly crafts market, crafts not made by "local" producers were banned. This decision was aimed at keeping ethnic handicrafts imported from Latin America and elsewhere from competing with locally produced goods. At the same time, a number of individuals and churches sell crafts to help support refugees and other impoverished craft producers from El Salvador and Guatemala.

Glossary of Kuna and Spanish Terms

Boldface entries are Kuna words. Entries in *italics* are Spanish.

akkwet, akkweti (Sp., *acudiente*):   person or couple who looks after or manages a household; host or sponsor of a visitor
arkar (Sp., *vocero*):   chief's spokesperson; second class of officers in village leadership
asuolo: "nose gold"; refers to women's gold nose rings
bicha: interior skirt
bolis: small plastic bags filled with frozen Kool-Aid
cacique: regional chief of Kuna Yala
cambombia: a large seashell
chalupa: sloop or sailboat
chicha: home-brewed alcoholic drink, consumed in celebrations also called *chicha*. Compare **inna**.
comarca: Panamanian name for native reserve or territory, as in Comarca de Kuna Yala
congreso: village or regional assembly or gathering
corregimiento: electoral and administrative district
finca: farm
guineo: banana
ibedi: household head
ikko inna: needle **inna**, a nose-piercing ceremony for a baby girl
ikor: Zanthoxylum
inna: an alcoholic beverage made primarily from burned corn and sugarcane; also refers to the celebration during which the beverage is drunk. Compare *chicha*.
inna muttikkit: night **inna**, a villagewide celebration of a girl's first menstruation
inna neka: a communal house where an **inna** celebration is held
inna suit: long **inna** (three to five days), usually held to celebrate the first time a girl's hair is cut short like an adult woman's

inna tunsikkalet: short **inna** (two days) similar to the long **inna**

kobe: to drink (**kobet**, a drink)

kurgin: special gifts or abilities

macharetkit: manlike (woman)

madu: bread

madun(nu):   plantain, plantain drink

mageb: *Bixa orellana*, the tree fruit from which the red paint called *annatto* or *achiote* in Spanish (**nisar** in Kuna) is made

maquiladora: transboundary seamstress

masi: food, plantains or bananas

mergi: someone from the United States

mola: Kuna woman's blouse; blouse panels and other cloth items sewn with **mola** designs; clothing in general

molita: little **mola**

monte: forest, bush, countryside

mormaknamaloe: go sew **molas**

morsan: cloth

musue: red scarf Kuna women use to cover their heads

muu: grandmother

naba: a gourd; **naba** or **nabawala** is a gourd tree (*Crescentia*)

neg ibed: owner of the house

nele (pl. **nerkan**):   "seer"

nuedi: good

ochi: sweet drink, often chocolate

olikwa: sweetened drink made from ground cocoa beans and corn

ome: woman

omekit: womanlike man

onmakketneka: gathering house

orroz kinnit: red rice

panemaloe: see you tomorrow

plátano: plantain

pozo: hole

saburrette: wraparound skirt

sakla: village chief

salu: river snails

sappan: firewood

saptur: a tree, *Genipa americana*, and a black dye made from its fruit

sigabula: a type of tiny fish (named for its hairy beard)

sippu: white

sociedades: voluntary associations

sualipet: Kuna police officer

tule: Kuna people; a person

tule masi: literally "Kuna food"; refers to a dish made from plantains, coconut milk, and fish

ulu: dugout canoe

waga: a non-Kuna person

wini: multicolored beads that Kuna women wrap in long strands around their forearms and lower legs

References

Kuna History and Ethnography

Alvarez, Robert
  1969 "Arbaeit Pukidara: Projections and Follow up for the Cooperativa de Productoras de *Mola* de San Blas, Panama." Unpublished Peace Corps Report.
Barahona, Nedelka Araceli, and Rosa Ameilia Yáñez
  1979 "Cooperativa de Producción y Mercadeo de Molas de San Blas R.L." Universidad de Panama. Graduation thesis. University of Panama.
Bourgois, Philip
  1988 "Conjugated Oppression: Class and Ethnicity among Guaymi and Kuna Banana Workers." *American Ethnologist* 15 (2): 328–348.
Breslin, Patrick, and Mac Chapin
  1984 "Conservation Kuna-Style." *Grassroots Development: Journal of the Inter-American Foundation* 8 (2): 26–35.
Brown, Judith
  1980 "Sex Division of Labor among the San Blas Cuna." *Anthropological Quarterly* 43 (2): 57–63.
Brown, Lady Richmond
  1925 *Unknown Tribes, Uncharted Seas.* New York: D. Appleton.
Chapin, Mac
  1970 *Pab igala: historias de la tradición kuna.* Panama: Centro de Investigaciones Antropológicas, Universidad de Panamá.
  1983 "Curing among the San Blas Kuna of Panama." Ph.D. dissertation. University of Arizona.
  1990 "The Silent Jungle: Ecotourism among the Kuna Indians of Panama." *Cultural Survival Quarterly* 14 (1): 42–45.
  1991 "How the Kuna Keep Scientists in Line." *Cultural Survival Quarterly* 15 (4): 32.
Controlaría General de la República
  1960 Censos nacionales de 1960. República de Panamá.
  1970 Censos nacionales de 1970. República de Panamá.
  1980 Censos nacionales de 1980. República de Panamá.
Costello, Richard
  1971 "Some Preliminary Findings on the Economic Structure of a San Blas Community." *Actas del II Simposio Nacional de Antropología, Ar-*

queología y Etnohistoria de Panamá. Panama: University of Panama/
INAC.

1975   "Political Economy and Private Interests in Río Azúcar: An Analysis of Economic Change in a San Blas Community." Ph.D. dissertation.
University of California, Davis.

1982   "New Economic Roles for Cuna Males and Females: An Examination of Socioeconomic Change in a San Blas Community." In *Sex Roles
and Social Change,* pp. 70–87. Edited by Christine Loveland and Franklin
Loveland. Urbana: University of Illinois Press.

Cullen, Edward
1853   *Isthmus of Darién Ship Canal.* London: Effingham Wilson.
1868   "The Darién Indians." *Transactions of the Ethnological Society of
London* (vol. 6).

De Puydt, Lucien
1868   *Account of Scientific Explorations in the Isthmus of Darién in the
Years 1861 and 1865.* London: Journal of the Royal Geographical Society
(vol. 38).

Duke, James A.
1968   *Darién Ethnobotanical Dictionary.* Columbus, Ohio: Battelle Me-
morial Institute.

Falla, Ricardo
1979a   *El tesoro de San Blas: turismo en San Blas.* (Cuaderno 5, Serie El
Indio Panameño.) Panama: Centro de Capacitación Social.
1979b   *Historia kuna, historia rebelde: la articulación del Archipiélago
Kuna a la nación panameña.* (Cuaderno 4, Serie El Indio Panameño.) Panama: Centro de Capacitación Social.

Gamio de Alba, Margarita
1957   *La mujer indígena de Centro América.* Mexico City: Instituto Indigenista Interamericano.

Hart, Francis Russell
1929   *The Disaster of Darien: The Story of the Scots Settlement and the
Causes of Its Failure, 1699–1701.* Boston & New York: Houghton Mifflin.

Hartmann, Gunther
1980   *Molakana: Volkskunst der Cuna, Panama.* Berlin: Museum für
Volkerkunde.

Hatley, Nancy Brennan
1976   "Cooperativism and Enculturation among the Cuna Indians of San
Blas." In *Enculturation in Latin America,* pp. 67–94. Edited by Johannes
Wilbert. Los Angeles: Latin American Center Publications, University of
California at Los Angeles.

Helms, Mary
1981   "Cuna Molas and Coclé Art Forms: Reflections on Panamanian Design Styles and Symbols." Working Papers in Traditional Arts 7. Philadelphia: Institute for the Study of Human Issues.

Herlihy, Peter
1989   "Panama's Quiet Revolution: Comarca Homelands and Indian
Rights." *Cultural Survival Quarterly* 13 (3): 17–24.

Herrera, Francisco
1972 "Aspectos del desarrollo económico y social de los indios Kunas de San Blas." *América Indígena* 32 (1): 113–138.

Hirschfeld, Lawrence A.
1976 "A Structural Analysis of the Cuna Arts." In *Ritual and Symbol in Native Central America*, pp. 43–56. Edited by Philip Young and James Howe. University of Oregon Anthropological Papers, no. 9. Eugene: University of Oregon, Dept. of Anthropology.
1977 "Cuna Aesthetics: A Quantitative Analysis." *Ethnology* 16 (2): 147–166.

Holloman, Regina
1969 "Developmental Change in San Blas." PhD dissertation. Northwestern University.
1975 "Ethnic Boundary Maintenance, Readaptation, and Societal Evolution in the San Blas Islands of Panama." In *Ethnicity and Resource Competition in Plural Societies*, pp. 27–40. Edited by Leo Despres. Paris: Mouton.
1976 "Cuna Household Types and the Domestic Cycle." In *Frontier Adaptation in Lower Central America*, pp. 131–149. Edited by Mary Helms and Franklin Loveland. Philadelphia: Institute for the Study of Human Issues.

Howe, James
1974 "Village and Political Organization among the San Blas Cuna." Ph.D. dissertation. University of Pennsylvania.
1975 "Notes on the Environment and Subsistence Practices of the San Blas Cuna." Working Papers on Peoples of Central America, no. 1. MIT, Cambridge, Mass. Photocopy.
1976 "Communal Land Tenure and the Origin of Descent Groups among the San Blas Cuna." In *Frontier Adaptation in Lower Central America*, pp. 152–163. Edited by Mary Helms and Franklin Loveland. Philadelphia: Institute for the Study of Human Issues.
1982a "Kindling Self-Determination among the Kuna." *Cultural Survival Quarterly* 6 (3): 15–17.
1982b "Kuna Split-Island Villages: The Development of a Twentieth-Century Dual Organization." Paper, 44th International Congress of Americanists, Manchester, England, September.
1985 "Marriage and Domestic Organization among the San Blas Cuna." In *The Botany and Natural History of Panama.* Edited by William D'Arcy and Mireya Correa A. St. Louis: Missouri Botanical Garden.
1986a "Native Rebellion and U.S. Intervention in Central America: The Implications of the Kuna Case for the Miskito." *Cultural Survival Quarterly* 10 (1): 59–65.
1986b *The Kuna Gathering: Contemporary Village Politics in Panama.* Austin: University of Texas Press.
1990 "Mission Rivalry and Conflict in San Blas, Panama." In *Class, Politics and Popular Religion in Mexico and Central America*, pp. 143–166.

Edited by Lynn Stephen and James Dow. Society for Latin American Anthropology Publication Series, vol. 10.
Forthcoming. "A People Who Would Not Kneel: Panama, the United States and the San Blas Kuna."
Howe, James, and Lawrence A. Hirschfeld
1981 "The Star Girls' Descent: A Myth about Men, Women, Matrilocality, and Singing." *Journal of American Folklore* 94 (373): 292–322.
Langebaek, Carl Henrik
1991 "Cuna Long Distance Journeys: The Result of Colonial Interaction." *Ethnology* 30:371–380.
McCosker, Sandra
1976 "San Blas Cuna Indian Lullabies: A Means of Informal Learning." In *Enculturation in Latin America*, pp. 67–94. Edited by Johannes Wilbert. Los Angeles: Latin American Center Publications, University of California at Los Angeles.
Marshall, Donald Stanley
1950 "Cuna Folk: A Conceptual Scheme Involving the Dynamic Factors of Culture, as Applied to the Cuna Indians of Darien." Unpublished honors thesis. Harvard University.
Moore, Alexander
1984 "From Council to Legislature: Democracy, Parliamentarianism, and the San Blas Cuna." *American Anthropologists* 86:28–42.
Nordenskiöld, E., with Rubén Pérez Kantule, S. Henry Wassén, eds.
1938 *An Historical and Ethnological Survey of the Cuna Indians.* Comparative Ethnographical Studies 10. Göteborg: Etnografiska Museum.
Olien, Michael D.
1988 "After the Indian Slave Trade: Cross-Cultural Trade in the Western Caribbean Rimland." *Journal of Anthropological Research* 44:41–66.
Parker, Ann, and Neal Parker
1977 *Molas: Folk Art of the Cuna Indians.* New York: Clarkson N. Potter.
Prestán, Arnulfo
n.d. "Historia del estudio del proyecto turístico de San Blas."
Puig, Manuel María
1948 *Los indios cunas de San Blas.* Colón: Talleres de "El Independiente."
Restrepo Tirado, Ernesto
1887 "Un viaje al Darién: apuntes de carretera." Bogotá.
Reynolds, Patricia
1968 Peace Corps Termination Report. Nargana, San Blas, Panama. Unpublished manuscript.
Roberts, Orlando
1827 *Narrative of Voyages and Excursions on the East Coast and in the Interior of Central America.* Edinburgh: Constable and Co.
Rose, Hugh
1929 [1698] *Journal or Diary of the Most Remarkable Things That Happened during the Scots African and Indian Fleet . . .* (Reprinted as

Appendix II in F. R. Hart, *The Disaster of the Darien.*) Boston and New York: Houghton Mifflin.

Salvador, Mari Lyn

1976a "Molas of the Cuna Indians: A Case Study of Artistic Criticism and Ethno-Aesthetics." Ph.D. dissertation. University of California, Berkeley.

1976b "The Clothing Arts of the Cuna of San Blas, Panama." In *Ethnic and Tourist Arts*, pp. 165–182. Edited by Nelson H. H. Graburn. Berkeley & Los Angeles: University of California Press.

1978 *Yer Dailege! Kuna Women's Art.* New Mexico: Maxwell Museum of Anthropology.

Shatto, Gloria

1972 "The San Blas Cuna Indian Sociedad as a Vehicle of Economic Development." *Journal of Developing Areas* 6 (3): 383–398.

Sherzer, Dina, and Joel Sherzer

1976 "Mormaknamaloe: The Cuna *Mola.*" In *Ritual and Symbol in Native Central America*, pp. 21–42. Edited by Philip Young and James Howe. University of Oregon Anthropological Papers, no. 9. Eugene: University of Oregon, Dept. of Anthropology.

Sherzer, Joel

1983 *Kuna Ways of Speaking.* Austin: University of Texas Press.

Stier, Frances Rhoda

1979 "The Effect of Demographic Change on Agriculture in San Blas, Panama." PhD dissertation. University of Arizona.

1982 "Domestic Economy: Land, Labor and Wealth in a San Blas Community." *American Ethnologist* 9 (3): 519–537.

1983 "Modeling Migration: Analyzing Migration Histories from a San Blas Cuna Community." *Human Organization* 42:9–22.

Stout, David

1946 "Land Tenure and Other Property Concepts among the San Blas Cuna." *Primitive Man* 19 (3/4): 63–80.

1947 *San Blas Cuna Acculturation: An Introduction.* New York: Viking Fund.

Swain, Margaret

1977 "Cuna Women and Ethnic Tourism: A Way to Persist and an Avenue to Change." In *Hosts and Guests: The Anthropology of Tourism*, pp. 71–81. Edited by Valene Smith. Philadelphia: University of Pennsylvania Press.

1978 "Aligandi Women: Continuity and Change in Cuna Female Identity." Ph.D. dissertation. University of Washington.

1982 "Being Cuna and Female: Ethnicity Mediating Change in Sex Roles." In *Sex Roles and Social Change*, pp. 102–123. Edited by Christine Loveland and Franklin Loveland. Urbana: University of Illinois Press.

Tice, Karin

1982 "Marketing Molas: Women's Options and Strategies in Kuna Yala (San Blas), Panama." Paper, 44th International Congress of Americanists, Manchester, England.

1988   "Expropriación de las artesanías kunas: nuevos contextos sociales del uso, producción y el mercado." Paper, "Cultura, Capital y Comercio," Escuela Nacional de Antropología and CIESAS, Mexico City.

1989a   "Indigenous Leadership, Social Scientists and International Foundations: The Social Organization of Research and Practice in San Blas, Panama." Paper, Society for Applied Anthropology meetings, Santa Fe, N.M.

1989b   "Gender, Capitalism and Egalitarian Forms of Social Organization in San Blas, Panama." Ph.D. dissertation. Columbia University.

n.d.   "Conflict and Resolution: Events Leading up to the Expropriation of a Foreign-operated Hotel in Kuna Yala (San Blas, Panama)."

Torres de Araúz, Reina

1974   *Etnohistoria cuna.* Panama: Dirección Nacional del Patrimonio Histórico/INAC.

Torres de Ianello, Reina

1957   *La mujer cuna de Panamá.* Mexico City: Instituto Indigenista Interamericano.

Wafer, Lionel

1903 [1699]   *A New Voyage and Description of the Isthmus of America.* Edited by George Parker Winship. Cleveland: Burrows Bros.

Wali, Alaka

1984   "Kilowatts and Crisis among the Kuna, Choco, and Colonos: The National and Regional Consequences of the Bayano Hydroelectric Complex in Eastern Panama." Ph.D. dissertation. Columbia University.

Young, Philip, and James Howe

1976   "Ritual and Symbol in Native Central America." University of Oregon Anthropological Papers, no. 9. Eugene: University of Oregon, Dept. of Anthropology.

Other References

Appadurai, Arjun (ed.)

1986   *The Social Life of Things: Commodities in Cultural Perspectives.* Cambridge: Cambridge University Press.

Babb, Florence

1989   *Between Field and Cooking Pot.* Austin: University of Texas Press.

Barker, Garry

1991   *The Handicraft Revival in Southern Appalachia, 1930–1991.* Knoxville: University of Tennessee Press.

Bauch, Elizabeth

1981   "Rural Artisans in Peru." Paper, American Anthropological Association meetings.

Benería, Lourdes

1979   "Reproduction, Production and the Sexual Divison of Labor." *Cambridge Journal of Economics* 3 (2): 203–225.

Benería, Lourdes (ed.)

1982   *Women and Development.* New York: Praeger.

Benería, Lourdes, and Martha Roldán
1987   *The Crossroads of Class and Gender: Industrial Homework, Sub-contracting and Household Dynamics in Mexico City.* Chicago: University of Chicago Press.

Bennholdt-Thomsen, Veronika
1981   "Subsistence Production and Extended Reproduction." In *Of Marriage and the Market*, pp. 16–29. Edited by Kate Young et al. London: CSE Books.

Blackwood, Evelyn
1984   "Sexuality and Gender in Certain Native American Tribes: The Case of Cross-Gender Females." *Signs: Journal of Women in Culture and Society* 10:27–42.

Boserup, Ester
1970 *Women's Role in Economic Development.* New York: St. Martin's.

Bossen, Laurel
1984   *The Redivision of Labor.* Albany: State University of New York Press.

Bottomley, Anthony
1965   "The Fate of the Artisan in Developing Countries." *Social and Economic Studies* 14 (2): 194–203.

Bourque, Susan, and Kay Warren
1981   *Women of the Andes.* Ann Arbor: University of Michigan Press.

Collier, John
1949   *The Awakening Valley.* Chicago: University of Chicago Press.

Cook, Scott
1984   *Peasant Capitalist Industry.* New York: University Press of America.

Cook, Scott, and Leigh Binford
1990   *Obliging Need: Rural Petty Industry in Mexican Capitalism.* Austin: University of Texas Press.

Croll, Elizabeth J.
1981   "Women in Rural Production and Reproduction in the Soviet Union, China, Cuba and Tanzania: Socialist Development Experiences. *Signs* 7 (2): 361–374.

Davis, Shelton
1977   *Victims of the Miracle.* New York: Cambridge University Press.

Deere, Carmen Diana, and Magdalena León de Leal
1981   "Peasant Production, Proletarianization and the Sexual Division of Labor in the Andes." *Signs* 7 (2): 338–360.

di Leonardo, Micaela
1991   *Gender at the Crossroads of Knowledge.* Berkeley & Los Angeles: University of California Press.

Ehlers, Tracy
1990   *Silent Looms.* Boulder, Colo. : Westview.

Engels, F.
1972 [1884]   *Origin of the Family, Private Property, and the State.* Edited by E. Leacock. New York: International.

Etienne, Mona
    1980   "Women and Men, Cloth and Colonization: The Transformation of
    Production-Distribution Relations among the Baule (Ivory Coast)." In
    Women and Colonization, pp. 214–238. Edited by Mona Etienne and
    Eleanor Leacock. New York: J. F. Bergin.
Etienne, Mona, and Eleanor Leacock
    1980   *Women and Colonization*. New York: J. F. Bergin.
Feldman, Shelley
    1991   "Still Invisible: Women in the Informal Sector." In *The Women and
    International Development Annual*, Vol. 2. Edited by Rita S. Gallin and
    Anne Ferguson. Boulder: Westview.
Fernández-Kelly, María Patricia
    1983   *For We Are Sold, I and My People*. Albany: State University of New
    York Press.
Frank, André Gunder
    1967   *Capitalism and Underdevelopment in Latin America*. New York:
    Monthly Review.
Gailey, Christine Ward
    1987   *Kinship to Kingship: Gender Hierarchy and State Formation in the
    Tongan Islands*. Austin: University of Texas Press.
Gallin, Rita S., and Anne Ferguson
    1991   "Conceptualizing Difference: Gender, Class and Action." In *The
    Women and International Development Annual*, Vol. 2. Edited by Rita S.
    Gallin and Anne Ferguson. Boulder: Westview.
Garay Castillo, Gloria, and José Medina Pérez
    1981   "La actividad artesanal en el Perú." *América Indígena* 41 (2):
    211–230.
García Canclini, Néstor
    1982   *Las culturas populares en el capitalismo*. Havana: Ediciones Casa
    de las Américas.
    1993   *Transforming Modernity: Popular Culture in Mexico*. Trans. Lidia
    Lozano. Austin: University of Texas Press.
Goody, Esther
    1982   *From Craft to Industry*. Cambridge: Cambridge University Press.
Graburn, Nelson
    1976   *Ethnic and Tourist Arts: Cultural Expressions from the Fourth
    World*. Berkeley & Los Angeles: University of California Press.
Harris, Olivia, and Kate Young
    1981   "Engendered Structures: Some Problems in the Analysis of Repro-
    duction." In *The Anthropology of Pre-Capitalist Societies*, pp. 109–147.
    Edited by J. Karn and J. Lobera. London: Routledge and Kegan Paul.
Healey, Kevin, and Elayne Zorn
    1982–1983   "Lake Titicaca's Campesino-controlled Tourism." In *Grass-
    roots Development* 6 (2)/7 (1): 3–10.
Helms, Mary
    1976   "Symbols and Society: Comments on Ritual and Symbolism of In-
    digenous Central America." In *Ritual and Symbol in Native Central*

America, pp. 125–141. Edited by Philip Young and James Howe. University of Oregon Anthropological Papers, no. 9. Eugene: University of Oregon, Dept. of Anthropology.

Leacock, Eleanor
1981a   *Myths of Male Dominance*. New York: Monthly Review.
1981b   "History, Development and the Division of Labor by Sex: Implications for Organization." *Signs* 7 (2): 474–491.

Leacock, Eleanor, and Helen Safa (eds.)
1981   "Special Issue: Development and the Sexual Division of Labor." *Signs* 7 (2): 265–512.

——— et al.
1986   *Women's Work: Development and the Division of Labor by Gender*. South Hadley, Mass.: Bergin and Garvey.

Littlefield, Alice
1979   "The Expansion of Capitalist Relations of Production in Mexican Crafts." *Journal of Peasant Studies* 6 (4): 471–488.

Mackintosh, Maureen
1981   "Gender and Economics: The Sexual Division of Labor and the Subordination of Women." In *Of Marriage and the Market*, pp. 1–15. Edited by Kate Young, Carol Wolkowitz, and Roslyn McCullagh. London: CSE.

McLellan, David (ed.)
1977   *Karl Marx: Selected Writings*. Oxford: Oxford University Press.

Manduly, Julio
1980   "Dependent Capitalism and Beyond." *Latin American Perspectives* 7 (2 & 3): 57–74.

Mencher, Joan, and Anne Okongwu (eds.)
1993   *Where Did All the Men Go? Female-Headed/Female-Supported Households in Cross-Cultural Perspective*. Boulder: Westview.

Menchú, Rigoberta
1984   *I, Rigoberta Menchú: An Indian Woman in Guatemala*. London: Verso and NLB.

Mies, Maria
1982   *The Lace Makers of Narsapur: Indian Housewives Produce for the World Market*. London: Zed.

Nash, June
1993   *Crafts in Global Markets: Changes in Artisan Production in Middle America*. Albany: State University of New York Press.

Nash, June, and María Patricia Fernández-Kelly (eds.)
1983   *Women, Men and the International Division of Labor*. Albany: State University of New York Press.

Nash, June, and Helen Safa
1986   *Women and Change in Latin America*. South Hadley, Mass.: Bergin and Garvey.

Novelo, Victoria
1976   *Artesanías y capitalismo en México*. Mexico City: Instituto Nacional de Antropología e Historia.

Orlove, Benjamin
   1974   "Urban and Rural Artisans in Southern Peru." *International Journal of Comparative Sociology* 15:193–231.
Ortner, Sherry, and Harriet Whitehead (eds.)
   1981   *Sexual Meanings: The Cultural Construction of Gender and Sexuality.* Cambridge: Cambridge Univeristy Press.
Roseberry, William
   1989   *Anthropologies and Histories.* New Brunswick, N.J.: Rutgers University Press.
   1992   "Consumer Choice, Flexible Accumulation and the Rise of Boutique Coffees." Paper, American Anthropological Association meetings, December, San Francisco, Calif.
Sabogal Wiesse, José
   1978   "El campesino-artesano en el Perú." *América Indígena* 38 (1): 207–218.
Sacks, Karen
   1982   *Sisters and Wives: The Past and Future of Sexual Equality.* Urbana: University of Illinois Press.
Salomon, Frank
   1973   "Weavers of Otavalo." In *Peoples and Cultures of Native South America*, pp. 463–492. Edited by Daniel Gross. New York: Doubleday/ Natural History.
Schneider, Jane
   1992   "In and Out of Polyester: A Look at Moments of Fashion Change." Paper, American Anthropological Association meetings, December, San Francisco, Calif.
Sider, Gerald
   1986   *Culture and Class in Anthropology and History.* Cambridge: Cambridge University Press
Stephen, Lynn
   1991a   *Zapotec Women.* Austin: University of Texas Press.
   1991b   "Culture as a Resource: Four Cases of Self-managed Indigenous Craft Production in Latin America." *Economic Development and Culture Change* (July): 101–130.
Stoler, Ann
   1977   "Class Structure and Female Autonomy in Rural Java." In *Women and National Development*, pp. 74–89. Edited by the Wellesley Editorial Committee. Chicago: University of Chicago Press.
Stolke, Verena
   1981   "Women's Labours: The Naturalisation of Social Inequality and Women's Subordination." In *Of Marriage and the Market*, pp. 30–48. Edited by Kate Young et al. London: CSE.
Torres de Araúz, Reina
   1975   "Profesionalismo femenino en Panamá: proyecciones económicas y sociales." In *Mujer en América Latina*, vol. 2, pp. 85–97. Edited by María del Carmen Elu de Leñero. Mexico City: Secretaría de Educación Pública.

Weiner, Annette
1980 "Stability in Banana Leaves: Colonization and Women in Kiriwina Trobriand Islands." In *Women and Colonization*, pp. 270–293. Edited by Mona Etienne and Eleanor Leacock. New York: J. F. Bergin.

Williams, Walter
1986 *The Spirit and the Flesh: Sexual Diversity in American Indian Culture*. Boston: Beacon.

Wolf, Eric
1982 *Europe and the People without History*. Berkeley & Los Angeles: University of California Press.

Yudelman, Sally
1987 *Hopeful Openings: A Study of Five Women's Development Organizations in Latin America and the Caribbean*. West Hartford, Conn.: Kumarian.

Index